Brussels

Belgium

EVERYMAN
CITY GUIDES

EVERYMAN CITY GUIDES

ISBN 1-85715-614-5

First published April 2000

Originally published in France by Nouveaux Loisirs, a subsidiary of Gallimard, Paris 1999, and in Italy by Touring Editore, Srl., Milano 1999.

SERIES EDITORS
Seymourina Cruse/Marisa Bassi
BRUSSELS EDITION: Lucie Milledrogues with the assistance of Maude Papillon and Sandrine Duviller
PROJECT MANAGER: Olivier Canavaso/Octavo
GRAPHICS
Élizabeth Cohat, Yann Le Duc
LAYOUT: Eric Sabot, Valerie Saingarraud
MINI-MAPS, MAPS OF THE AREA: Edigraphie
STREET MAPS: Touring Club Italiano
PRODUCTION
Catherine Bourrabier

Translated by Simon Knight and typeset by The Write Idea in association with First Edition Translations Ltd, Cambridge, UK

Printed in Italy by Editoriale Lloyd

Authors Aller & Retour
BRUSSELS

Things you need to know:
This section was written in consultation with the personnel of OPT Wallonie-Bruxelles and Toerisme Vlaanderen.

Where to stay: Yannick Penagos (1)
A multi-media reporter and writer, Y. Penagos specializes in tourism, lifestyle topics and local traditions. He has contributed to a number of Everyman and Knopf guides.

Where to eat: Louis Willems (2)
Born at Ixelles in 1928, L. Willems works as a journalist. He joined the staff of the *Libre Belgique* in 1969 and filed reports from many countries before becoming editor of the paper's 'Bonne Table' column, devoted to food and drink. A confirmed gastronome, he helped found the magazines *Ambiance* and *Culinaire*, of which he is now editor-in-chief. For the RTBF, he hosts a television program devoted to cookery, and has published many books on this subject.

After dark :
Luc Gilson (3)
A journalist for Belgian television, over the last few years L. Gilson has go to know the shakers and movers of Brussels nightlife. Originally from Wallonia, now settled in Brussels, he casts a fresh eye over the nocturnal activities of his adopted city.

Isabelle Ghislain (4)
A freelance journalist, I. Ghislain has already contributed to many guides and other publications. In love with Brussels, she goes out of her way to help others discover the cultural activities and nightlife of her native city.

What to see and Further afield : Jacques Maget (5)
A journalist with *Touring* magazine, J. Maget is also a photographer and has written many articles on Belgium. Author of a cyclists' guide to Belgium, he has a regular Saturday afternoon spot on RTBF, when he comments on the latest developments in tourism. His special enthusiasms are discovering towns on foot, real food and drink, and the cooks who feature local produce on their menus.

Where to shop : Brigitte Tabary (6)
A journalist who writes the 'Tourisme' and 'Agenda culturel' columns in the women's monthly magazine Gael, B. Tabary has lived in Brussels for the last thirty years – plenty of time to get to know the city's stores and boutiques.

Key

- ☎ telephone number
- fax number
- ● price or price range
- opening hours
- credit cards accepted
- credit cards not accepted
- toll-free number
- @ e-mail/website address
- ★ tips and recommendations

Access

- subway station(s)
- bus
- private parking
- parking attendant
- no facilities for the disabled
- train
- car
- boat

Hotels

- telephone in room
- fax in room on request
- minibar in room
- television in room
- air-conditioned rooms
- 24-hour room service
- caretaker
- babysitting
- meeting room(s)
- no pets
- breakfast
- open for tea/coffee
- restaurant
- live music
- disco
- garden, patio or terrace
- gym, fitness club
- swimming pool, sauna

Restaurants

- vegetarian food
- view
- formal dress required
- smoking area
- bar

Museums and galleries

- on-site store(s)
- guided tours
- café

Stores

- branches, outlets

The Insider's Guide is made up of **9 sections** each indicated by a different color.

Things you need to know (mauve)
Where to stay (blue)
Where to eat (red)
After dark (pink)
What to see (green)
Further afield (orange
Where to shop (yellow
Finding your way (purp
Business factfile (whit

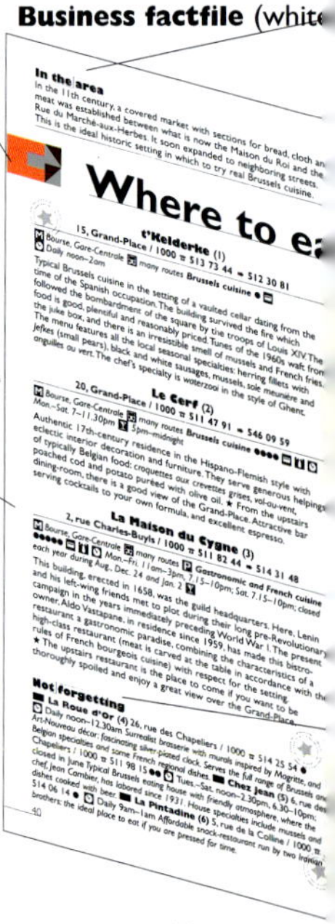

Practical information is given for each particular establishment: opening times, prices, ways of paying, different services available

"Good value!" The star sign indicates modestly priced hotels and restaurants.

How to use this guide

> **In the area**
> In the 11th century, a covered meat was established between

> Where to stay
> After dark ➥ 62 ➥ 64
> to see ➥ 80 ➥ 82

The section **"In the area"** refers you (➥ 00) to other establishments that are covered in a different section of the guide but found in the same area of the city.

> **Grand-Place** **A** B2

The small map shows all the establishments mentioned and others described elsewhere but found "in the area", by the color of the section.

The name of the district is given above the map. A grid reference (**A** B-C 2) enables you to find it in the section on Maps at the end of the book.

> ood: *croquettes aux crevettes grises*
> tato puréed with olive oil. ★ Fr

Hot tips, indicated by a star ★, contains advice from the author: the best rooms, recommended dishes, views not to be missed…

> **Not forgetting**
> **La Roue d'Or (4)** 26, rue

The section "Not forgetting" lists other useful addresses in the same area..

The opening page to each section contains an index ordered alphabetically (Getting there), by subject or by district (After dark) as well as useful addresses and advice.

The section "Things you need to know" covers information on getting to Brussels and day-to-day life in the city.

Theme pages introduce a selection of establishments on a given topic.

The "Maps" section of this guide contains 6 street plans of Brussels followed by a detailed index.

Time difference

Belgium is 1 hour ahead of GMT. At noon in Belgium it is 11am in London and 6am in New York, except for short periods in March and October, when the clocks change.

Getting there

Electricity supply

As in other European countries, the mains supply is 220 volts, and wall sockets are two-pin. You will therefore need an adaptor for an electric razor or other appliance.

Public holidays

Public holidays in Belgium are the same as in other Catholic countries. The National Holiday is July 21, the festival of the French Community September 27. On these days most stores and businesses close, though museums are open.

Belgian Tourist Office in the UK
24h/24h information and brochure line ☎ 0891 887799 ➡ 020 7629 0454
Belgian Tourist Office in the US
780 Third Avenue, Suite 1501, New York, NY 10017 ☎ 212 758 8130
➡ 212 355 7675

40 Things you need to know

Formalities
All visitors, except citizens of the EU with a national identity card, must have a valid passport. The expiry date of US passports must not be earlier than three months after the date of departure from Belgium.

Health
Citizens of the EU should take an E111 form, in case urgent medical treatment is needed while in Belgium ➡ 15. Other visitors should have appropriate medical insurance.

Motorists
Motorists must carry a driver's license, vehicle registration document, green card insurance, first aid kit and red triangle.

INDEX A-Z

Basic facts

Thanks to Eurostar, Brussels is only 3h 15 mins from London. Amsterdam, Cologne and Paris are easily accessible by the Thalys network. The Belgian capital is also connected by high-speed (TGV) train services, via Lille, with major French cities (Lyons, Montpellier, Rennes, Bordeaux).

Getting there

By train
Eurostar

Undoubtedly the most convenient and comfortable means of reaching Brussels from London. Fares are similar to those of scheduled airlines but do check on availability of leisure, excursion and weekend tickets at much reduced prices. The journey takes 3h15min. Check-in closes 20 mins before departure. Reservations are essential. Up to 10 departures Mon.–Sat. (8 Sun.) from Waterloo International, London.

☎ 0990 186 186
From outside UK
00 + 44 123 3617 575
@ *http://www.eurostar.com*

In Brussels
Eurostar information
☎ *08 36 35 35 39*

Thalys

A practical high-speed rail network set up by the French, Belgian, German and Dutch railroad companies, linking destinations in these countries at very competitive prices and with frequent departures. The trains are recognizable by their red livery. Seats must be reserved, and you would do well to book early, especially for the wide range of reduced fares.

Information, reservations

In UK
Rail Europe Travel Centre
179 Piccadilly
London W1V 0BA
☎ 0990 848 848

In Belgium
Information
☎ *0800 95 777 (freephone)*
Reservations
☎ *0900 10 177 (6.05 BEF/12 s)*
🕒 *Mon.–Fri. 7am–9pm; Sat., Sun. 9am–5.30pm*

Reservations can be made at approved travel agents and at the ticket offices of major railroad stations.

Reaching the center of Brussels

By train
Just take a northward-bound SNCB train (in the direction of Namur, Antwerp, Liège, Ghent or the airport). The same trains also stop at the Bruxelles-Nord, Quartier-Léopold and Schuman stations. Thalys tickets are also valid for the onward journey from the Gare du Midi to the Gare Centrale (550 yds from the Grande-Place).
Journey time: 5 to 12 mins.

By taxi
There are two taxi ranks, one on your right if you take the Rue de France exit from the Gare du Midi; the other also on your right if you take the Avenue de Fonsny exit.

By subway, bus or tram
There is a subway entrance in the main hall of the station itself, and another at the Avenue Fonsny exit. Bus and tram stops are in the Rue Couverte.
Journey time: 10 to 20 mins.

By car
There are car rental agencies in the main hall of the Gare du Midi, in the Eurostar, Thalys and TGV arrivals area.

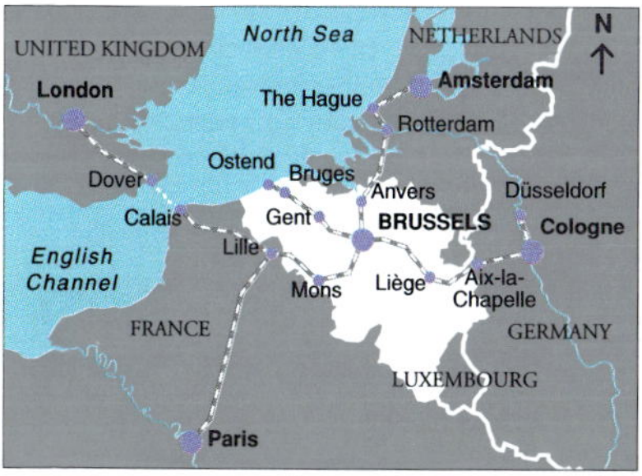

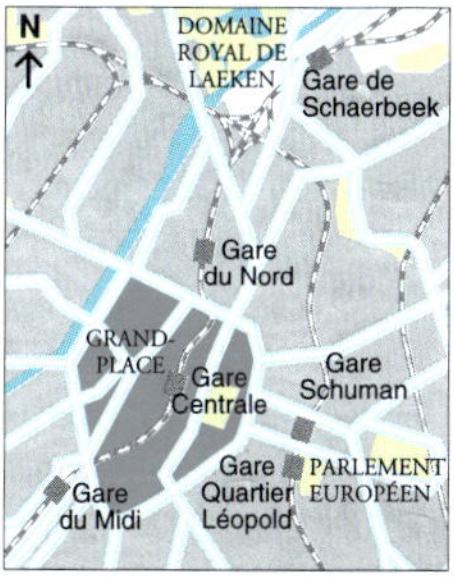

Avis
☎ *527 17 05*
➠ *539 13 62*
Europcar
☎ *522 95 73*
➠ *522 85 21*
Hertz
☎ *524 31 00*
➠ *523 88 61*

SNCB

General information (Société nationale des chemins de fer belges)
80, Rue du Progrès/ 1210
The state railways carry passenger traffic within Belgium and to destinations abroad.
International number
☎ *08 36 35 35 35 (2.23 FRF/min)*
The logo of the SNCB is a blue 'B' in a blue circle.
There is no point in reserving a seat for journeys within Belgium. Nor do you need to validate your ticket prior to departure, as you do in France.
Bruxelles-Midi (1) (Brussel-Zuid)
2, rue de France / 1070
Arrivals and departures
Eurostar *(to London),* ***Thalys*** *(to Paris, Cologne and Amsterdam)*
Bureau de change
In the main hall, near the Rue de France exit.
Telephones
In the main hall, going toward the Avenue Fonsny exit, and in the secondary hall, near the escalators.
Left luggage
Opposite the Rue de France exit.
Gare Centrale (2) (Centraal Station)
2, carrefour de l'Europe / 1000
550 yds from the Grande-Place *(domestic departures).*
Bruxelles-Nord (3) (Brussel-Noord)
85, rue du Progrès / 1210 (domestic and international departures to the north)
Other stations
In the Bruxelles-Capitale metropolitan area.
Bruxelles-Quartier-Léopold / Léopoldswijk (4) *(departures for Luxembourg)*
Schuman (5) *(for the European Institutions)*
Schaarbeek / Schaerbeek (6) *(for motor-rail and sleeping-car trains)*
Lost property
Inform the next station or the station where your train terminates.
SNCB
☎ *555 25 25*

In UK

Belgian National Railways
10 Greycoat Place, London SW1P 1SB
☎ *020 7233 0360*

Belgian Embassy in US

330 Garfield Street NW, Washington DC 20008
☎ *202-333-6900*
➠ *202-333-3079*

Belgian Embassy in UK

103 Eaton Square, London SW1W 9AB
☎ *020 7470 3700*
➠ *020 7259 6213*

US Embassy in Belgium

Regentlaan 27 / Boulevard du Regent, B-1000 Brussels
☎ *(02) 512 2210*
➠ *(02) 511 9652*

British Embassy in Belgium

85 Rue Arlon, 1040 Brussels
☎ *(02) 287 6211*
➠ *(02) 287 6360*

Basic facts

Both British Airways and Sabena have frequent scheduled flights between London (Heathrow and Gatwick) and Brussels. Sabena also has regular flights from London City Airport. Flying time is about 1h. There are direct daily flights to Brussels from most of the main gateway cities in the US.

Getting there

Arriving by air

Information

Switchboard
☎ 723 23 45
🕒 24h/24h

Departures and arrivals information
🕒 *7am–10pm*
☎ *753 39 13*
Office in the departure hall.

Customs
☎ *753 48 50*

Airport police
☎ *753 70 00*

Lost luggage
(lost in terminal). In the arrivals hall, near the luggage carousels.
🕒 *8am–4pm*
(lost on the aircraft)
☎ *723 39 29*
☎ *(lost in the airport)*
753 68 20

Gendarmerie
☎ *753 25 05*

Left luggage
☎ *723 06 16*
Level 0, on the left coming from the terminal via the Diamant.
● *100 to 300 BEF for 24h*

Duty-free
Level 2, in the arrivals hall; since July 1999, restricted to non-EU travelers.
● *Maximum permitted value: 90 EURO (3,800 BEF/ 92 USD)*

Postal services
Arrivals hall
🕒 *Mon.–Fri. 8am–7pm*
☎ *720 07 36*

Telephones
Coin-operated booths are difficult to find. Telephone cards (Télécard) are on sale at airport news-stands.

Bureaux de change
You can change money in the departure and arrivals halls, and near the luggage carousels and duty-free store. There are cash dispensers in the arrivals hall and on the Promenade.

Airlines

From the US
Sabena Belgian World Airlines
☎ *800-955-2000*
American Airlines
☎ *800-433-7300*
United Airlines
☎ *800-241-6522*
Delta Airlines
☎ *800-241-4141*
Continental Airlines
☎ *800-525-0280*

From the UK

British Airways
Frequent departures from Heathrow and Gatwick

In London
Reservations
☎ *0345 222111*
Flight information
☎ *0990 444000*
🕒 *24h/24h*

Sabena
Frequent departures from Heathrow and Gatwick.

In London
☎ *020 8780 1444*
➟ *020 8780 1502*

In Brussels
☎ *511 90 30*
☎ *723 23 23*
Reservations
☎ *509 25 11*
At the airport
☎ *723 60 10*

Getting to the city center

By train
The Airport City Express service links the airport with Bruxelles-Nord, Bruxelles-Midi and Bruxelles-Centrale stations. Tickets can be bought at the station ticket offices or at the airport (level 0).

Information
☎ *733 24 40*
🕒 *5.30am–11.45pm. Trains depart every 15 mins, in either direction. Traveling time 15 to 25 mins.*
● *1st class one-way 140 BEF, 2nd class one-way 90 BEF. Tickets cannot be purchased on the train.*

By bus
Hotels and tour operators run shuttles; local authorities in the outlying areas run their own bus services. The terminus is under the arrivals hall (access by elevator from the Diamant). There are no bus services into the city center; take the train.

Flying time varies according to the location of the airport. It is also possible to fly direct to Paris and major French cities.

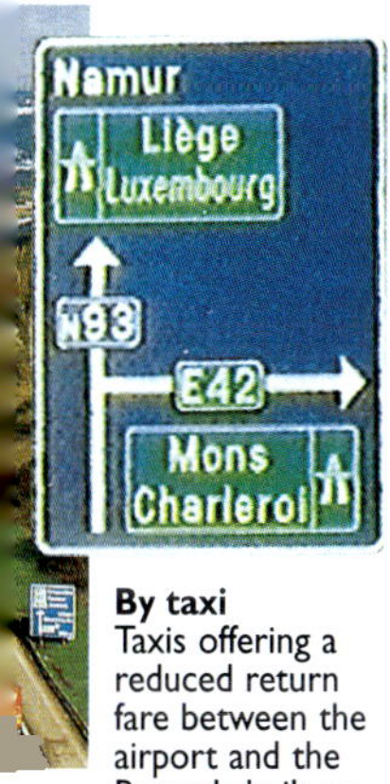

By taxi
Taxis offering a reduced return fare between the airport and the Brussels built-up area (valid for two months) are distinguished by a square sticker in the upper right-hand corner of the windshield showing a white airplane on an orange background. The taxi rank is at the exit from the arrivals hall. It is advisable to take a licensed taxi (blue and yellow sticker).
● *The ride from the airport to the city center costs approximately 1,000 BEF*

Airport hotels

Sheraton Brussels Airport
Aéroport de Bruxelles-National / 1930 Zaventem
☎ 725 10 00
➠ 725 11 55
● 10,400 BEF to 12,400 BEF
Within walking distance of the airport.

Sofitel Brussels Airport
15, Bessenveldstraat 1831 Diegem
☎ 713 65 56
➠ 721 43 45
● 9,500 BEF
On a bus route into the city center.

Novotel Brussels Airport
1, Olmenstraat / 1831 Diegem
☎ 725 30 50
➠ 721 39 58
● 2,500 BEF to 5,450 BEF
Free shuttle service from the airport.

Holiday Inn Brussels Airport
7, Holydaystraat / 1831 Diegem
☎ 720 58 65
➠ 720 41 45
● 3,300 BEF to 9,390 BEF
Free shuttle service from the airport.

Car rental

Agencies are located together in the arrivals hall.

Avis
☎ 720 09 44
➠ 725 93 35
⏲ Daily 6.30am–11.30pm

Budget Rent-a-Car
☎ 720 80 50
➠ 721 19 70
⏲ Daily 7.30am–11pm

Eurodollar / ABC
☎ 753 24 82
➠ 753 24 80
⏲ Daily 7.30am–9pm

Europcar
☎ 721 11 78
➠ 725 79 24
⏲ Daily 6.30am–11.30pm

Hertz
☎ 720 60 44
➠ 720 36 36
⏲ Daily 6.30am–11pm

By bus

Eurolines
Two (three July, August) departures daily. Journey takes about 10h but it is the cheapest way to reach Brussels from London. Check in 1h before departure.

Information and reservations
For debit/credit card bookings
☎ 0990 14 32 19
⏲ Mon.– Sat. 8.30am–7pm
@ http://eurolines.co.uk

Europabus
The Belgian agency of Eurolines.
80, rue du Progrès / 1210
Ⓜ Nord
☎ 253 52 05
➠ 253 66 94
⏲ Mon.–Fri. 9am–6pm

Via the Channel Tunnel

Cars go on purpose-built carriers between Folkestone and Calais. The UK terminal is situated off junction 11A on the M20. The French terminal is reached via junction 13 on the A16 motorway. The journey time is 35 minutes platform to platform. 24h/24h service; fares vary depending on time and date. It is advisable to book ahead, especially at peak times.
Le Shuttle
☎ 01303 273 300
0990 51 52 53
0990 35 35 35
Brussels is served by national motorways A1, A3, A4, A7, A10 and A12. Belgian motorways are free, illuminated at night and signposted in green. Brussels is approached from the southwest by the N5 and N6 national highways. The speed limit is 75mph on motorways, 56mph on other roads, and 30mph in built-up areas. In the Brussels area, towns may be indicated by their Flemish names on signposts, for example: Paris (Parÿs), Lille (Rijsel), Mons (Bergen), Brussels (Brussel), Liège (Luik), Namur (Namen) and Antwerp (Antwerpen).

Basic facts

Brussels has an excellent public transport network. The eastern and western districts are linked by subway, and the lines are extended by a 'Pré-Métro' system of trams running underground. At street level, the whole city is covered by tram and bus routes. In the historic center, the most

Getting around

STIB (MIVB)

(Société de transports intercommunaux bruxellois)
This company runs public transport (subways, buses and trams) in the Bruxelles-Capitale metropolitan area.

Informations STIB sales agencies
In subway and 'Pré-Métro' stations.

Midi
M *Gare du Midi*
Mon.–Fri. 7.30am–5pm; on the first Sunday of each month 8am–2pm

Anspach
M *De Brouckère*
31, rue de l'Évêque / 1000
Mon.–Fri. 8.30am–5.15pm; Sat. 11am–6pm

Rogier
M *Rogier*
Mon.–Fri. 8.30am–5.15pm; Sat. 9.30am–5.15pm

Porte de Namur
M *Porte de Namur*
Mon.–Fri. 8.30am–5.15pm; Sat. 9.30am–5.15pm

A map of the network is available free of charge from subway stations, information offices and tourist reception centers. Public transport is generally operative from 6am to midnight. Buses do not run after this time.

Tickets
With one ticket, you can transfer between the subway, buses and trams for a period of one hour. Tickets can be purchased at subway stations, at STIB sales agencies, from news-stands, some newsagents, tourist reception centers (OPT and TIB ➡ 15 only one-day-travel and ten-journey cards) and even at the Thalys bar and on Eurostar trains.

- *ticket for a one-way journey: 50 BEF, for ten journeys: 340 BEF, for a whole day: 130 BEF. There are also monthly travel cards, useful for longer visits.*

Subway

Subway stations are indicated by the 'M' symbol (white on a blue background).

Subway art
For the last twenty years, contemporary artists have been invited to decorate the Belgian subway system. Individual stations bear the stamp of Pol Bury, Jean-Michel Folon, Pierre Alechinsky, Christian Dotremont, and others. Comic strips also feature prominently. The walls of the Stockel station were painted with lively frescos of familiar characters by the Hergé Studios. At Porte-de-Hal, Schuiten expresses its remarkable vision of the city. *Brochures are available free of charge from the OPT, the TIB, and STIB information offices. There are also guided tours run by STIB guides (by appointment).*

Buses and trams

Though slower than the subway during rush hours, buses and trams enable you to get to know the city. Stops are indicated by a red and white sign but you need to signal to the driver. The 'Pré-Métro' is an underground tram system designed to avoid congestion in the city center.

Taxis

There are taxi ranks in many locations (railroad stations, hotels and near the Grand-Place), or you can call for a taxi.

Fares
- ***Basic charge*** *95 BEF (with a supplement of 75*

pleasant way to get around is on foot or by bicycle.

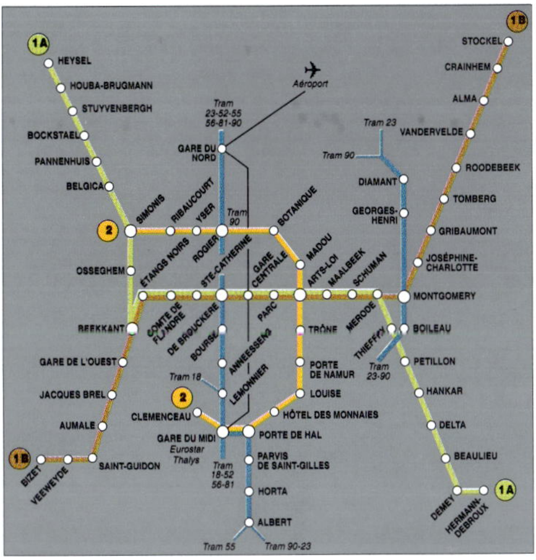

BEF at night)

Fare per km (0.6 mile)

38 BEF in the Brussels built-up area, 76 BEF outside city limits

One hour's waiting

600 BEF

Tipping

Service is included in the fare shown on the taximeter, but it is normal to round this up.

Complaints

CCN-Service régional des taxis et limousines
80, rue du Progrès, bât. 1, niv. 15 / 1030

Taxi companies

🕒 **24h/24h**

ATR
☎ *647 22 22*

Autolux
☎ *411 41 42*

Taxis Bleus
☎ *268 00 00*

Taxis Orange
☎ *513 62 00*

Taxis Verts
☎ *349 49 49*

By bicycle and on water

Bicycle hire

Pro Vélo
Ⓜ Porte de Namur
32 A, rue Ernest-Solvay / 1050
☎ *502 73 55*
➠ *502 86 41*
🕒 *Mon.–Fri. 9am–6pm*
Guided tours.

By boat

Cruises on the canals of Brussels and the Brabant region.

Brussels by Water
2 bis, quai des Péniches / 1000
☎ *420 59 20*
➠ *420 59 21*

Driving in Brussels

Avoid the Petite Ceinture (inner circle of boulevards), the Ring Road (the orbital road taking in the outer suburbs) and motorway access roads during rush hours (8–10am / 5–7pm). It is difficult to find a parking place around the Bourse and the Avenue Louise. Use underground parking lots.

Parking lots

🕒 24h/24h
● *390 BEF/24h*

Agora (Grand-Place)
104, rue du Marché-aux-Herbes / 1000
☎ *513 33 18*

Monnaie
Place de la Monnaie / 1000
☎ *217 04 67*

Pœlaert
Rue E.-Allard, place Poelaert / 1000
🕒 *Mon.–Sat. 7am–8pm, Sun. 10am–7pm*

Traffic information

Gendarmerie
☎ *642 66 66*

Radio frequencies
Radio 21 : 93,2
Première : 92,5

Roadside assistance

Royal Automobile Club de Belgique
53, rue d'Arlon / 1040
☎ *287 09 11/12*

SOS dépannage
☎ *(078) 15 20 00*

Touring Club de Belgique
44, rue de la Loi / 1040
☎ *233 22 11*

Touring secours
☎ *(070) 34 47 77*

Getting out of Brussels

By train

Train times and information
☎ *555 25 25*

The main towns of Belgium are served by Intercity (IC) and Interregional (IR) SNCB trains, which are scheduled to leave at the same time every hour. In the tourist season, there are direct trains from Brussels to the Belgian coast and the Ardennes.

● *To save money on day trips, get a 'B-Excursion' ticket, which includes the cost of transportation and admittance to a tourist attraction.*

By bus

The SNCB rail network is complemented by the TEC (Walloon Brabant) and DeLijn (Flemish Brabant) bus networks.

TEC
☎ *010 23 53 53*

DeLijn
☎ *526 28 28*

Basic facts

Most stores and other establishments are open from Monday to Saturday, 9am–6pm, often with a lunch break between noon and 2pm. Post offices and banks close early in the afternoon, as well as on Saturdays and Sundays. However, most have cash dispensers. Be warned:

Getting by

Money

You can withdraw money from cash dispensers, or pay bills with a credit card. If your card is lost or stolen, contact:

American Express
◷ *24h/24*
☎ *676 23 23*

Visa, Mastercard and Eurocard
◷ *24h/24*
☎ *70 34 43 55*

Currency

The unit of currency is the Belgian franc (BEF). Notes come in 100, 200, 500, 1,000, 2,000 and 10,000 BEF denominations. There are also _, 1, 5, 20 and 50 BEF coins.

Changing money

● *£1 = c. 61 BEF; 1 EURO = c. 40.33 BEF; $1 = c. 35 BEF. Banks charge a commission ranging from 100 to 1,000 BEF, depending on the amount changed, so it is advisable to use cash dispensers or bureaux de change (commission ranging from 55 to 400 BEF).*

Best Change
2, rue de la Colline / 1000
◷ *24h/24*
☎ *511 45 53*

Gare Centrale
◷ *daily 7am–9pm*
☎ *511 46 96*

Gare du Midi
◷ *daily 6.45am–10pm*
☎ *521 12 84*

Gare du Nord
◷ *Daily 7am–10pm*
☎ *203 39 14*

Générale de Banque
12, rue de la Colline / 1000
☎ *513 02 47*

GWK change
88, rue du Marché-aux-Herbes / 1000
☎ *502 23 82*

Banks
◷ *Mon.–Fri. 9am–3.30pm*
Outside the city center, some banks are open on Saturday mornings.

Tipping

Service is included in restaurant and hotel prices and in taxi fares. Still it is acceptable to give a tip as a way of showing your appreciation.

The media

Belgian newspapers

Belgium embraces three communities – French-speaking, Flemish-speaking and German-speaking – which explains why there are so many newspapers, although the trend is toward concentration.

French-language dailies

Le Soir, La Libre Belgique and *La Dernière Heure.*

Flemish-language dailies

Het Laaste Nieuws, De Standaard and *De Morgen.*

German-language dailies

The most important is *Grenz Echo.*

Others

The International Herald Tribune, Wall Street Journal and British dailies. *The Bulletin* is an English-language weekly, sold mainly in Brussels.

International news agencies

News agencies center on the European institutions.

International Press Centre (IPC)
1, bd Charlemagne / 1040
☎ *285 08 00*

Radio

There are three national radio stations: RTBF (serving the French-speaking community), Radio 1 (Flemish-speaking) and BRF (German-speaking).

Television

National channels

French community: RTBF, Sport 21 and Arte.
Flemish-speaking community: TV1 and TV2.
Local channel: TV Bruxelles.

Commercial channels

RTL-Tvi (French language), VTM and TV4 (Flemish). Cable:

on July 21, the National Holiday, banks and shops are closed. But museums stay open.

34 programs can be received.

Tourist offices

Tourist reception and information office (OPT...) (1)
Maison du tourisme
63, rue du Marché-aux-Herbes / 1000
☎ *504 03 90*
➠ *504 02 70*
@ *www.belgique-tourisme.net ; www.toervl.be*
🕒 *Mon.–Fri. 9am–6pm; Sat., Sun. 9am–1pm, 2–6pm / July, Aug. closes daily at 7pm / Nov.–Apr. closes on Sunday afternoons.*
M *Gare-Centrale*
Tourist office for Brussels and the whole of Belgium.

TIB – Brussels tourist information office (2)
Hôtel de ville, Grand-Place / 1000
☎ *513 89 40*
➠ *514 45 38*
🕒 *Daily 9am–6pm (except in winter: Sun. 10am–2pm)*

Lost property

For items lost in public places, contact the district police station or the **Division Centrale de Bruxelles (3)**
30, rue du Marché-au-Charbon / 1000
☎ *517 96 11*
For items lost on buses, trams or in the subway:
STIB lost property office
15, avenue de la Toison-d'Or / 1050
☎ *515 23 94*

Telephones

Belgacom headquarters
17, bd de l'Impératrice / 1000
☎ *540 60 11*

Dialing codes

Dial 02 for the Bruxelles-Capitale metropolitan area when calling from elsewhere. Within the area, simply dial the seven-digit number.

Between Brussels and the UK/US

Calls to the UK from Brussels: 00 + 44 + STD code (without initial 0) + local number.
Calls to the US from Brussels: 00 + 1 + area code + seven-digit number.
Calls to Brussels from the UK and US: 00 or 010 + 32 + 2 + seven-digit number.

Operator services

National directory inquiries
☎ *1307*
International directory inquiries
☎ *1304*
Operator-connected international calls
☎ *1324*

Public telephones

Coin-operated telephones (20 BEF) are now few and far between. Buy a telephone card (Télécard) from a news-stand, post office or railroad station. Call rates are displayed in telephone booths.

Internet

Cyber Théâtre
➡ **64**
Avenue de la Toison-d'Or / 1000
A large café where you can surf the net.
Some hotels have facilities for receiving e-mail.
● *Self-service Internet connections.*

Postal services

Post offices

🕒 *Mon.–Fri. 9am–5pm*
Some offices are open on Friday evenings and Saturday mornings.

Central post office (4)

Place de la Monnaie
🕒 *Mon.–Sat. 8am–8pm*

Stamps

● *17 BEF for mail to EU countries*

Info-poste

☎ *226 23 10*

Alcohol

You have to be over 18 to buy or drink alcoholic liquor.

Emergency services

Fire and ambulance
☎ *100*
Police and gendarmerie
☎ *101*
Red Cross
☎ *105*
Duty doctors
☎ *479 18 18*
Emergency dentists
☎ *426 10 26*
☎ *428 58 88*

Where to stay

'Aparthôtels'
Self-catering studios and apartments. Convenient for frequent or long stays. Very popular with the staff of European institutions and multinational companies.

• *For a two-room apartment, one night: 2,500 to 5,400 BEF, one week: 15,000 to 34,000 BEF, one month: 40,000 to 120,000 BEF.*

Les Citadines
61–63, avenue de la Toison-d'Or / 1050
☎ 543 53 53 ➠ 543 53 00.

Aparthotel Lambermont
18, allée des Freesias / 1030
☎ 246 02 11 ➠ 246 02 00

Résidence Parnasse
8, rue d'Italie / 1050
☎ 505 98 00 ➠ 505 99 00

Résidence Sabina
78, rue du Nord / 1000
☎ 218 26 37 ➠ 219 32 39

Many hotels also offer self-catering accommodation.

No need to pay over the odds

Brussels has hotels to suit every taste and pocket. If you are on a tight budget, check out some of the addresses below. Bed & Breakfasts, youth hostels (*jeugdherberg* in Flemish) and *centres d'hébergement* (budget accommodation) offer clean, simple facilities at affordable prices.

42 Hotels

THE INSIDER'S FAVORITES

Youth hostels

● *with set meal and double room for the night: 550 BEF/person* [breakfast] *included*

Auberge de jeunesse Bruegel
2, rue du Saint-Esprit / 1000
☎ 511 04 36 ➡ 512 07 11

Auberge de jeunesse Jacques-Brel
30, rue de la Sablonnière / 1000
☎ 218 01 87 ➡ 217 20 05 [wheelchair access]

Auberge de jeunesse Jean-Nihon
4, rue de l'Éléphant / 1080
☎ 410 38 58 ➡ 410 39 05

Centres d'hébergement

● *double room for the night: 520 to 570 BEF/person* [breakfast] *included*

Hôtel de jeunes-Sleepwell
Espace du Marais, 23, rue du Damier / 1000 ☎ 218 50 50 ➡ 218 13 13

Centre Vincent-Van-Gogh
8, rue Traversière / 1030
☎ 217 01 58 ➡ 219 79 95

Bed & Breakfast

An inexpensive friendly solution, staying in a private house.

● *double room for the night: 1,500 to2,700 BEF, depending on facilities* [breakfast] *included*

Bed & Brussels
2, rue Gustave-Biot / 1050
☎ 646 07 37 ➡ 644 01 14
@ www.BnB-Brussels.be ;
E-mail : BnBru@IBM.net
Around a hundred addresses in Brussels and its suburbs.

Bed & Breakfast-Taxistop
28, rue du Fossé-aux-Loups / 1000
☎ 223 22 31 ➡ 223 22 32
@ www.taxistop.belf
Addresses in all parts of Belgium.

International campsite

● *200 BEF (space) + 200 BEF/person/ night* [clock] *ouvert July-Aug*
205, chaussée de Wavre / 1050
☎ 640 79 67 ➡ 648 24 53

INDEX BY PRICE

5 LEVELS OF HOTEL PRICES
Double rooms in the tourist season
● less than 3,200 BEF
●● 3,200–4,300 BEF
●●● 4,400–6,500 BEF
●●●● 6,600–10,000 BEF
●●●●● more than 10,000 BEF

In the area

A capital city of charm and tradition, Brussels still has its secrets and surprises. Some hotels, like the famous Amigo, located in the old city center, invite you to explore the heart of the place. Not a stone's throw from the Grand-Place, and the city, chocolate and lace museums.

Where to stay

a

b

c

d

Châteaux et Hôtels de Charme - ILA Group

6, chaussée de Boondael / 1050 ☎ 647 29 23 ➟ 647 42 51
@ www.ILA-chateau.com

Bruges: hotel ***De Tuilerieen*** *(a), hotel* ***De Orangerie*** *(b) and hotel* ***Prinsenhof*** *(c); Brussels: hotel* ***Amigo*** *(d and 1 on facing page); Berlare–Ghent: hotel* ***Briel***

The International Lodging Association was the brainchild of a former pupil of the Paris hotel school and former luxury hotel and restaurant owner, Richard C. Cabouret, who still manages the organization. The ILA is an association of establishments offering that indefinable extra something which distinguishes them from their rivals. And the founder still scours the countryside to find the 'right' hotel owners. The final selection depends very much on cuisine, environment and level of comfort. 'I tend to look for strengths, rather than applying fixed criteria,' he explains. His role is to point you to the hotels where he feels comfortable, basing his choice on his own experience and sensitivity. The association includes 200 hotels in Europe, the United States, Canada and Africa – a selection of establishments managed by caring professionals wanting to offer you the best possible service with modesty, courtesy and a smile, all in a convivial atmosphere. If you love old castles, unusual places, charming hotels and doing your own thing, have a look at the ILA brochure, or visit their web-site, to make your choice and book an unforgettable vacation.

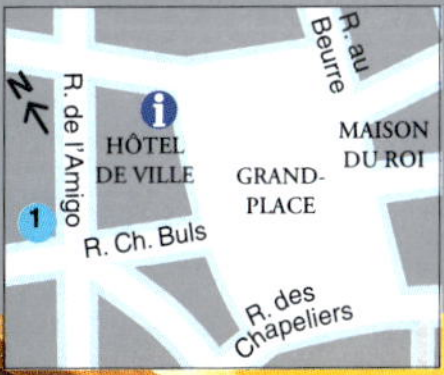

L'amigo (1)

1-3, rue de l'Amigo / 1000 ☎ 547 47 47 ➠ 513 52 77

Bourse *many routes* ***178 rooms*** *(7 suites)* ●●●● *included*

www.hotelamigo.com

This was the name given by the Spanish occupiers to the state prison which once stood on this site. They confused the Flemish word *vrunte*, which means 'lock-up' with *vriend – amigo* in Spanish. It was not until the 20th century that the cold cells were replaced by the comfortable rooms of one of the city's most elegant hotels, which stands in an extension of the Grand-Place. The modern visitor, entering the opulent interior, receives a friendly, courteous welcome. The Spanish Renaissance atmosphere is enhanced by Flemish and Aubusson tapestries, and paintings by Dutch and Italian masters. The signatures in the visitors' book bear witness to the frequent visits of international celebrities. The spacious apartments are decorated with taste and elegance in the Louis XV and Louis XVI styles. Close your door and you lose all sense of being in a hotel. The height of luxury is to occupy the suite on the sixth floor, with its terrace and splendid view of the Gothic spire of the Hôtel de Ville (Town Hall). At the Amigo, the affable manager and diligent staff have created an atmosphere that will make your stay an occasion to remember. Book a special-rate romantic weekend to experience the gracious setting and privileged air of a truly great hotel.

In the area

Here we are on the Grand-Place, the finest theater in the world according to Jean Cocteau. It was here that Arthur Rimbaud and Paul Verlaine first met, on July 10, 1873. And it was in the Maison des Brasseurs that Verlaine eventually shot and wounded his friend. ■ Where to eat ➥ 40 ➥ 42

Where to stay

Sema Hôtel (2)

6-8, rue des Harengs / 1000 ☎ 514 07 60 ➠ 548 90 39

M *Gare-Centrale* *many routes* ***11 rooms*** *(1 suite)* ●● *included*

Eleven comfortable rooms, including a suite with its own terrace, have been created in this old private house, which derives its warm atmosphere from wooden beams, good lighting and quality fabrics. Its trump cards are a pleasant, restful setting, privacy and a central location in a cobbled lane at the very heart of old Brussels.

Mozart (3)

15a, rue du Marché-aux-Fromages / 1000 ☎ 502 66 61 ➠ 502 77 58

M *Gare-Centrale* *many routes* ***47 rooms*** ● *included*

The Rue du Marché aux Fromages with its restaurants and café terraces may be a busy place, but the moment you enter the hotel you are in an oasis of calm. As you might expect from the name, the strains of classical music greet you in the newly designed reception area. A wealth of reproduction furniture, exposed beams and copies of Old Masters adorn the hotel's corridors and 47 standard rooms, which are served by elevator.

Aris (4)

78-80, rue du Marché-aux-Herbes / 1000 ☎ 514 43 00 ➠ 514 01 19

M *Gare-Centrale* *many routes 55 rooms* ●●● *included*

In a privileged position beside the Galeries Saint-Hubert, the Aris was opened only recently, with 55 comfortable, modern rooms. The sense of newness combined with the sobriety of contemporary furniture and fresh green plants creates a pleasant atmosphere. ★ Some of the rooms on the top floor have views over the old center of Brussels and a corner of the Grand-Place.

Matignon (5)

10-12, rue de la Bourse / 1000 ☎ 511 08 88 ➠ 513 69 27

M *Bourse* *many routes* ***37 rooms*** ●● *included*

Near the Bourse, on the same side of the street as the celebrated Le Cirio brasserie, the Matignon is a quiet, pleasant hotel right in the city center. Recently refurbished in a simple, traditional style, the comfortable bedrooms are decorated in pastel shades. Some have a mezzanine level with two extra beds, to accommodate four people. Its excellent quality/price ratio and prominent position make this hotel one of the most sought in its category. The ground-floor brasserie has a good-quality menu, and murals based on posters by Toulouse-Lautrec.

Not forgetting

■ **La Légende (6)** 35, rue du Lombard / 1000 ☎ 512 82 90 ➠ 512 34 93
●● *La Légende, completely modernized and refurbished, is within a stone's throw of Mannekin-pis. The façade has been renovated and the 26 bedrooms equipped with double glazing and new furniture. Discreet comfort in a district of major hotels.*

After dark ➥ 62 ➥ 64 ➥ 70 ➥ 72 What to see ➥ 80 ➥ 82 Where to shop ➥ 126 ➥ 128 ➥ 130 ➥ 138

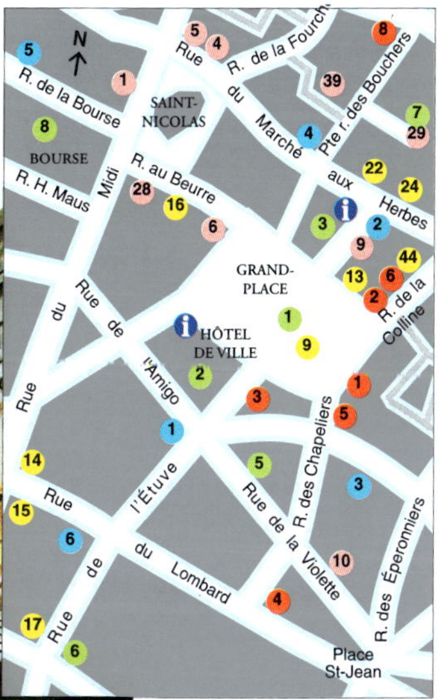

2

A portrait of Mozart graces the hotel that bears his name. Classical music also contributes to the atmosphere of dignified charm.

4

5

In the area

Right by the central rail station, the cathedral of Saints-Michel-et-Gudule, which Victor Hugo called the purest expression of Gothic architecture, is now isolated from the district it served. You can visit the Romanesque crypt, where the relics of Saint Gudule are preserved. ■ Where to

Where to stay

Madeleine (7)

22, rue de la Montagne / 1000 ☎ 513 29 73 ➠ 502 13 50

M *Gare-Centrale* *many routes* ***52 rooms*** ●● *included*

A short walk from the Grand-Place, this 17th-century residence has been turned into a no-frills hotel with 52 bedrooms of different sizes. The larger 'executive' rooms are more comfortable and more expensive. Though the Madeleine is rather uninspiring, it has the great advantage of being in the old part of Brussels.

Le Dix-septième (8)

25, rue de la Madeleine / 1000 ☎ 502 57 44 ➠ 502 64 24

M *Gare-Centrale* *many routes* ***24 rooms*** ●●●● *extra*

This gabled building was the residence of a Spanish ambassador in the early 18th century. The reception rooms, decorated with carved wooden medallions, crystal chandeliers and Louis XVI paneling, cast a spell on visitors the moment they cross the threshold. A grand staircase leads to the spacious bedrooms, each named after a famous Belgian painter. They feature antique furniture, parquet floors and curtains and bed-covers in rich, pastel-colored fabrics. There are exposed beams in the bedrooms on the top floor, and sculpted chimney-breasts add to the general air of elegance. A warm welcome and impeccable service complete the picture.

Arenberg (9)

15, rue d'Assaut / 1000 ☎ 501 16 16 ➠ 501 18 18

M *Gare-Centrale* *many routes* P ***155 rooms*** *(6 suites)* ●●●● *included*

This hotel has recently been renovated – with a fair degree of success. The décor is a celebration of the comic strip genre, whose heroes and heroines have sprung off the page to adorn the walls. In corridors and bedrooms, lithographs of front covers and inner pages serve as a reminder that Brussels is the capital of this art form. The Espadon bar/restaurant offers Belgian specialties in a setting dominated by a mural and model of the supersonic airliner from the adventures of *Blake and Mortimer.*

Méridien (10)

3, carrefour de l'Europe / 1000 ☎ 548 42 11 ➠ 548 47 35

M *Gare-Centrale* *many routes* P ***224 rooms*** *(12 suites)* ●●●●● *included*

Standing at the Carrefour de l'Europe, the Méridien is emblematic of Brussels: a cross-roads where northern and southern Europe meet, and ancient and modern clash and mix. The sumptuous, Victorian-style lobby sets the tone with its wealth of marble, shrubs, softly lit lounges and a piano playing in the evening.

Not forgetting

■ **Ibis Grand Place Centre (11)** 100, rue du Marché-aux-Herbes / 1000 ☎ 514 40 40 ➠ 514 50 67 ●●● *A high-class hotel, well situated and efficient.*

stay ➥ 24 ■ Where to eat ➥ 40 ➥ 42 ■ After dark ➥ 62 ➥ 64 ➥ 70 ➥ 72 ■ What to see ➥ 82 ■ Where to shop ➥ 126 ➥ 130 ➥ 138

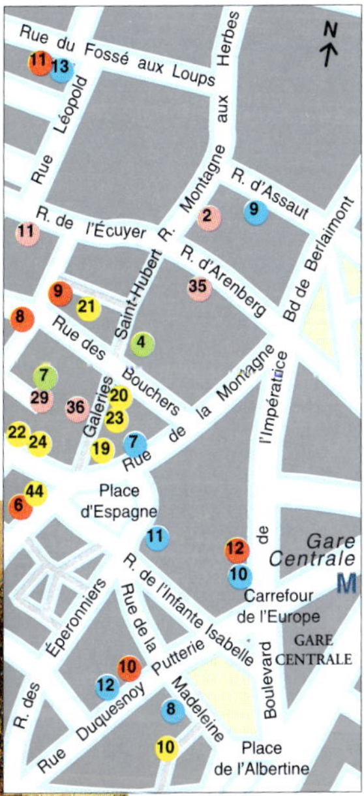

8

10

9

In the area

The curving Rue du Marché-aux-Herbes, in the center of this district, was once the main thoroughfare of the old town. It linked the ducal palace on Coudenberg hill – now the site of the Place Royale – with the River Senne and its port facilities.

Where to stay

Royal Windsor (12)

5, rue Duquesnoy / 1000 ☎ 505 55 55 ➠ 505 55 00

M *Gare-Centrale* *many routes* P **266 rooms** *(40 suites)* ●●●●● *extra* *sauna*

This large hotel stands on the Îlot Sacré, halfway between the Grand-Place and the main railroad station. Service and facilities are perfection itself, with a real concern for all-round excellence. The Royal Windsor belongs to the Leading Hotels of the World chain, well known for its rigorous standards, which guarantee a level of accommodation worthy of a top luxury hotel. Each apartment is decorated in its own style, with the very best in furniture and facilities. * From the window of penthouse room n° 441, there is a view of the Rue du Marché-aux-Fromages and, in the background, the spire of the Hôtel de Ville – an impressive sight when illuminated at night. Begin your evening in the Waterloo piano-bar, then move on to one of the two restaurants (the Windsor Arms or Les 4 Saisons ➠ 42). The round table under the dome is a delightful setting in which to sample the excellent fare in the second of these venues. You can end the evening with a nightcap downstairs in the very chic Griffin's disco.

Radisson SAS (13)

47, rue du Fossé-aux-Loups / 1000 ☎ 227 30 40 ➟ 217 40 85

Gare-Centrale *many routes* ***281 rooms** (18 suites)* ●●●●●
extra *sauna*

Ideally situated within easy walking distance of the comic-strip museum, the Théâtre de la Monnaie and the Grand-Place, reached via the Galeries Royales. Behind its modern façade this luxury hotel offers a welcome fit for an old-fashioned king. Once inside, you find yourself in an air-conditioned garden with a high glass roof and goldfish ponds. The hotel and restaurants are arranged around this naturally lit feature, where vegetation runs riot. Choose your floor and style of accommodation to suit your mood: Scandinavian, Italian or Oriental. Each area is designed with comfort and efficiency in mind: the fitness club with sauna, solarium and jacuzzi; the Bar Dessiné with its comic-strip décor; the Atrium, which offers Belgian and Scandinavian specialties. The Sea Grill ➥ 42 has become one of Belgium's most renowned restaurants, thanks to the skills and advice of the great French chef Yves Mattagne, a specialist in seafood cuisine. At weekends, the hotel offers various discover-Brussels packages at reduced rates (including tours in quest of beer and comic-strip murals).

In the area

Sainte-Catherine and Saint-Géry are swinging districts, with way-out night clubs, cafés and restaurants, the workshops of avant-garde Belgian artists and dynamic boutiques. The old meat market in the Place Saint-Géry, built in 1881, is the last vestige of a former way of life. ■ Where to eat ➥ 44

Where to stay

Welcome (14)

5, rue du Peuplier / 1000 ☎ 219 95 46 ➠ 217 18 87

Sainte-Catherine *many routes* **6 rooms ●** *included* *sauna*

This hotel is managed by Sophie and Michel Smeesters, who proudly claim it to be the smallest in Brussels. (There are plans to increase the number of bedrooms from 6 to 10.) The turn-of-the-century building is kept in perfect order, along with the Truite d'Argent restaurant ➥ 44. A friendly, welcoming hotel offering excellent facilities.

Atlas (15)

30, rue du Vieux-Marché-aux-Grains / 1000 ☎ 502 60 06 ➠ 502 69 35

Sainte-Catherine *many routes* **88 rooms ●●** *included*

The historic Place Sainte-Catherine exerts it charm and the Atlas hotel, which overlooks the square, benefits from the attractive location. Changes are afoot, and it is clear that the management aim to provide a high standard of comfort and service. The immense breakfast room is clean, quiet and well-lit. An interesting feature is its stone wall, a vestige of the town's original fortifications.

Astrid (16)

11, place du Samedi / 1000 ☎ 219 31 19 ➠ 219 31 70

De Brouckère *many routes* **100 rooms ●●●** *included*

This hotel, which opened in 1995, is close to the fish market, a place of bustling activity by day and by night. The rooms are pleasant, the furniture in a contemporary Scandinavian style, the atmosphere friendly. ★ The generous hot and cold buffet provided at breakfast time will set you up for the day's work or sightseeing program.

Noga (17)

38, rue du Béguinage / 1000 ☎ 218 67 63 ➠ 218 16 03

Sainte-Catherine *many routes* **19 rooms ●** *included*

This is a delightful little hotel, efficiently run by a friendly, enthusiastic owner. Frédéric scours the antique shops to find the furniture and artifacts which grace the bedrooms, each beautifully decorated in its own original style. Here is a proprietor who devotes himself entirely to his occupation and the well-being of his customers. The result is a loyal clientele, recruited by personal recommendation: you would do well to book in advance. Apparently, Noga means 'flash of light'.

Not forgetting

■ **Saint-Nicolas (18)** 32, rue du Marché-aux-Poulets / 1000 ☎ 219 04 40 ➠ 219 17 21 ● *An unpretentious but pleasant hotel in a central location, hidden away between the Place Saint-Géry and the Grand-Place. Comfortable rooms with simple décor.*

■ After dark ➥ 68
■ What to see ➥ 82 ➥ 84
■ Where to shop ➥ 126
➥ 132 ➥ 138

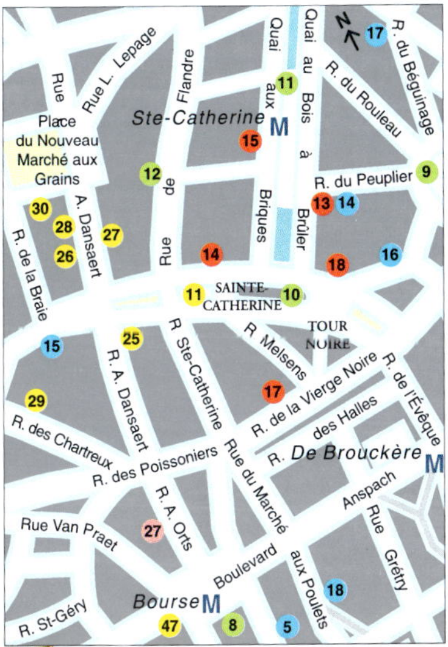

15

17

14

The Noga lays on a buffet breakfast to suit every taste and appetite, from tea or coffee to charcuterie …

16

In the area

In Place de Brouckère, you will no longer find the women in crinolines looking in shop windows nor the omnibuses with men in top hats that Jacques Brel used to sing about. Today, the great thoroughfare created by Burgomaster Anspach in the 18th century is brightly illuminated with

Where to stay

Le Plaza (19)

118-126, boulevard Adolphe-Max / 1000 ☎ 227 67 00 ➠ 227 67 20

Ⓜ *Rogier* *many routes* **P** ***193 rooms*** *(22 suites)* ●●●●● *included*

@ *RESERVATIONS@leplaza-brussels.be*

This palace, built in 1930 on the lines of the George V hotel in Paris, was a favorite with French film stars of the Signoret/Jouvet era, and even welcomed Winston Churchill and his famous cigar. Renovated throughout in 1996, it now boasts 193 very elegant, spacious rooms, furnished in the Louis-Philippe style and fitted with modern communications equipment. Quality fabrics, period paneling, gleaming bathrooms and faultless service earn high marks for this hotel, which has achieved an intelligent mix of authenticity and modernity: marble tiles, sumptuous chandeliers, a real Gobelin tapestry in the lobby, and the bar-restaurant with its trompe-l'œil cupola. The management team and attentive staff go out of their way to ensure that you enjoy your stay. The adjacent auditorium of the old Plaza theater, with its balcony and loggias in the Andalusian style, has been transformed into an amazing reception area to complement the very fine basement rooms. Special terms for weekend visits.

shop signs and attracts a cosmopolitan crowd.

■ Where to eat ➥ 48

■ After dark ➥ 64 ➥ 66 ➥ 72

22

20

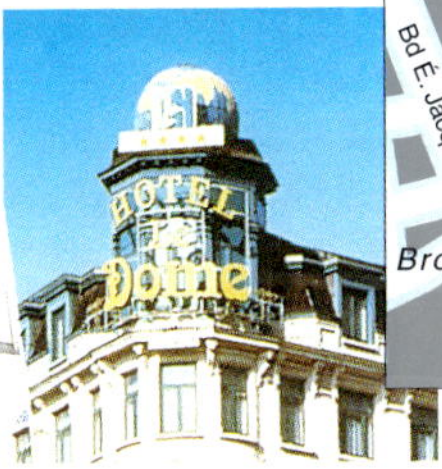

21

Art Hôtel Siru (20)

1, place Rogier / 1000 ☎ 203 35 80 ➡ 203 33 03

M *Rogier* *many routes* P ***101 rooms*** ●●● *included* *608, 708*

The owners have made this hotel into a gallery of contemporary art – not just a place to spend the night. Behind the neon-lit façade by Fernand Flauch are 101 original rooms in which Belgian artists and craftsmen have been given a free hand. A comfortable hotel with a difference.

Dome I et II (21)

12-13, boulevard du Jardin-Botanique / 1000 ☎ 219 41 61 ➡ 218 41 12

M *Rogier* *many routes* ***125 rooms*** *(15 suites)* ●●● *included*

The majestic Art-Nouveau façade of this building, erected in 1902, overlooks the Place Rogier. A south wind seems to have blown through the former Hôtel Cecil, bringing Spanish management and warmth, with attentive staff only too happy too meet your every need. The warm tones of fabrics and wall coverings create a cozy atmosphere. A buffet breakfast is served in the very fine Art-Deco dining-room.

Metropole (22)

31, place De Brouckère / 1000 ☎ 217 23 00 ➡ 218 02 20

M *De Brouckère* *many routes* P ***410 rooms*** *(3 suites)* ●●●● *Le Metropole* ➥ *64* *included*

An opulent palace with Belle Époque décor, once patronized by Sacha Guitry and still very popular with visiting celebrities. With its marbles, wooden paneling, mirrors, columns and profusion of gilt bronzes, the hotel is a rare jewel – an unusual feature of Brussels' architectural heritage.

Not forgetting

■ **Jolly Hotel Atlanta (23)** 7, bd A.-Max / 1000 ☎ 217 01 20 ➡ 217 37 58 ●●●● *A fine Art-Deco façade, matched by splendid Italian hospitality.*

In the area

When the city was developed for modern traffic, the main north-south boulevard was wished on the Botanical Garden. The vast glasshouses were transformed into a cultural center ➥ 68 ➥ 86, but fortunately the park has retained its fine trees and sculptures by Charles Van den

Where to stay

Sheraton Brussels Hotel & Towers (24)

3, place Rogier / 1210 ☎ 224 31 11 ➥ 224 34 56

Rogier *many routes* ***507 rooms*** *(43 suites)* ●●●●● *extra* *from the 30th floor*
Sheraton, Brussels National Airport / 1930 Zaventem @ *www.sheraton.com/brussels*

Beyond the Place Rogier, the northern district with its new high-rise buildings has been taken over by corporate interests. At the foot of this business district stands the Sheraton with its 30 floors, 507 bedrooms (215 for non-smokers), 43 suites, modular reception room (the largest in town), and round-the-clock service. The aim is clear: to create the best, most comfortable hotel in Brussels, with the finest facilities. Great efforts have been made in this direction. Even the classic enamel work of the bathrooms have been replaced with more fashionable marble and the very latest in faucets and fittings. ★ Between the 25th and 30th floors is an almost separate business hotel, offering reception arrangements, offices, a library, and bedrooms with excellent service and facilities. The Sheraton aims to establish a loyal clientele, which includes even the very young: some of the children's rooms have been decorated by Laura Ashley and are equipped with toys. On the top floor are a fabulous swimming pool and fitness club. This is a good place to sip a cocktail and admire the extensive view of the city. Another favorite spot is the Rendez-vous piano bar with its Chesterfield sofas and soft lighting – the ideal place for a quiet chat before or after a meal at the Crescendo ➥ 48.

Stappen and Constantin Meunier.

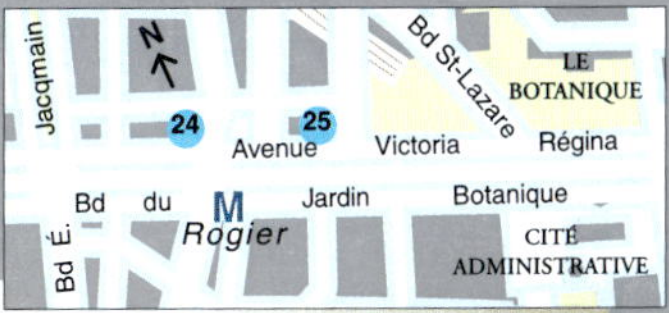

Crown Plaza Brussels (25)

3, rue Gineste / 1210 Bruxelles ☎ 203 62 00 ➠ 203 55 55

M *Rogier* *many routes* ***358 rooms*** *(6 suites)* ●●● *included*
sauna *www.crowneplaza.com*

A new name for the Hôtel Palace, a celebrated Brussels institution since the beginning of the century. In the lobby is a display illustrating some of the local history, with photographs of stars who have patronized the hotel. In a privileged location overlooking the Botanical Garden and close to the city-center attractions, the hotel has built up a loyal business and tourist clientele and is committed to modernizing and improving its facilities as a matter of course. A glance in the direction of the bar and high-ceilinged dining-room with its Art-Deco features will give you an immediate sense of the general atmosphere and originality of the place. The recently refurbished bedrooms on the 17th floor are highly functional and attractive. The others are still furnished in 1920s style. ★ If you have always wanted to sleep in a princess's bed, here is your chance. The amazing Grace Kelly suite has been preserved intact, with its made-to-measure furniture and the Monaco coat of arms above the bed-head. The staff are at pains to ensure you enjoy your stay.

In the area

Atop the Colonne du Congrès stands a statue of Leopold I, first King of the Belgians. Designed by the architect Joseph Poelaert, it was erected in 1859 to commemorate the national congress which proclaimed Belgian independence and adopted the 1831 constitution.

Where to stay

Astoria (26)

103, rue Royale / 1000 ☎ 227 05 05 ➟ 217 11 50

M *Botanique* *tram 92, 93* P ***104 rooms** (14 suites)* ●●●● *extra*

With its wooden paneling, alcoves, ornate moldings, wall-lights and mirrors, this Belle Époque palace has lost nothing of its former splendor, retaining a style found in very few European hotels. The monumental entrance, supported by 20 Corinthian columns in solid granite, leads into a neo-Victorian lobby resplendent with gilt decoration. The majestic staircase provides a setting worthy of Maurice Chevalier, inviting you to come on up and indulge your wildest fantasies. The Pullman bar is a faithful reconstruction of the Golden Arrow express train, with exotic hardwoods, marquetry, copper fittings, leather chairs and soft lighting.

Congrès (27)

42-44, rue du Congrès / 1000 ☎ 217 18 90 ➟ 217 18 97

M *Madou* *tram 92, 93* P ***53 rooms*** ● *included*

Welcoming and unpretentious, this hotel's 53 standardized rooms occupy two former private houses in a quiet street. Friendly service, a generous breakfast and private car parking are other points in its favor.

Léopold (28)

35, rue du Luxembourg / 1050 ☎ 511 18 28 ➟ 514 19 39

M *Trône* *many routes* P ***96 rooms** (4 suites and 8 apartments)* ●●● *extra* *sauna, solarium*

Located between the Trône subway station and the Léopold district railroad station, this new hotel is one of several that have grown up around the European Parliament building. To attract the well-heeled clientele frequenting this institution, everything is impeccably organized and comfortable, including the sauna-solarium, Pastabar and terraced café, which is very popular in summertime. ★ For long stays, the hotel has 8 split-level apartments.

Stanhope (29)

9, rue du Commerce / 1000 ☎ 506 91 11 ➟ 512 17 08

M *Trône* *many routes* P ***50 rooms** (25 suites)* ●●●● *extra* *sauna*

Between the Palais Royal and the European Parliament, this large mansion was the first five-star hotel in Brussels. The stars have lost nothing of their shine, as upper-class British style and sophistication still convey an image of quality and prestige. Each bedroom is decorated in its own original style. The décor of the excellent restaurant is inspired by the Royal Pavilion in Brighton. The bay windows overlook a pleasant garden courtyard and, in the background, a discreet penthouse ideal for a romantic weekend.

Not forgetting

■ **Tasse d'Argent (30)** 48, rue du Congrès / 1000 ☎ 218 83 75 ➟ 218 83 75 ● *A small, modestly priced hotel, clean and quiet.*

- Where to eat ➥ 48 ➥ 52
- After dark ➥ 66 ➥ 68 ➥ 70 ➥ 74
- What to see ➥ 80 ➥ 82
- Where to shop ➥ 136 ➥ 138

26

28

28

29

In the area

In a swish residential district, the Avenue Louise and the Boulevard de la Toison-d'Or are the chic shopping streets of the upper town. Be sure to carry on down to the Place Brugmann, where the florists and fashionable boutiques are concentrated. ■ Where to eat ➥ 54

Where to stay

Hilton (31)

38, boulevard de Waterloo / 1000 ☎ 504 11 11 ➡ 504 21 11

M *Porte-Louise* 34 ; *tram 91, 92, 93, 94* P ***430 rooms** (33 suites)* ●●●●● *included* @ *www.hilton.com*

This prestigious hotel, whose name is synonymous with elegance, luxury and comfort, is located in the smartest part of Brussels. Its 27 floors dominate the city's skyline, offering fine views of the whole built-up area and the Heysel in the distance. It has 430 rooms, including 33 ultra-comfortable suites and junior-suites, with quality furniture and the latest facilities. Warm-hued curtains and covers, together with the soft lighting, create a sense of well-being. ★ The top three floors form a separate hotel, with direct elevators and independent reception facilities, geared to the needs of businessmen and women.
You can also eat well at the Hilton. There is a celebrated restaurant, la Maison du Boeuf ➥ 54. and the Café d'Egmont – a brasserie with a corner devoted to Alfred Hitchcock, featuring stills from films such as *The Birds*, photographs of Grace Kelly and Cary Grant, statuettes, books and busts. The brasserie caters specially for cinema-goers.
Finally, if you want to relax, you can enjoy live music in the bar until late at night, or you may prefer to try the fitness club on the 16th floor. The Hilton's slogan is most appropriate: 'An exceptional palace in an exceptional city.'

After dark ➡ 64
Where to shop ➡ 134 ➡ 136 ➡ 138

32

34

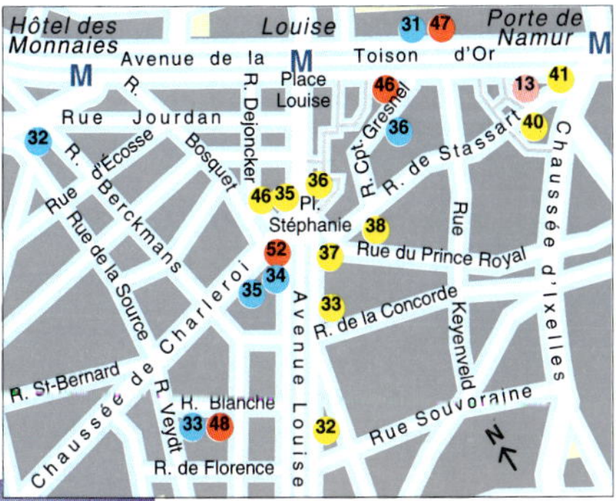

35

Les Bluets (32)

124, rue Berckmans / 1060 ☎ 534 39 83 ➠ 543 09 70

M *Hôtel-des-Monnaies* ***10 rooms*** ● *extra*

In this pleasant district, you will easily recognize the Bluets – or Bleuets – by its display of flowers. The owners welcome you into their tastefully decorated town house, where the antique furniture, knick-knacks, marble chimney-breasts, curtains crocheted by Mme Baez and flowers on the veranda soon make you feel at home. The attractive rooms are all different and very reasonably priced.

De Boeck's (33)

40, rue Veydt / 1050 ☎ 537 40 33 ➠ 534 40 37

M *Louise* *tram 91, 92* P ***50 rooms*** ● *included*

Located in a quiet street off the Avenue Louise, this hotel has character. It is popular with foreign visitors, who appreciate its atmosphere of affordable luxury. From the large, brightly lit lobby, an attractive staircase leads to the upper floors. The refurbished bedrooms are spacious and comfortable, decorated in restful pastel shades. Breakfast is served in the conservatory.

Not forgetting

■ **Conrad international (34)** 71, avenue Louise / 1050 ☎ 542 42 42 ➠ 542 42 00 ●●●●● *The hotel's elegant façade is emblematic of this smart district, where street and square bear the names of the princesses Louise and Stéphanie, the daughters of Leopold II. The Conrad boasts 269 luxurious rooms, a gastronomic restaurant and a delightful patio. A top-of-the-range, American-style hotel, with a price-list to match.* ■ **Manos (35)** 100-104, chaussée de Charleroi / 1060 ☎ 537 96 82 ➠ 539 36 55 ●●● *You will love the spacious garden, where hens lay the fresh eggs served at breakfast. The décor is elegant, with crystal chandeliers, Persian carpets, marble and gilding. The recently refurbished bedrooms are decorated in the Louis XV and Louis XVI styles.* ■ **Argus (36)** 6, rue du Capitaine-Crespel / 1050 ☎ 514 07 70 ➠ 514 12 22 ●● *This pleasant hotel with its discreet Art-Deco features is ideally situated just a short walk from the Louise railroad station. Contemporary paintings enliven the brightly lit rooms. Friendly atmosphere and affordable prices.*

Although most of the city's hotels are grouped together inside the 'pentagon', or inner ring of boulevards, there are a few more isolated establishments which have much to commend them, in both tourist and business districts.

Where to stay

Montgomery (37)
134, avenue de Tervueren / 1150 ☎ 741 85 11 ➟ 741 85 00

M *Montgomery* P *61 rooms (2 suites)* ●●●● *extra* *suites* @ *www.hotel@montgomery.be*

Do not be fooled by the modern appearance of the façade. Staying at the Montgomery is like staying in the traditional comfort of a grand English country house. As soon as you set foot inside the building, the influence of a woman's hand is evident in the harmonious details of the décor: the choice and positioning of the furniture in the public areas, the subtle lighting, the vases of flowers, fruit bowls and chocolates – elegant touches to please the eye. Then there is the cozy drawing-room with its fireplace, large bookcases and deep settees, all reminiscent of an old English manor house – comfort and elegance combined. The bedrooms are well equipped and there is a choice of three types of décor: cottage, British with floral-pattern fabrics, or colonial. You can dine at La Duchesse restaurant ➥ 52, whose French chef specializes in sunny Mediterranean cuisine. The hotel also offers some very attractive deals at weekends.

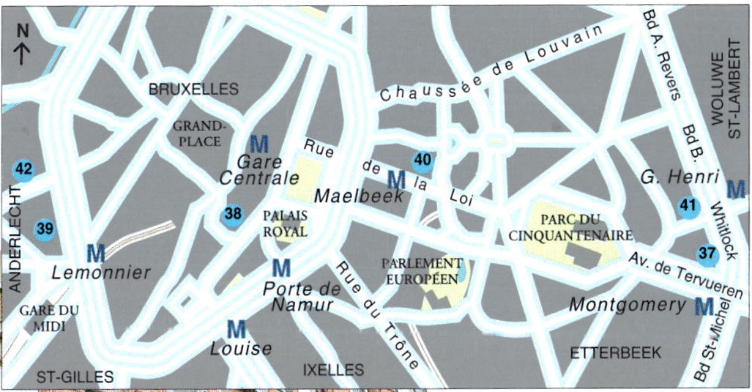

40

39

Jolly Hôtel du Grand Sablon (38)

Place du Grand-Sablon / 1000 ☎ 512 88 00 ➟ 512 67 66

20, 34, 48, 95, 96 ; tram 92, 93, 94 ***201 rooms*** *(6 suites)* ●●●●● *included*

In the 17th century this building sheltered the monks of Aywières abbey. Taken over by the pottery manufacturer Boch, it eventually became the fine hotel you see today. An Italian decorator, Laura Marzotto, designed the pink and beige entrance with Rosso Verona and Botticino marble cladding, which goes so well with the bas-reliefs. Inviting covers and curtains and classical-style furniture are features of the spacious bedrooms.

Ustel (39)

6-8, square de l'Aviation / 1070 ☎ 520 60 53 ➟ 520 33 28

Gare-du-Midi, Lemonnier ***94 rooms*** *(5 suites)* ●● *included*

This comfortable building with its imposing red-brick façade has only recently been converted into a hotel. Beyond the bar is a quiet inner courtyard with a large terrace. An interesting restaurant has been installed in the 19th-century building which once controlled the lock on the River Senne.

Not forgetting

■ **Dorint (40)** 11-19, bd Charlemagne / 1070 ☎ 231 09 09 ➟ 230 33 71 ●●●● *The Dorint combines comfort, art and culture: contemporary furniture, glass roofs to ensure natural lighting and a wonderful bar.* ■ **Armorial (41)** 101, bd Brandt-Whitlock / 1200 ☎ 734 56 36 ➟ 734 50 05 ● *A stylish, cozy hotel with 15 bedrooms furnished with antiques..* ★ *Ask for one of the very quiet rooms at the rear.* ■ **Van Belle (42)** 39-43, chaussée de Mons / 1070 ☎ 521 35 16 ➟ 527 00 02 ● *A friendly hotel where you can luxuriate in front of an open fire.*

Le Pain Quotidien
'Daily Bread': a chain of bakeries selling delicious tartines (open sandwiches) and other snacks. ⏲ *Mon.–Fri. 7.30am–7pm; Sat., Sun. 8am–7pm*

Where to eat

Dishes you must sample

Anguilles au vert (eels with herbs).
Asperges à la flamande (asparagus with mashed hard-cooked egg, butter, parsley and nutmeg).
Carbonade (a rich beef stew made with onions and beer).
Caricoles en bouillon (winkle soup).
Choux de Bruxelles en velouté (Brussels sprouts in a cream sauce).
Cougnou (sugarloaf, a Christmas specialty).
Croquettes aux crevettes grises (potato croquettes with shrimp; also made with mussels or herring).
Chicons (Belgian endive).
Faisan or **poulet à la brabançonne** (stuffed pheasant or chicken, served with Belgian endive).
Jets de houblon (hop shoots).
Moules marinières (mussels cooked in their own juice with onions).
Œufs meulemeerster (eggs, tomatoes and shrimp, served hot).
Pain à la grecque (a crisp pancake with superfine sugar and spices).
Pavé des brasseurs (châteaubriand steak with beer sauce).
Pistolet (crusty round roll).
Queue de boeuf à la gueuze (oxtail cooked in gueuze beer).
Tartine de fromage blanc (slice of bread with white cheese, accompanied by kriek beer).
Waterzooi (creamy chicken or sea food soup).

Brussels: a city of big eaters

Belgian cuisine is essentially French, seasoned with some native inventions (sauces made with beer, for example) and influenced by the customs of the various nations that have occupied the territory over the centuries (Spain, Austria, the Netherlands). Specifically Flemish cuisine is characterized by fish and sea food, and an abundance of vegetables.

64 Restaurants

THE INSIDER'S FAVORITES

INDEX BY TYPE

SPECIALTY AND PRICE
● less than 1,000 BEF
●● 1,000–1,250 BEF
●●● 1,300–1,500 BEF
●●●● 1,550–2,000 BEF
●●●●● more than 2,000 BEF

In the area

In the 11th century, a covered market with sections for bread, cloth and meat was established between what is now the Maison du Roi and the Rue du Marché-aux-Herbes. It soon expanded to neighboring streets. This is the ideal historic setting in which to try real Brussels cuisine.

Where to eat

t'Kelderke (1)

15, Grand-Place / 1000 ☎ 513 73 44 ➠ 512 30 81

M *Bourse, Gare-Centrale* *many routes* ***Brussels cuisine*** ●
Daily noon–2am

Typical Brussels cuisine in the setting of a vaulted cellar dating from the time of the Spanish occupation. The building survived the fire which followed the bombardment of the square by the troops of Louis XIV. The food is good, plentiful and reasonably priced. Tunes of the 1960s waft from the juke box, and there is an irresistible smell of mussels and French fries. The menu features all the local seasonal specialties: herring fillets with *Jefkes* (small pears), black and white sausages, mussels, *sole meunière* and *anguilles au vert*. The chef's specialty is *waterzooi* in the style of Ghent.

Le Cerf (2)

20, Grand-Place / 1000 ☎ 511 47 91 ➠ 546 09 59

M *Bourse, Gare-Centrale* *many routes* ***Brussels cuisine*** ●●●●
Mon.–Sat. 7–11.30pm *5pm–midnight*

Authentic 17th-century residence in the Hispano-Flemish style with eclectic interior decoration and furniture. They serve generous helpings of typically Belgian food: *croquettes aux crevettes grises, vol-au-vent,* poached cod and potato puréed with olive oil. ★ From the upstairs dining-room, there is a good view of the Grand-Place. Attractive bar serving cocktails to your own formula, and excellent espresso.

La Maison du Cygne (3)

2, rue Charles-Buyls / 1000 ☎ 511 82 44 ➠ 514 31 48

M *Bourse, Gare-Centrale* *many routes* P ***Gastronomic and French cuisine*** ●●●●● *Mon.–Fri. 11am–3pm, 7.15–10pm; Sat. 7.15–10pm; closed each year during Aug., Dec. 24 and Jan. 2*

This building, erected in 1658, was the guild headquarters. Here, Lenin and his left-wing friends met to plot during their long pre-Revolutionary campaign in the years immediately preceding World War I. The present owner, Aldo Vastapane, in residence since 1959, has made this bistro-restaurant a gastronomic paradise, combining the characteristics of a high-class restaurant (meat is carved at the table in accordance with the rules of French bourgeois cuisine) with respect for the setting.
★ The upstairs restaurant is the place to come if you want to be thoroughly spoiled and enjoy a great view over the Grand-Place.

Not forgetting

■ **La Roue d'Or (4)** 26, rue des Chapeliers / 1000 ☎ 514 25 54 ● Daily noon–12.30am *Surrealist brasserie with murals inspired by Magritte, and Art-Nouveau décor: fascinating silver-plated clock. Serves the full range of Brussels and Belgian specialties and some French regional dishes.* ■ **Chez Jean (5)** 6, rue des Chapeliers / 1000 ☎ 511 98 15 ●● Tues.–Sat. noon–2.30pm, 6.30–10pm; closed in June *Typical Brussels eating house with friendly atmosphere, where the chef, Jean Cambier, has labored since 1931. House specialties include mussels and dishes cooked with beer.* ■ **La Pintadine (6)** 5, rue de la Colline / 1000 ☎ 514 06 14 ● Daily 9am–1am *Affordable snack-restaurant run by two Iranian brothers: the ideal place to eat if you are pressed for time.*

■ Where to stay ➡ 18 ➡ 20 ■ After dark ➡ 62 ➡ 64 ■ What to see ➡ 80 ➡ 82 ■ Where to shop ➡ 126 ➡ 128 ➡ 138

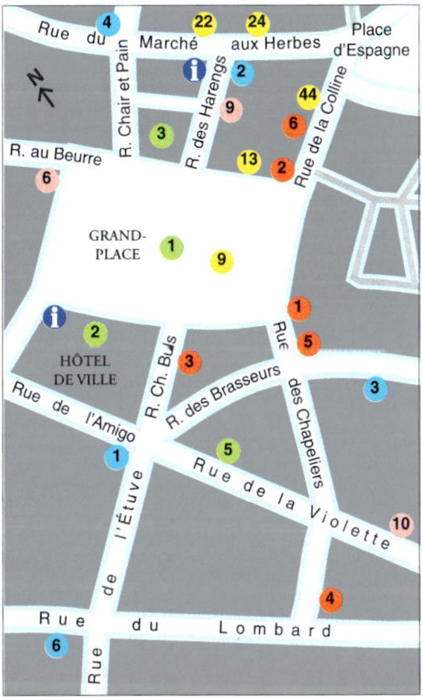

1

3

4

5

In the area
This area is the 'belly' of Brussels, with a whole string of restaurants in close proximity. ■ Where to stay ➡ 20 ➡ 22 ➡ 24 ■ After dark ➡ 62 ➡ 64 ➡ 66 ➡ 70 ➡ 72 ■ What to see ➡ 80 ➡ 82 ■ Where to shop ➡ 126 ➡ 128 ➡ 130 ➡ 138

Where to eat

Le Pou qui tousse (7)

49, place de la Vieille-Halle-aux-Blés / 1000 ☎ 512 28 71 ➡ 511 39 71

Gare-Centrale, Bourse *many routes* ***Sea food and Sardinian specialties*** ●● *Mon., Tues, and Thurs.–Sun. noon–2pm, 6–10pm; Wed. noon–2pm; closed in July, on Christmas Day and Jan. 1.*

Since it was founded in 1970, this restaurant has campaigned on behalf of Italian regional cuisine, combining high-quality ingredients, originality and a sense of fun. Enjoy such dishes as *risotto al nero di seppia* or *penne alla vernaccoia*, served with some excellent Italian wines.

Aux Armes de Bruxelles (8)

13, rue des Bouchers / 1000 ☎ 511 55 50 ➡ 514 33 81

Gare-Centrale, De Brouckère *many routes* ***Brussels cuisine*** ●●● *Tues.–Sun. noon–11.15pm*

This establishment, the best in the district, serves traditional Brussels fare – authentic recipes and quality ingredients. It combines a Belgian-style brasserie and a restaurant able to accommodate large parties. The *patronne* presides at the cash desk, in the grand tradition of Parisian brasseries. The spotless kitchen opens onto the dining-room, and the food is served in friendly fashion by an army of waiters and waitresses. Here was born the cry 'un complet, un!', shorthand for 'Bring me a plate of mussels and French fries, and a draft pilsner lager'! Book ahead to avoid disappointment. Good selection of wines and beers.

L'Ogenblik (9)

1, galerie des Princes / 1000 ☎ 511 61 51 ➡ 513 41 58

Bourse, Gare-Centrale *many routes* ***French cuisine, Belgian specialties*** ●●● *Mon.–Thurs. noon–2.30pm, 7pm–midnight; Fri., Sat. noon–2.30pm, 7pm–12.30am*

A tight-packed bistro-brasserie with dining-rooms on two levels, open kitchen, white-marble tables and benches around the wall. Founded in 1973, L'Ogenblik (Flemish for 'brief moment') launched a fashion for Parisian-style bistros, quite different from the traditional Belgian café-bistro. Its success is due to good basic food and no-nonsense service.

Not forgetting

■ **Les 4 Saisons (10)** Royal Windsor Hôtel, 5, rue Duquesnoy / 1000 ☎ 505 51 00 ●●●●● Mon.–Fri, noon–2.30pm, 7–10pm; Sat. 7–10pm *Interesting French cuisine: lobster salad, langoustines with wild mushrooms and, the specialty, whole sea-bass grilled with rosemary and garlic oil.* ■ **Sea Grill Radisson (11)** SAS Hôtel, 47, rue du Fossé-aux-Loups / 1000 ☎ 227 31 20 ●●●●● Mon.–Fri. noon–2.30pm, 7–10.30pm; Sat. 7–10.30pm; *closed on public holidays. Founded seven years ago in collaboration with Jacques Le Divellec, Parisian high-priest of fish cookery, the Sea Grill is now run by Le Divellec's disciple, Yves Matagne. Fish and sea food cooked and presented to the very highest standard.* ■ **L'Épicerie (12)** Hôtel Méridien, 3, carrefour de l'Europe / 1000 ☎ 548 47 16 ●●●● Daily noon–2.30pm, 7–10.45pm *David Martin came from the Arpège restaurant in Paris, having trained under Alain Passard. He is a great enthusiast for spices and exciting new combinations. He won the Prosper Montagné Award to become Belgium's top chef in 1998.*

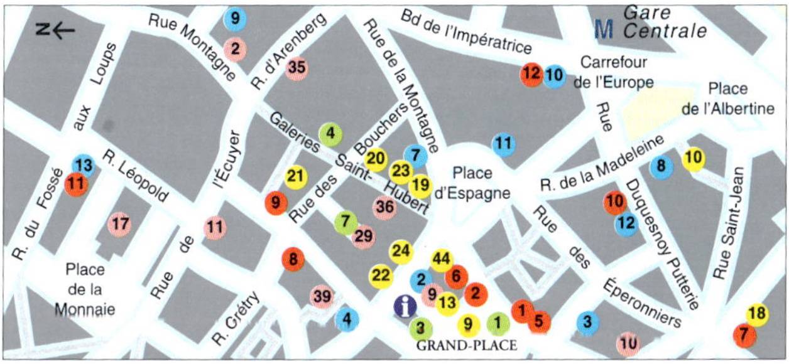

9

8

10

le Pou qui Tousse

12

In the area

A hundred years ago, trawlers fishing the North Sea came as far as Brussels to unload their catches here at the Vismet (fish market). The love of fish and sea food has endured, though sadly the boats disappeared when the River Senne was covered over. ■ Where to stay ➥ 26 ■ What to see ➥ 84

Where to eat

La Truite d'Argent (13)

23, quai au Bois-à-Brûler / 1000 ☎ 219 95 46 ➠ 217 18 87

M *Sainte-Catherine* 🚌 *many routes* P **Sea food ●●●●** ▭ 🕒 *Mon.–Fri. noon–2.30pm, 7–11pm; Sat. 7–11pm* ✱ ⇔ *Welcome hotel* ➥ *26*

This attractive 19th-century house with wooden paneling has just celebrated its hundredth anniversary as a restaurant, serving fish and game in season. A meeting place for politicians in the 1970s, the décor has remained the same but the menu has become more varied, including such delights as foie-gras ravioli and sea-bass braised with fresh thyme. There is a good selection of wines, and a knowledgeable wine waiter.

La Belle Maraîchère (14)

11, place Sainte-Catherine / 1000 ☎ 512 97 59 ➠ 513 76 91

M *Sainte-Catherine* 🚌 *many routes* P **Sea food ●●** ▭ 🕒 *Mon., Tues. and Fri.–Sun. noon–2.30pm, 6–10pm*

An old local bistro, converted into a restaurant in 1973 and renovated with respect for its former friendly atmosphere and regional cookery. North Sea specialities: skate and crab pâté with a hot sauce, clarified butter (a must) and fishermen's stew *(marmite des pêcheurs).*

Jacques (15)

44, quai aux Briques / 1000 ☎ 513 27 62 ➠ 270 13 00

M *Sainte-Catherine* 🚌 *many routes* **Sea food ●●** ▭ 🕒 *Mon.–Sat. noon–2.30pm, 6.30–10.30pm; closed in July and on public holidays*

An excellent family-run restaurant specializing in sea food, which in 1967 took over a traditional Brussels bistro. Managed by people who know a thing or two about fish, this restaurant is always crammed with loyal customers. The atmosphere is unfailingly warm and friendly.

Le Loup Gallant (16)

4, quai aux Barques / 1000 ☎ 219 99 98 ➠ 219 99 98

M *Sainte-Catherine* 🚌 *many routes* **French cuisine and sea food ●●●** ▭ 🕒 *Tues.–Sat. noon–2pm, 7–10pm* ✱

The Loup Gallant is one of the glories of Brussels. Here, Daniel Molmans has perfected his own versions of such Mediterranean favorites as *bouillabaisse* and *rascasse au pistou* (scorpion fish), without neglecting the local mussels, shrimp and soles.

Not forgetting

■ **Au Thé de Pékin (17)** 16-24, rue de la Vierge-Noire / 1000 ☎ 513 46 42 ● 🕒 Daily noon-3pm, 7–11pm *Modern Chinese cuisine, serves excellent teas.*

■ **La Moulière (18)** 23, place Sainte-Catherine / 1000 ☎ 219 65 49 ● 🕒 winter: Mon.–Fri. 11.30am–2pm, 6.30–9.30pm; Sat. 6.30–9.30pm / summer Tues.–Fri. 11.30am–2pm, 6.30–9.30pm; Sat., Sun. 6.30–9.30pm *They have been serving mussels here since 1964. There must be a style to suit every taste: plain, in white wine, in a cream sauce, with green peppercorns…*

■ **In 't Spinnekopke (19)** 1, place du Jardin-aux-Fleurs / 1000 ☎ 511 86 95 ● 🕒 Mon.–Fri. noon–3pm, 6–11pm; Sat. 6–11pm *Old tavern dating from 1762, perfectly preserved, with a menu of 100 local Belgian beers used to concoct a wide range of dishes and sauces.*

Where to shop ➥ 126 ➥ 132

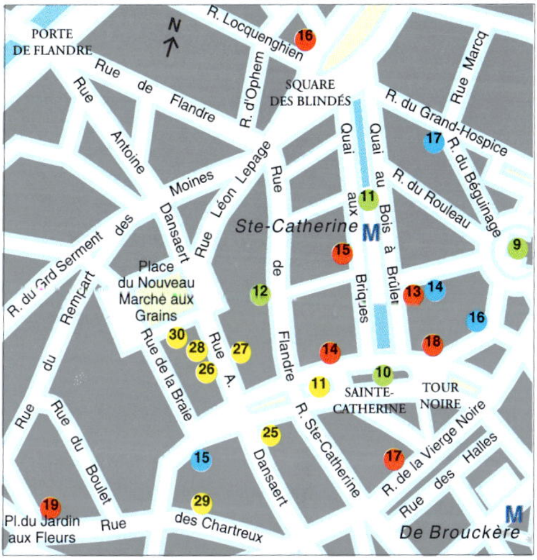

13

18 Mussels are prepared in over 30 different ways at the aptly named La Moulière.

13

In the area

This culinary itinerary covers various locations in the southern part of the historic center: from the Place Rouppe to Notre-Dame-de-la-Chapelle, then on to the Palais de Justice, the Place du Jeu-de-Balle and the Gare du Midi. ■ Where to stay ➡ 36 ■ After dark ➡ 64 ➡ 74

Where to eat

Comme chez soi (20)

23, place Rouppe / 1000 ☎ 512 29 21 ➡ 511 80 52

Anneessens *many routes* ***Gastronomic French cuisine*** ●●●●● *Tues.–Sat. noon–2pm, 7–10pm; closed in July, Dec. 25 and Jan. 1*

There is no need to introduce Pierre Wynants, one of the world's three or four top chefs, able to move a hungry gourmet to tears by the subtlety and finesse of his masterpieces. The food is served in an elegant Art-Nouveau setting, to complement the culinary experience. One of his very finest dishes is a North Sea lobster salad with black truffles *(salade parmentière au homard).*

Les Petits Oignons (21)

13, rue Notre-Seigneur / 1000 ☎ 512 47 38 ➡ 512 41 30

20, 48, 95, 96 ***French cuisine*** ● *Mon.–Sat. noon–2.30pm, 7–11pm; closed during Aug.*

This charming restaurant is housed in a listed 17th-century building, decorated with modern paintings. The chef performs gastronomic miracles: try the smoked foie gras, or the poisson royal with aromatic herbs or an olive oil-based emulsion. The intimate atmosphere of the small dining-room with its open fire is ideal for a romantic, candlelit dinner.

Les Brigittines (22)

5, place de la Chapelle / 1000 ☎ 512 68 91 ➡ 512 69 57

20, 48, 95, 96 ***Brasserie*** ●●● *Mon.–Thurs noon–2.30pm, 7–11pm; Fri. noon–2.30pm, 7pm–midnight; Sat. 7pm–midnight; closed during Aug.*

A good restaurant will have a number of points in its favor: harmonious setting, atmosphere, warm welcome, quality cuisine, reasonable prices... This is certainly true of Les Brigittines, a Belle Époque brasserie with wooden paneling. Specialties include steamed Danish cod with leeks, and rabbit-liver pâté.

Chez Maria (23)

50, avenue Clemenceau / 1070 ☎ 521 31 99

Clemenceau *20, 82* ***Specialist in red meat*** ●● *Mon.–Fri, noon–2.30pm, 7–10pm; Sat. 7–10pm; closed during July and on public holidays*

This restaurant has specialized in red meat for the last forty years. In the days of Maria Delenatte, in the 1980s, all the carnivores of the kingdom gathered here to enjoy her steak tartare. The restaurant is located near the Cureghem slaughterhouse, so supplies of top-quality meat are guaranteed.

Not forgetting

■ **Les Trois Chicons (24)** 9, rue des Renards / 1000 ☎ 511 55 83 ●● Tues.–Sun. noon–2.30pm, 6.30pm–2am *In the heart of the Marolles district, this restaurant serves dishes not found elsewhere:* stoemp à la bruxelloise, *Jeu-de-Balle meatballs,* endive au gratin. ■ **Au Stekerlapatte (25)** 4, rue des Prêtres / 1000 ☎ 512 86 81 ● Tues.–Sun. 7pm–1am *Frequented by media personalities, the strong points of this very Belgian restaurant are its grilled pigs' trotters and Brussels capon. The food is as tasty as the gossip.*

What to see
➥ 88 ➥ 100
Where to shop
➥ 124 ➥ 126 ➥ 138

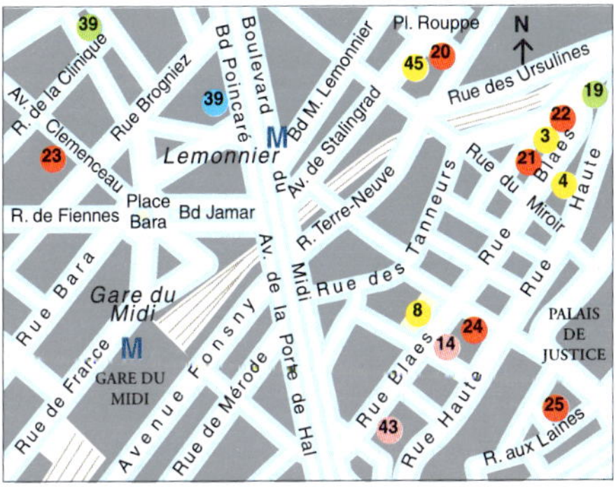

20

21

25

AU STEKERLAPATTE

The Stekerlapatte, open until late, is a good place to have a meal after going to the theater or seeing a movie.

22

In the area

Parallel with the Boulevard Adolphe-Max, the Rue Neuve is nowadays a bustling commercial thoroughfare. It leads to the Place des Martyrs.
■ Where to stay ➡ 28 ➡ 30 ➡ 32 ■ After dark ➡ 64 ➡ 66 ➡ 68 ➡ 70 ➡ 72 ■ What to see ➡ 84 ➡ 86 ■ Where to shop ➡ 138

Where to eat

Crescendo (26)

Hôtel Sheraton, 3, place Rogier / 1210 ☎ 224 32 05 ➡ 224 34 56

Rogier many routes ***International cuisine*** ●● *Daily noon–11pm* ***Buffet*** *daily noon–2.30pm 8pm–midnight*

The team from the former Comte des Flandres is now installed in the Sheraton's most popular restaurant, the Crescendo, which has undergone a complete face-lift. It resembles a chic bistro, with open-plan kitchen and dining area. Many of the dishes are of Mediterranean origin.

Alban Chambon (27)

Hôtel Metropole, 1, place De Brouckère / 1000 ☎ 217 23 00 ➡ 218 02 20

De Brouckère many routes ***French cuisine*** ●●● *Mon.–Fri. noon–2.30pm, 7–10pm; closed on public holidays*

The restaurant is named for the French architect who designed the hotel at the end of the 19th century. The gilt-and-marble décor may be of historical interest, but the kitchen is unashamedly modern, presided over by Dominique Michou. His creations are of the highest standard: potato petals with truffles and langoustines roasted with lemon juice, fillet of pike perch with caviar, sautéed *aiguillettes* of barbary duckling, and his exceptional *cuisse de foie gras*.

De Ultieme Hallucinatie (28)

316, rue Royale / 1210 ☎ 217 06 14 ➡ 217 72 40

Botanique 58, 92, 93, 94 ***Restaurant : French bourgeois cuisine*** ●●●● *Mon.–Fri. noon–2.30pm, 7–10.30pm; Sat. 7–10.30pm* ***Brasserie*** ●●● *Mon.–Fri. 11am–2.30pm; Sat., Sun. 3pm–2.30am Terrace*

The restaurant would be well worth visiting just for its Art-Nouveau decoration, designed by Paul Hamesse in 1904 and perfectly preserved. Specialties include lobster with bisque sauce and tagliatelle with smoked salmon. ★ If your funds are limited, try the magnificent brasserie with its vast conservatory and beer counter, where the food is good and quickly served.

Au Brabançon (29)

75, rue de la Commune / 1210 ☎ 217 71 91

Madou 29, 59, 63 ***Brussels cuisine*** ● *Mon.–Fri. noon–3pm, 7–9.30pm; Sat. 7–9.30pm; closed on public holidays*

Now approaching 78, Marie-Jeanne Lucas has a wealth of experience of old country recipes involving the lavish use of butter, and of preparing horsemeat (the Brabançon is a breed of horse). She also has a prodigious knowledge of every variety of charcuterie. Be sure to book ahead.

Not forgetting

■ **Les Dames Tartine (30)** 58, chaussée de Haecht / 1210 ☎ 218 45 49 ●● Tues.–Fri. noon–2pm, 7–9.30pm; Sat. 7–9.30pm *Excellent French cuisine combining tradition and creativity, beautifully presented.*

■ **Le Temps présent (31)** Hôtel Crowne-Plaza, 3, rue Gineste / 1000 ☎ 203 62 00 ●● Daily noon–2.30pm, 6–11pm *Classic cuisine with an Italian slant, in the setting of a palace built in the 1920s.*

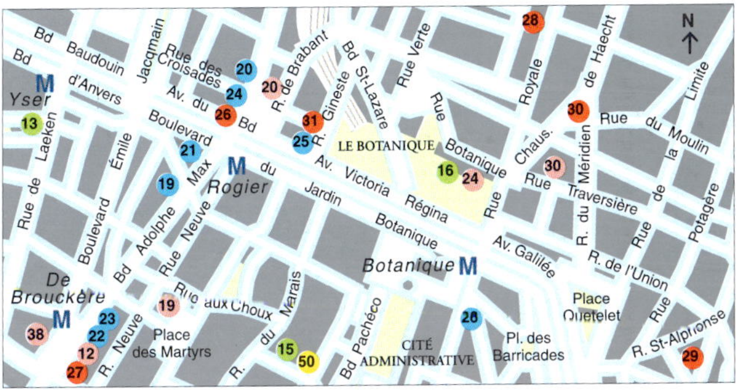

26

27

28

The Ultieme Hallucinatie's décor is all Art Nouveau, from the windows to the smallest decorative details, such as this statue in the dining-room.

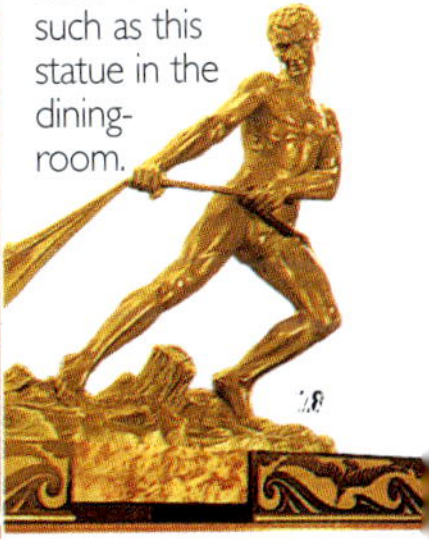

30

In the area

Beyond the Place du Petit-Sablon, be sure to visit the Rue des Laines, saved from the wrecker's ball in 1995. Lined on one side by fine pre-19th-century townhouses and mansions, on the other by a series of 26 residences (1905) built by the Duc d'Arenberg. ■ Where to stay ➥ 36

Where to eat

Trente Rue de la Paille (32)

30, rue de la Paille / 1000 ☎ 512 07 15 ➡ 514 07 15

20, 34, 48, 95, 96 ; tram 92, 93, 94 ***French cuisine*** ●●● *Mon.–Fri. noon–2.30pm, 7–11.30pm; closed July 15–Aug. 15 and public holidays.*

André Martiny, the chef, is skilled in the art of creative harmonization, presenting two kinds of meat or fish on the same plate, with a final mouth watering touch of acidity. Some excellent Alsatian wines.

L'Écailler du Palais Royal (33)

18, rue Bodenbroeck / 1000 ☎ 512 87 51 ➡ 511 99 50

20, 34, 48, 95, 96 ; tram 92, 93, 94 P ***Gastronomic cuisine and sea food*** ●●●●● *Mon.–Sat. noon–2.30pm, 7–11pm; closed on public holidays.*

An elegant setting, sophisticated cuisine, impeccable service, and a first-class wine list… and, if you are on a tight schedule, the snack bar offers a *plat du jour* chalked up on a small blackboard. The house specialties, depending on season, include lobster ravioli and *turbot en écailles de pommes de terre.*

Au Vieux Saint-Martin (34)

38, place du Grand-Sablon / 1000 ☎ 512 64 76 ➡ 512 92 92

20, 34, 48, 95, 96 ; tram 92, 93, 94 ***Brussels cuisine*** ●●● *Daily 10am–midnight* *At the Duc d'Arenberg (below), La Marie-Joseph, Canterbury*

This is the in place for those who work in the Sablon area or like to come in the evening, before or after going to a show. The setting is that of a modern Belgian-style brasserie, but with an additional touch of luxury: the paintings on the walls are by Alechinsky. Service is prompt, the espresso coffee excellent, and the food varied.

La Canne à Sucre (35)

12, rue des Pigeons / 1000 ☎ 513 03 72 ➡ 353 06 29

20, 34, 48, 95, 96 ; tram 92, 93, 94 ***Cuisine from the island of Martinique*** ●●● *Tues.–Sat. 7.30–10pm; closed on public holidays* *live Caribbean music on Fri. and Sat.*

Have you ever eaten *cyriques?* – land crabs prepared West-Indian style! Here, everything is exotic: original, spicy, freshly prepared in a cheerful, noisy atmosphere. Back home, this would be described as an 'îlet', a corner of paradise in the urban jungle of Brussels. The specialties include Creole black pudding, fricassee of lambis, pilaf, fried chicken, and a choice of 400 different rum cocktails.

Not forgetting

■ **La Tour d'y Voir (36)** 8, place du Grand-Sablon / 1000 ☎ 511 40 43 ●●● Tues.–Fri. noon–3pm, 7.30–11pm; Sat., Sun. 7.30pm–midnight *This striking restaurant is housed on the first floor of a former chapel, an interesting setting for the new chef's first-class French cuisine.* ■ **Chez Marius en Provence (37)** 1, place du Petit-Sablon / 1000 ☎ 5512 27 89 ●●●● Mon.–Sat. noon–2.30pm, 7–10.30pm *Mediterranean-style food, rustic décor and convivial atmosphere.*

■ **Au Duc d'Arenberg (38)** 9, place du Petit-Sablon / 1000 ☎ 511 14 75 ●●●●● Mon.–Sat. noon–2.30pm, 7–10.30pm *A chic restaurant based on Parisian models. Dishes include quenelles of pike and roast Breton cockerel.*

■ After dark ➥ 70
■ What to see ➥ 92
■ Where to shop ➥ 124

32

33

34

The Tour d'y Voir has taken over a 16th-century chapel. The stained glass of the windows is more recent, dating from the early years of Belgian independence (1830).

36

In the area

In this district of squares, gardens and open-air sculpture, you will find a fascinating concentration of Art-Nouveau residences. A striking example is the façade of the Maison Saint-Cyr at no. 11 Square Ambiorix.

■ Where to stay ➥ 32 ➥ 36 ■ What to see ➥ 94 ➥ 96 ➥ 104

Where to eat

Chez Callens (39)

73, rue du Commerce / 1000 ☎ 512 08 43 ➡ 512 46 04

M *Trône* 🚌 *many routes* ***Bourgeois cuisine*** ● ▭ 🕒 *Mon.–Fri. noon–3pm, 6–10pm*

Founded in 1952, surrounded by government offices, this restaurant has become something of an institution. The warm, friendly atmosphere engulfs you as you settle down to read the menu, designed in the days of the present owners' parents. Specialties include *anguilles au vert*, homemade sauerkraut, and duck breasts with blackcurrants.

Stirwen (40)

15-17, chaussée Saint-Pierre / 1040 Etterbeek ☎ 640 85 41

M *Schuman* 🚌 *28, 36, 67* ***French regional cuisine*** ●●● ▭ 🕒 *Mon.–Fri. noon–2pm, 7.30–9.30pm; Sat. 7.30–9.30pm*

As well as the Stirwen, Alain Troubat manages the Trefle à 4, the celebrated restaurant at the Château du Lac, Genval. Here, assisted by Laurent Brouwers, he serves his native Breton dishes and other French regional specialties. There is also an excellent wine list.

Perry's Grill (41)

137, rue de Froisart / 1040 Etterbeek ☎ 230 62 78

M *Schuman* 🚌 *28, 36, 67* ***French cuisine*** ●● ▭ 🕒 *Mon.–Fri. noon–3pm, 7–10pm; closed during Aug. and on public holidays*

Opened in 1980, this restaurant is a rendezvous of Belgian and EU civil servants. This need not prevent you from going there to sample the cuisine of Jean-Louis Genot, at his best when preparing local dishes. The atmosphere is friendly.

L'Atelier européen (42)

21, rue Franklin / 1000 ☎ 734 91 40 ➡ 735 35 98

M *Schuman* 🚌 *28, 36, 67* ***French cuisine*** ●● ▭ 🕒 *Mon.–Fri. noon–2.30pm, 7–10pm; closed during Aug.*

Installed in an old warehouse, this restaurant and its cold buffet (eat as much as you like) are well known to all those who make regular visits to Brussels on EU business. European functionaries and local residents engage in noisy, animated discussion of the latest Euro-scandals. A sight to be seen.

Not forgetting

■ **Nico Central Brussels (43)** 19, rue du Parnasse / 1050 ☎ 505 25 78 ●●● 🕒 Mon.–Fri. noon–2.30pm, 6.30–10.30pm; Sat. 6.30–10.30pm *A chic brasserie-restaurant, one of a chain launched by Nico Ladenis of the highly rated Park Lane Hotel, London.* ■ **Takésushi (44)** 12, rue Joseph-Stevens / 1000 ☎ 230 56 27 ●● 🕒 Sun.–Fri. noon–2.30pm, 7–10.30pm *The local Japanese restaurant, friendly, competent and scrupulously observant of the culinary principles of the Land of the Rising Sun.* ■ **La Duchesse (45)** Montgomery, 134, av. de Tervuren / 1150 ☎ 741 85 00 ●●●● 🕒 Mon.–Fri. noon–2.30pm, 7–10pm *Creative French cuisine featuring some unusual dishes, especially ones using fish.*

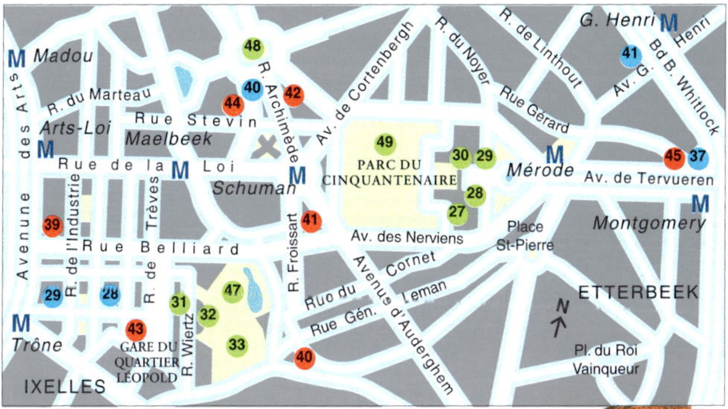

39

41

40

The Atelier européen, approached by a leafy alley, puts on a daily cold buffet, from which you can eat your fill. It also serves a range of hot dishes à la carte.

42

In the area

The Avenue Louise was laid out in 1864 to link the city center with the Bois de la Cambre. A mile and a half long and 180 ft wide, it was soon lined with desirable residences. Victor Horta showed what he was capable of, building a palatial mansion for the industrialist Solvay in

Where to eat

Adrienne Toison d'Or (46)

1a, rue du Capitaine-Crespel / 1050 ☎ 511 93 39 ➡ 513 69 79

Louise 34 ; tram 91, 92, 93, 94 ***Hot and cold buffet*** ● *Mon.–Sat. noon–2.15pm, 6.30–10pm; Sun. noon–2.15pm*

Without a doubt, the top buffet in Brussels, offering an incredible choice of dishes, whether fish, sea food, meat, cheese or desserts, seemingly in endless supply. ★ Begin with the main table, devoted to sea food, which is generally known as the 'aircraft-carrier' because of its strange shape.

Maison du Bœuf (47)

Hilton, 38, boulevard de Waterloo / 1000 ☎ 504 11 11 ➡ 504 21 11

Louise 34 ; tram 91, 92, 93, 94 P ***French cuisine*** ●●●● *Daily noon–2.30pm, 7–10.30pm*

The Maison du Boeuf has exceptionally well qualified staff: the cook is Michel Theurel, maître cuisinier de Belgique, president of the Académie Culinaire de France, and a disciple of Escoffier; the maître d'hôtel, named Belgium's top wine waiter in 1982, is highly skilled in matching wines and dishes. You will enjoy the creative style of cuisine. One of Theurel's inventions is steak tartare fried in olive oil and topped with caviar. Delicious!

Le Chem's (48)

14, rue Blanche / 1000 ☎ 538 14 94

Louise tram 91, 92, 93, 94 ***Moroccan cuisine*** ●● *Mon.–Fri. noon–2pm, 7–10.30pm; Sat. 7–10.30pm*

With a little imagination, you might think you were in Marrakech. Have you heard of *briouats kefta*? – puff pastry stuffed with pan-fried ground lamb and eggplants. Couscous is, of course, better known, but how about *tajine* of young pigeon cooked with apples, pears and almonds, or *pastilla*?

La Quincaillerie (49)

45, rue du Page / 1050 ☎ 538 25 53 ➡ 539 40 95

54 ; tram 81, 82, 91, 92 ***Brasserie-style cuisine*** ●● *Mon.–Fri. noon–2.30pm, 7pm–midnight; Sat., Sun. 7pm–midnight*

This switched-on restaurant is installed in a 1903 hardware store, strikingly renovated but still with the original shelving and steel staircases. The chef has a clear understanding of what his customers are looking for: local dishes, interesting flavors, and fast service, accompanied by first-class wines.

Not forgetting

■ **La Porte des Indes (50)** 455, av. Louise / 1000 ☎ 374 78 81 ●●● Mon.–Sat. noon–2.30pm, 7–10.30pm; Sun. 7–10.30pm *Fragrant, sophisticated Indian cuisine, spiced with curry, nutmeg and saffron.* ■ **Maison Félix (51)** 14, av. Washington / 1050 ☎ 345 66 93 ●●● Tues.–Sat. noon–3.30pm, 7–9.30pm *The authentic taste of grandmother's home recipes: roast John Dory with thyme or Vendée pigeon baked in a crust of sea salt.* ■ **La Maison de Maître (52)** Hôtel Conrad, 71, avenue Louise / 1050 ☎ 542 47 16 ●●● Tues.–Fri. noon–2pm, 7–10pm; Sat. 7–10pm *Excellent Provençal and Mediterranean dishes.*

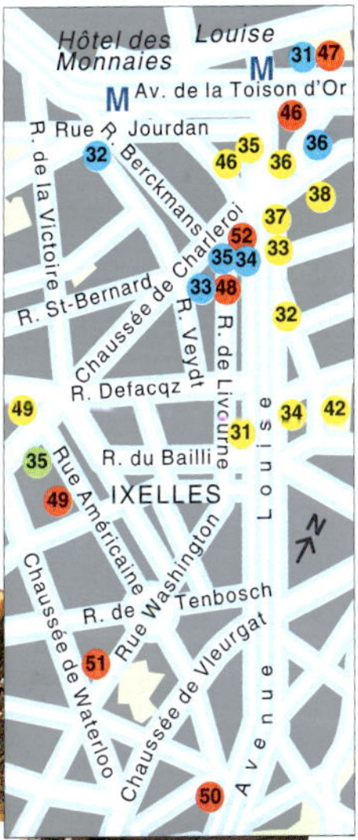

1894–8 (no. 224), for which he designed all the furniture and silverware.

■ Where to stay ➥ 34 ■ What to see ➥ 98
■ Where to shop ➥ 134 ➥ 136 ➥ 138

46

49

47

50

On the ground floor of the Maison Félix is a delicatessen where you can buy freshly cooked food to take out.

51

In the area

A 304-acre area of park and woodland, the Bois de la Cambre was laid out by the city of Brussels in 1862, under the direction of the architect Édouard Keilig. It is a magnificent achievement. ■ After dark ➥ 66 ➥ 74 ■ What to see ➥ 98 ➥ 104 ■ Where to shop ➥ 138

Where to eat

La Truffe noire (53)

12, boulevard de la Cambre / 1050 ☎ 640 44 22 ➟ 647 97 04

tram 23, 90, 93, 94 ***French and Italian gastronomic cuisine*** ●●●●● *Mon.–Fri. noon–3pm, 7–11pm; Sat. 7–11pm*

Luigi Ciciriello may have many interests, but truffles are certainly his great passion. Here they are served up in every conceivable way: with sea salt, *en papillote*, grated, in thin flakes with fish, as an accompaniment to meat, bringing out the full flavor of poultry and cheese. The white variety, which comes from Piedmont in October, is served with pasta in a delicious creamy sauce.

Gri-Gri (54)

16, rue Basse / 1180 ☎ 375 82 02 ➟ 375 27 46

41, 43, 60 ; tram 92 ***Congolese and African cuisine*** ● *Tues.–Fri. and Sun. noon–3pm, 6.30–midnight; Mon. and Sat. 6.30–midnight*

The Congolese patronne, Augustine, having achieved great success with her celebrated *moambes* – jugged chicken with *saka-saka* – has extended her repertoire to several other sub-Saharan countries. She simply recruited a cook from each country, who presents her favorite dish. Get to know the cooking of Senegal, Dahomey, Ivory Coast, Chad or Angola, as you sway to the rhythm of the *djembe*.

La Brasserie Georges (55)

259, avenue Churchill / 1180 ☎ 347 21 00 ➟ 344 02 45

38 ; tram 23, 90 ***Brasserie-style cuisine*** ●● *Daily 11.30am–3pm, 7pm–12.30am*

Facing the Bois de la Cambre, Georges Neefs has recreated every aspect of an authentic brasserie. You are greeted by the deafening din coming from the always busy dining area. There is a classic, high-quality brasserie menu and the produce on the shellfish stall is the freshest in town, thanks to the establishment's direct contacts with the oyster farmers of Brittany, Normandy, Colchester and Zeeland. They serve draft beers.

La Brasserie Marebœuf (56)

445, avenue de la Couronne / 1050 ☎ 648 99 06 ➟ 648 38 30

95, 96 ; tram 23, 90 ***Brasserie-style cuisine*** ● *Mon.–Thurs. noon–2.30pm, 7pm–midnight; Fri., Sat. noon–2.30pm, 7pm–1am*

The establishment combines Belgian dishes, such as braised calf's brain and croquettes, with the sea food plateau, sauerkraut and other fare more typical of a French brasserie. One of the specialties is a fish sauerkraut of the kind prepared in Alsace, the owner's home area. Being near the university, this brasserie tends to attract a younger clientele.

Not forgetting

■ **Blue Elephant (57)** 1120, chaussée de Waterloo / 1180 ☎ 374 49 62 ● Sun.–Fri. noon–2.30pm, 7–10,30pm; Sat. 7–10.30pm *First-class Thai cuisine in a fabulous garden.* ■ **La Villa Lorraine (58)** 28, chaussée de la Hulpe / 1000 ☎ 374 31 63 ●●●●● Mon.–Sat. noon–2.30pm, 7–9.30pm *Excellent French cuisine, awarded a Michelin star.*

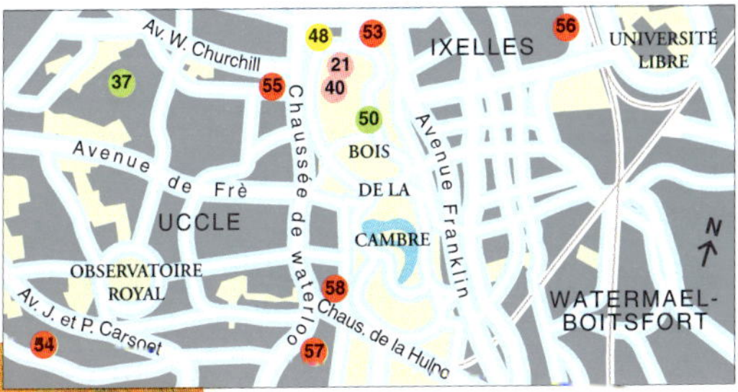

Below, Luigi Ciciriello, director of the Truffe Noire, and chef de cuisine, Aziz Bhatti.

53

54

58

In the area

At the end of the Boulevard Léopold-II, the immense silhouette of the national basilica of the Sacré-Coeur rises above the cityscape of Brussels. Begun in 1905, but soon interrupted by World War I, the building was not really finished until 1969! Controversial on account of

Where to eat

Bruneau (59)

75, avenue Broustin / 1083 ☎ 427 69 78 ➠ 425 97 26

M *Simonis* 🚌 *49, 87 ; tram 19* ***Gastronomic cuisine*** ●●●●● ▭
🕒 *Thurs.–Mon. noon–2.30pm, 7–10pm; Tues. noon–2.30pm*

The very finest cuisine, imaginatively prepared and presented. Perhaps it would be better to say no more, and leave you to discover the delicious flavors and fragrances on offer in this restaurant. For a real treat, try the chef's succulent stuffed scallops, or what is described as a '*jalousie*' of calf sweetbreads.

Claude Dupont (60)

49, avenue Vital-Riethuisen / 1083 ☎ 426 00 00 ➠ 426 65 40

M *Simonis* 🚌 *49, 87 ; tram 19* ***Gastronomic cuisine*** ●●●●● ▭
🕒 *Wed.–Sun. noon–2pm, 7–10pm*

Claude Dupont set up his restaurant in this comfortable, attractively decorated villa in 1971. The food he serves is classy, creative and sophisticated, but nonetheless filling, flavorsome, harmonious and presented in a way which makes your mouth water. The charming *patronne* presides over the dining-room. Try the filet of charolais with duck-liver pâté and green peppercorns.

Béguine des Béguines (61)

168, rue des Béguines / 1080 ☎ 414 77 70 ➠ 414 77 70

🚌 *85 ; tram 82* ***Belgian cuisine*** ● ▭ 🕒 *Tues.–Fri. noon–2.30pm, 6.30–9.30pm; Sat. 6.30–9.30pm; Sun. noon–2.30pm*

In the early 1960s, a number of chefs developed a Belgian style of cuisine based on beer. The dishes were not so much cooked in beer – a commonplace in many countries – but served with delicious sauces made with beer rather than the more normal wine. The idea was to find the beer perfectly suited to each type of food, in terms of taste and fragrance. Michel David is still engaged on this quest.

Auberge de l'Isard (62)

1, parvis Notre-Dame / 1020 ☎ 479 85 64 ➠ 479 16 49

M *Bockstael* 🚌 *81, 94* ***French and Belgian cuisine*** ●●● ▭ 🕒 *Tues.–Sat. noon–2.30pm, 7–10pm; Mon.-Sun. noon–2.30pm*

In the 1980s, when still a young couple, the Taildemans set up in this turn-of-the-century house, which stands halfway between the Royal Crypt and the Royal Palace. Nowadays, their roles are well established: he continues to develop the culinary art, creating dishes of French and Belgian inspiration; she welcomes the guests with unfailing courtesy. You must try the liver cutlet, served with an apple-and-pear sauce.

Not forgetting

■ **San Daniele (63)** 6, av. Charles-Quint / 1083 ☎ 426 79 23 ●●●● 🕒 Tues.–Sat. noon–2.30pm, 7–10.30pm; Sun., Mon. noon–2.30pm *Classic Italian dishes served with excellent wines.* ■ **Les Baguettes Impériales (64)** 70, av. Jean-Sobieski / 1020 ☎ 479 67 32 ●●●●● 🕒 Mon. and Wed.–Sat. noon–2.30pm, 7–10.30pm; Sun. noon–2.30pm *Vietnamese cuisine of a high standard.*

its Byzantine architecture, the sanctuary is nonetheless impressive: 548 ft long and 282 ft high.

■ What to see ➥ 100 ➥ 102

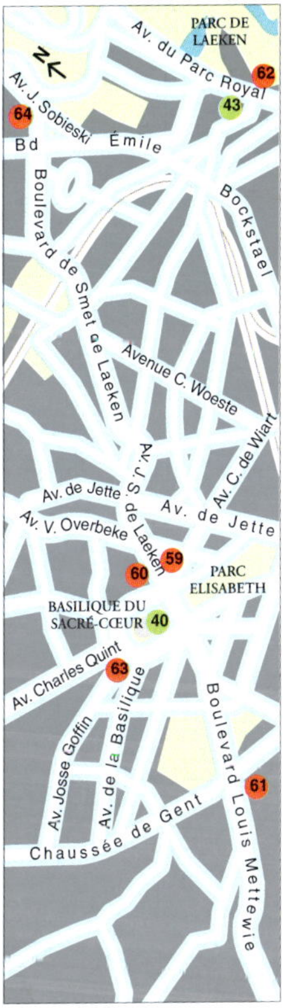

59

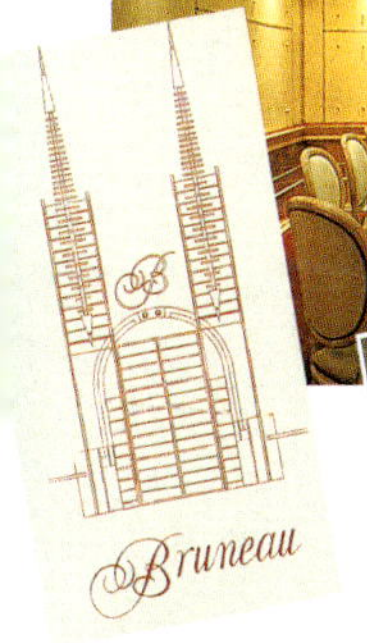

Rediscover some delicious old-fashioned flavors chez Claude Dupont. 60

63

Kladaradatsch

A brand new mini-cinema complex, combining the technical quality of major cinemas with the intimacy of small auditoria. You can also have something to eat and drink. *85, boulevard Anspach / 1000* ☎ *501 67 76* ➠ *501 67 77*
@ *e-mail : kladaradatsch kladaradatsch.be, site web : www.kladaradatsch.be*

After dark

Belgian beers

Local beers come in a wide range of flavors and colors.
Blanche a refreshing, cloudy beer made from wheat. Fragrant and low in alcohol.
Brunes dense, strong-tasting.
Faro a sweet, sugary lambic beer, interesting flavor.
Gueuze a blend of old and young lambic beers which has fermented a second time in the bottle. Frothy, fruity flavor.
Kriek a sweet, fruity lambic beer steeped in cherries.
Lambic a beer that has been left to ferment spontaneously (by exposure to air). Yeasty in taste, hard to find.
Rouges made with red barley and matured in oak casks. Fruity, sugary, slightly acid.
Trappiste a dense beer with a strong malt flavor and high alcohol content, originally brewed by the monks of Cistercian abbeys (Chimay, Orval, Rochefort).

Entertainment listings

Babel (monthly, 90 BEF), **Kiosque** (monthly, 60 BEF), **MAD** (Wednesday supplement to *Le Soir* newspaper, 30 BEF), **Park mail** (free bi-monthly, available in public places), **Tenue de ville** (monthly, 70 BEF), **The Ticket** (monthly, free from music shops), **Vlan** (free weekly news-sheet delivered on Wednesdays with the mail), **What's on** (English-language weekly, 90 BEF, Thursday supplement to *The Bulletin*).

45 Nights out

THE INSIDER'S FAVORITES

INDEX BY AREA

Belgium is the land of beer and Brussels is certainly not short of places where you can try the many types of local brew: *lambic*, *faro* (incorporating brown sugar), *kriek* (made with cherries), *gueuze*, and hundreds of other interesting Belgian beers. The range is enormous.

After dark

2

4

À la Bécasse (1)

11, rue Tabora / 1000 ☎ 511 00 06 ➠ 511 00 06

De Brouckère · *many routes* · *Daily 10am–1am*

Hidden away at the end of a cul-de-sac indicated with a sign in the shape of a woodcock *(bécasse)*, this tavern is nevertheless very popular with tourists wanting to try the local brew. The house specialty is '*lambic doux*', a sweeter type of *lambic* beer, served by the pitcher. Run by the same family since 1877, according to historians La Bécasse has been in the business of quenching people's thirst for several centuries. ★ It also serves traditional, country-style bread and cheese.

À la Mort Subite (2)

7, rue Montagne-aux-Herbes-Potagères / 1000 ☎ 513 13 18

De Brouckère, Bourse · *many routes* · *Daily 10.30am–2am*

More an institution than a café, La Mort Subite (Sudden Death, from the name of the famous beer served here in large quantities), with its wooden paneling, mildewy mirrors and old-fashioned – but magnificent – bar counter, has an ageless atmosphere. Tourists and regulars come here to drink *kriek*, *faro* and other types of *gueuze* beer.

Chez Moeder Lambic (3)

68, rue de Savoie / 1060 ☎ 539 14 19

Horta, Hôtel-des-Monnaies · *48; many tram routes* · *4pm–4am*

Rather off the beaten track but well worth a visit! More than a café, this is a veritable museum of Belgian and imported beers, serving over 1,200 different types: blond, brown and amber, as well as Trappist and abbey brews. ★ To kill time between rounds, you can read comic-strip books.

À l'Imaige Nostre-Dame (4)

8, rue du Marché-aux-Herbes / 1000 ☎ 219 42 49

De Brouckère · *many routes* · *Mon.–Thurs. 11.30am–1am; Fri., Sat. 11.30am–2.30am; Sun. 4pm–1am*

This is another old tavern tucked away at the end of a cul-de-sac, already well known at the turn of the 20th century, with an impressive list of special beers. If you ask him, the friendly young owner will be only too pleased to help you make your choice. The house specialty is Bourgogne des Flandres, a fine cask beer.

7

8

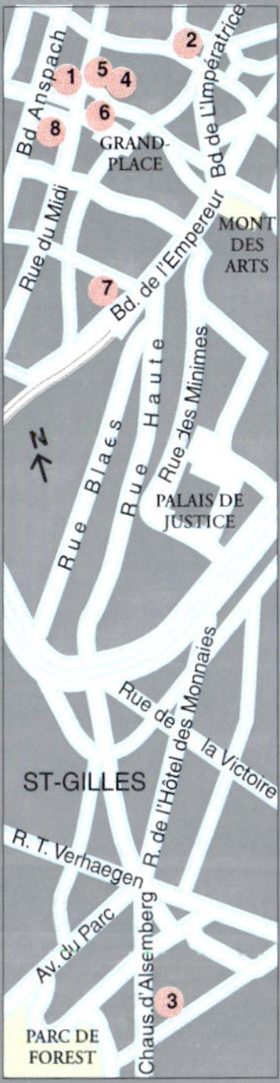

Au Bon Vieux Temps (5)

4, impasse Saint-Nicolas / 1000 ☎ 217 26 26

De Brouckère *many routes* *Sun.–Thurs. 11am–midnight; Fri., Sat. 11am–2am*

This is one of the oldest cafés in Brussels (17th century), with a wealth of wooden paneling reflecting the more gracious style of former days – the place for those who believe that Brussels' golden age lies in the past. The patronne even reserves the right to refuse entry. Her tavern is nevertheless known the world over.

Le Roy d'Espagne (6)

1, Grand-Place / 1000 ☎ 513 08 07

De Brouckère, Gare-Centrale *many routes* *10am–1am*

One of the most popular taverns on the Grand-Place, along with the Brouette, the Cerf and the Chaloupe d'Or. ★ When weather permits, try a cask ale out on the terrace, overlooking what Cocteau described as 'the finest theater in the world'. Or sit inside and enjoy a bowl of onion soup in old-style surroundings. But do not forget that the privilege of being on the Grand-Place will be reflected in the prices.

Not forgetting

La Fleur en papier doré (7) 55, rue des Alexiens / 1000 ☎ 511 16 59 Sun.–Thurs. 11am–1am; Fri., Sat. 11am–3am *If you are looking for local color, this tavern is well worth a visit. Founded by the Sisters of Charity in 1846, in the 1920s it became the meeting place of the Brussels Surrealists. This is still evident from the walls of its three small rooms, darkened by time and tobacco smoke, with their Dada pictures and graffiti.* **Le Falstaff (8)** 17-23, rue Henri-Maus / 1000 ☎ 511 87 89 Sun.–Thurs. 11.30am–3pm; Fri., Sat. 11.30am–5am *Designed by Houbion, a disciple of Horta, the Falstaff* weinstube *opened in 1903. The small tavern has since become a large brasserie typical of Brussels. A stained-glass window (1909), depicts the legendary Shakespearean character.*

If beer does not appeal to you, don't worry! Brussels is full of small bars which serve drinks other than the national brew. They range from the conventional to the bizarre, from bistros specializing in one type of drink to others where the décor is all-important. And there are plenty that are almost impossible to categorize – a good thing, too.

After dark

Le Cercueil (9)

10-12, rue des Harengs / 1000 ☎ 512 30 77 ➡ 513 33 61

M *De Brouckère, Gare-Centrale* *many routes* *Sun.–Thurs. 11am–3am; Fri., Sat. 11am–5am*

This bar is totally given over to the prince of darkness. You can drink your beer from a skull, and coffins do duty as tables. Then there are cocktails with such reassuring names as 'devil's sperm' or 'corpse juice', crowds of tourists, subdued lighting and suitable macabre canned music.

Goupil le Fol (10)

22, rue de la Violette / 1000 ☎ 511 13 96 ➡ 511 13 96

M *Gare-Centrale* *many routes* *Daily 8pm–4am*

Lulled by nostalgic old French songs, this ageless bistro weaves its spell. Old gramophone records are tacked to the walls, which are impregnated with the fragrance of fruit wines (the house specialty). The subdued atmosphere is ideal for a quiet chat with friends, putting the world to rights, or snogging on one of the beat-up old settees on the first floor.

Les Chemins du Sud (11)

43, rue de l'Écuyer / 1000 ☎ 514 37 03

M *De Brouckère, Gare-Centrale* *many routes* *Tues.–Thurs. 10pm–3am; Fri.–Sun. 10pm–6am*

The most 'underground' of Brussels' cafés looks more like a squat. There is even a small reception committee and you pay to get in. The clientele is very 'grunge'; the décor apparently from a junk shop. Liberally sprinkled with vodka and lime, the walls reverberate to soul or funk produced by the sound system or, if you come on the right day, played by one of the groups that sometimes perform here.

Le Metropole (12)

31, place De Brouckère / 1000 ☎ 219 23 84

M *De Brouckère* *many routes* *Sun.–Thurs. 9am–1am; Fri., Sat. 9am–2am*

The spacious covered terrace of this splendid hotel ➡ 29 always attracts a large crowd. Facing the busy square, the wicker chairs of the brasserie provide a vantage point from which to see and be seen. The Art-Deco interior is also worth a look.

Not forgetting

■ **CyberThéâtre (Avenue) (13)** 4, avenue de la Toison-d'Or / 1050 ☎ 500 78 11 @ info@nirvanet.net Mon.–Fri. 10am–1am; Sat. 11am–2am; Sun. 3pm–1am *Former movie theater, now a cyberspace temple with Blade-Runner-style décor and resident DJs. ★ Help is available for learning to surf the net.* ■ **De Skieven Architek (14)** 50, place du Jeu-de-Balle / 1000 ☎ 514 43 69 Daily 6am–7pm *In the heart of Marolles, this café bears the insulting nickname given to the architect of the Palais de Justice. The ideal place to have a drink after visiting the flea market.* ■ **Le Soleil (15)** 86, rue du Marché-au-Charbon / 1000 ☎ 513 34 30 Sun.–Thurs. 10am–1am; Fri., Sat. 10am–2am *Bistro in a former boutique, always busy in the evenings. ★ Sit out on the terrace in fine weather.*

15

N
SAINTE-CATHERINE
12
De Brouckère
R. des Chartreux
Bourse
R. Van Artevelde
11
Bd Anspach
CATHÉDRALE
GRAND-PLACE
9
Midi
Gare Centrale
Place Fontainas
15
du
10
Rue
Place St-Jean
Place de l'Albertine
Anneessens
Place Rouppe
MONT DES ARTS
Place du Grand Sablon
PALAIS ROYAL
Rue Haute
R. des Minimes
Rue de la Régence
Porte de Namur
Pl. du Jeu de Balle
14
PALAIS DE JUSTICE
JARDIN D'EGMONT
13

14

12

9

CAFE METROPOLE

Because Belgium is a relatively small country, it has always welcomed artistic productions from abroad. Theaters in Brussels therefore regularly feature seasons of foreign works. But Belgian authors and artists are also very creative, and increasingly their often innovative productions are delighting audiences abroad. Visit the major theaters for performances of

After dark

Théâtre royal du Parc (16)

3, rue de la Loi / 1000 ☎ 512 42 82 ➡ 512 80 98

Parc, Arts-Loi 60, 65, 66 ; tram 92, 93, 94 ***Matinée*** *3pm* ***Evening performance*** *8.15pm; closed June and July ● 200-900 BEF*

Brussels boasts a number of theaters. The Parc, opposite the Parliament building on the edge of the Parc Royal, features Belgian and foreign actors in an eclectic but traditional repertoire which includes Ionesco, Goldoni and Racine. As you might imagine, the auditorium has a gilded ceiling, balconies and red carpets. A program to rejuvenate this venerable institution began in March, 1999.

Théâtre royal de la Monnaie (17)

4, rue Léopold / 1000 ☎ 229 12 11 ➡ 229 13 80

De Brouckère many routes ***Performances*** *generally 8pm ●* ***Operas*** *300–3,200 BEF* ***Ballets*** *800 BEF* ***Concerts*** *250–1,100 BEF*

This building was the scene of Belgium's first revolutionary convulsions in 1830. Nowadays, it hosts opera, the ballets of Anna-Teresa De Keersmaeker, and recitals by great tenors. For the year 2000, La Monnaie is preparing for Wagner's *Ring* and a work by the Belgian composer Philippe Boesmans based on Shakespeare's *Winter's Tale*.

Le Public (18)

64-70, rue Braemt / 1210 ☎ 0800 944 44 ➡ 223 29 98

Madou 29, 63 ***Performances*** *Tues.–Sat. 8.30pm, Sun. 3.30pm; closed July 15–Aug. 15 ● 750 BEF dîner-spectacle ● 1 300 BEF*

A private theater which in a short time has performed the feat of attracting several thousand spectators each season. Its productions appeal to a wide audience: comedy, classic drama, vaudeville and more serious material. ★ It has recently opened a second restaurant, L'Aparté, where you can mull things over before or after the performance.

Théâtre de la Place des Martyrs (19)

22, place des Martyrs /1000 ☎ 223 32 08 ➡ 227 50 08

De Brouckère 65, 66, 71; many tram routes ***Performances*** *Wed.–Sat. 8.15pm, Tues. 7pm, Sun. 4pm ● 600 BEF fast food*

A converted movie theater, this venue is now home to the formerly itinerant Théâtre en Liberté company. The aim of the actors and their director, Daniel Scahaise, is to give drama a prominent place in the life of the city by making it accessible to a large audience. This includes staging revivals of some of the great classics.

Not forgetting

■ **Théâtre national de la Communauté française de Belgique (20)** 28, centre Rogier, place Rogier / 1210 ☎ 203 53 03 *Founded in 1945, the national theater is undoubtedly one of the pillars of Belgian theatrical life. The program includes major classics and new plays.* ■ **Théâtre de Poche (21)** Chemin du Gymnase, bois de la Cambre / 1000 ☎ 649 17 27 *This theater tackles controversial social issues (drugs, violence, etc.) and every year recruits young actors from the city's drama schools.*

both the classics and new plays, or look for more off-beat entertainment in some of the capital's smaller venues.

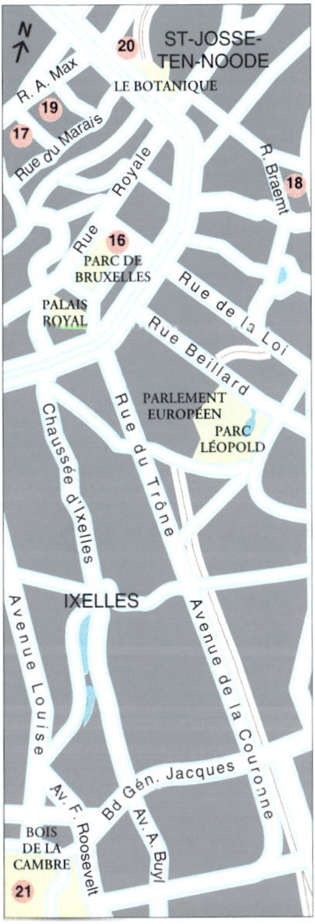

18

17

16

One of the works staged by the Théâtre de la Place des Martyrs during the 1998–99 season was Alexandre Dumas' ***The Three Musketeers***.

19

Belgium regularly plays host to the great names in international show business. The concerts of rock, soul, funk and rap artists, and French singers, are always attended by appreciative, well-informed Belgian audiences. At the same time, smaller venues offer 'alternative' but equally attractive styles of music.

After dark

Forest National (22)

Avenue Victor-Rousseau / 1190 ☎ 340 22 11 ➠ 340 22 19

54 ; tram 18, 52 **Box office** *24h/24 ☎ 0900 00 951* **Performances** *8pm or 8.30pm ● variable*

This is Brussels' largest concert hall, with seating for about 8,000. Most of the big stars perform here when visiting the city. They range from Eros Ramazzotti to Johnny Hallyday, by way of Deep Purple! With such irresistible attractions, you would do well to book in advance.

Ancienne Belgique (23)

110, boulevard Anspach / 1000 ☎ 548 24 24 ➠ 548 24 99

De Brouckère many routes **Box office** *Mon.–Fri. 10.30am–6.30pm; Sat. 10am–3pm ● 300–1,500 BEF*

This celebrated music hall has welcomed Trenet, Piaf and Brel... and given groups such as The Cure, The Clash and Red Hot Chili Peppers their first big break. At the end of 1997, it acquired a new auditorium, new acoustics and a café-restaurant. There is a consistency about the programing: groups and singers from Belgium and abroad, already famous or on the verge of success. The management seems to have an instinct for making the right choice.

Le Botanique (24)

236, rue Royale / 1210 ☎ 218 37 32 ➠ 219 66 60

Botanique many routes **Box office** *Daily 10am–6pm (10.30pm on concert evenings)* **Concerts** *8.30pm ● 350-450 BEF*

This vast tropical glasshouse has several auditoria, and performances are also staged outdoors. Among the regular high spots are the Parcours Chanté song festival, the Théâtre en Compagnie festival (productions by new theater companies), Scènes d'écran (devoted to arts in the audiovisual media), and in September the wonderful season of Nuits Botaniques when dozens of concerts are organized.

Le Cirque royal (25)

81, rue de l'Enseignement / 1000 ☎ 218 20 15 ➠ 219 59 58

Parc, Madou many routes **Box office** *Tues.–Sat. 11am–6pm* **Performances** *matinée 3pm or 4pm; evening 8pm or 8.30pm ● variable*

This auditorium is used for staging various types of show: productions by the Théâtre royal de la Monnaie (such as *Don Giovanni*) or the Jean-Vilar theater of Louvain-la-Neuve, comedy, concerts and children's theater. The theater-in-the-round format makes it easy to achieve the right setting for each production.

Not forgetting

■ **Lunatheater (26)** 20, square Sainctelette / 1000 ☎ 201 58 58 *Theater, dance, music and public lectures. ★ Literary café every first Monday in the month.*
■ **Beursschouwburg (27)** 22-28, rue Auguste-Orts / 1000 ☎ 513 82 90 *Concerts, exhibitions, lectures, local festivals... These bare brick walls have heard a thing or two. Although this is a Flemish venue, it has a warm welcome for people of the most varied backgrounds.*

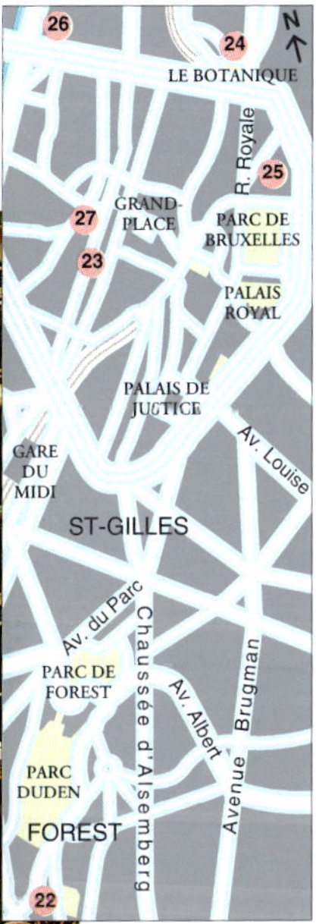

Le Botanique has three auditoria, including the semi-circular Rotonde (left).

24

25

26

27

If you still have doubts about the Bruxellois' appetite for having fun, darken the doors of a local cabaret. Whether their forte is putting up an amusing defense of local tradition or featuring young, up-and-coming artistes, there are plenty of places where you can have a laugh, sing along or swing to the music.

After dark

Chez Flo (28)

25, rue au Beurre / 1000 ☎ 513 31 52 ➠ 514 22 75

M *De Brouckère* *many routes* *7.30–11pm*

No doubt about it, Flo is to Brussels what Michou is to Paris. In this little house, located between the Grand-Place and the Bourse, Marilyn Monroe, Serge Gainsbourg, Dalida, Claude François, Piaf and others live again in the performances of talented drag artists. Michael Jackson, Prince and George Michael are also in on the fun. Performances worthy of the great Parisian music-halls, with four choices of menu: *Argent* (1,475 BEF), *Or* (1,950 BEF), *Prestige* (2,375 BEF) and *Privilège* (2,950 BEF, including a half bottle of champagne).

Théâtre royal de Toone (29)

21, Petit-Rue-des-Bouchers / 1000 ☎ 511 71 37 ➠ 218 55 78

M *Bourse, Gare-Centrale* *many routes* *Tues.–Sat. 8.30pm* ● *400 BEF*

Since 1830, the Toone family has kept alive the magic of adult puppet theater, staged in the Bruxellois dialect ➠ 82. The current puppet-master, Toone VII, performs thirty or so different plays with his marionettes, including the star turn, Woltje. ★ In addition, you can visit the museum, where elderly puppets spend their retirement, and there is a friendly little bar. Book for performances.

Le Travers (30)

11, rue Traversière / 1210 ☎ 218 40 86 ➠ 223 10 21

M *Botanique* *many routes* **Box office** *Mon.–Sat from 2pm*
Concerts *Mon.–Sat. 8.30pm* ● *300 BEF* @ *www.cyclone.be/travers/*

Renowned for its jazz, Le Travers also features other styles, such as rhythm 'n' blues, and world-wide ethnic music. Atmospheric jam sessions take place on Monday nights. Top Belgian and international musicians regularly perform here, and no two evenings are the same. If you are not a great jazz fan, a visit to Le Travers might make you think again.

La Samaritaine (31)

16, rue de la Samaritaine / 1000 ☎ 511 33 95 ➠ 242 60 53

20, 48 **Box office** *Tues.–Sat. from 7.30pm* **Performances** *8.30pm*
● *400 BEF*

A café-theater just as it ought to be. In Marolles, one of Brussels' most working-class districts, not far from the very chic Place du Sablon, a crumbling staircase leads down to a small, cellar-like room with bare brick walls. It may seat only a hundred or so people, but here you can discover talented young singers, comics and actors. Huguette, the patronne, organizes the program and shows you to your seat.

Not forgetting

■ **Le Comiqu'Art (32)** 1, rue de la Victoire / 1060 ☎ 537 69 37 *Café-theater featuring Belgian and international comedians, new faces and established stars.* ■ **La Soupape (33)** 26a, rue A.-Dewitte / 1050 ☎ 649 58 88 *This very French-style cabaret has recently celebrated its twentieth anniversary.*

N
LE BOTANIQUE
ST-JOSSE-TEN-NOODE
30
Bd A. Max
Boulevard Anspach
R. du Midi
29
28
GRAND-PLACE
Rue Royale
PARC DE BRUXELLES
Rue de la Loi
Rue Belliard
PALAIS ROYAL
31
R. des Minimes
R. de la Régence
Rue du Trône
PALAIS DE JUSTICE
Chaussée d'Ixelles
Avenue Louise
IXELLES
32
33
ST-GILLES

29

THÉATRE DE MARIONNETTES
TOONE
TOONE VII
GOUNOD
BIZET
SATIE
GEAL
FAUQUEZ
GHELDERODE
SHAKESPEARE
MOLIERE
DUMAS
FEVAL
CORNEILLE
ROSTAND
CONSCIENCE
ARISTOPHANE
ZEVACO
MARIONNETTES DE TRADITION POPULAIRE
BRUXELLES
N BOIS POUR NE PAS AIMER
BOIS AYANT UNE ÂME
Jean Cocteau

LA SAMARITAINE

31

28

If you want to see a movie in Brussels, you will be spoiled for choice. Every genre is well represented in the city's movie theaters: British, French, American, commercial, art... The programs, which change every Wednesday, are published in the daily papers. Most films are shown in the original version, with subtitles in both French and Flemish – an

After dark

Kinépolis (34)

20, boulevard du Centenaire / 1020 ☎ 474 26 00

Heysel; 84, 89 ; tram 23, 81; Daily showings 2.30pm, 5pm, 8pm, 10.30pm; ● 250 BEF; ☎ program 0900 00 555

Located in the Parc des Expositions, Kinépolis is a concrete monster with thirty auditoria, a temple to the seventh art. Its lack of soul is made up for by the wide choice of films, among which American and British blockbusters predominate. Coke and popcorn in profusion, as you would expect.

Cinéma NOVA (35)

3a, rue d'Arenberg / 1000 ☎ 511 27 74

De Brouckère, Gare-Centrale; many routes; depending on the program; ● 200 BEF; ☎ program 0900 29 550

Opened in January 1997 by a group of film buffs, this formerly derelict movie theater has been saved from certain death. A cheap-and-cheerful refurbishment, non-conformist programing and publicity stunts in the vicinity have brought back the spectators. One Thursday a month, there is an Open Screen session, when DJs play music to accompany the pictures. ★ On Fridays, the NOVA hosts a political debate – everyone's views welcome.

Arenberg Galeries (36)

26, galerie de la Reine / 1000 ☎ 512 80 63

De Brouckère, Gare-Centrale; many routes; Daily showings 2pm, 5pm, 7pm, 10pm; ● 200 BEF; ☎ program 0900 29 550

What distinguishes the Arenberg from other movie theaters is its policy of screening full-length art films and old favorites. It also runs a children's movie club to introduce young people to some of these treasures. Another unique feature of the Arenberg is its summer *Écran Total* program of classics and new material. ★ Thursday is Sneak Preview evening: you only find out the title of the movie when the opening credits begin to roll.

Musée du Cinéma (37)

9, rue Baron-Horta / 1000 ☎ 507 83 70

Gare-Centrale; 71, 60, 38 ; tram 92, 93, 94; ***Daily showings*** *6.15pm, 8.15pm, 10.15pm (talkies); 7pm, 9pm (silent movies); ● 60 BEF if paid in advance, 90 BEF on the day*

This museum is unique, showing five films a day: three talkies and two silent movies with live piano accompaniment, as in the good old days. ★ Before or after the show, you can also visit a permanent exhibition illustrating the history of the seventh art. Each month, there is a series of movies featuring a particular country, genre or director.

Not forgetting

■ **UGC De Brouckère (38)** 38, place De Brouckère / 1000 ☎ 0900 / 10 440
A very large movie theater showing both British/American and French productions.

■ **Actor's Studio (39)** 16, Petite-Rue-des-Bouchers / 1000 ☎ 0900 / 27 854
Located in the historic heart of the city, this theater screens movies made by the smaller European and American studios, retrospectives, major classics, etc.

aspect of Brussels' official bilingualism. Reduced rates on Mondays.

34

36

35

38

When it was renovated, the UGC retained the large auditorium of the former Eldorado theater with its magnificent 1930s décor.

Brussels has a thriving night life, and every taste is catered for, whether you are looking for techno music, a place to dance or an 80s-style club. Night spots do not open before 11pm, but the fun goes on well into the early hours.

After dark

Les Jeux d'hiver (40)

1, chemin du Croquet, bois de la Cambre / 1050 ☎ 649 08 64

38 ; tram 23, 90, 93, 94 Thurs.–Sat. ***Bar*** *9pm–dawn* ***Disco*** *0.30am–dawn* ● ***Admission*** *free* ***Drinks*** *200 BEF*

Les Jeux d'Hiver opened about ten years ago and is still a very popular venue, especially with the capital's more privileged young people. They size you up at the door, and you may be turned away if you do not make the grade. Inside, there is a long bar and a classic FM style of music. The two main events of the year are the club's anniversary celebration, in November, and the ball held on July 21, the national holiday.

Chez Johnny (Le Claridge) (41)

24, chaussée de Louvain / 1210 ☎ 227 39 99

M *Madou 29, 63, 65, 66 Fri., Sat. 10pm–5am* ● ***Admission*** *150 BEF* ***Drinks*** *150–250 BEF*

This is the place for those who want to jig about to the music of the 1980s and earlier. Johnny, the master of ceremonies, referees a mock duel between two DJs and is not averse to interrupting the music with the screen credits of cartoon movies or television series. The young, and not so young, work up a sweat to the music of U2 or even Abba, and no one takes themselves too seriously.

Le Bal (42)

47, boulevard du Triomphe / 1160 ☎ 644 93 91

M *Pétillon, Delta 34 ; tram 23, 90 Fri., Sat. 10pm–dawn* ● ***Admission*** *free* ***Drinks*** *150–200 BEF*

A former warehouse converted into a night club, opposite the VUB and ULB university campuses. The outside is painted purple red; the inside is cozy with an abundance of sofas. The denizens are of course rather on the young side, but for the more staid there is also the occasional thé-dansant. The decibel level is fairly restrained as Le Bal is located in a residential area.

Le Fuse / La Démence (43)

208, rue Blaes / 1000 ☎ 511 97 89 ➟ 512 89 67

M *Porte-de-Hal 20, 48 ; tram 23, 55, 90 Sat. 10pm–7am* ● ***Admission*** *300 BEF (Sat.: free 10–11pm* ***Drinks*** *150 BEF*

Open for business since April 1994, Le Fuse has lost none of its popularity, and no wonder. Each of the three floors is devoted to a different style of music: techno on the ground floor, house on the first, and jazz-funk-electro up top. The sophisticated insulation system stops them from drowning one another out. ★ Every evening, the consoles are manned by resident DJs or internationally famous guest stars.

Not forgetting

■ **Le Mirano Continental (44)** 38, chaussée de Louvain / 1210 ☎ 227 39 70 Fri., Sat. midnight–dawn *The one night club you must not miss, nirvana of dance and techno.* ■ **Who's Who's Land (45)** 17, rue du Poinçon / 1000 ☎ 511 93 88 Thurs.–Sat. 11pm–dawn *Large night club specializing in techno in a slightly out-of-the-way area, tends to attract the moneyed classes.*

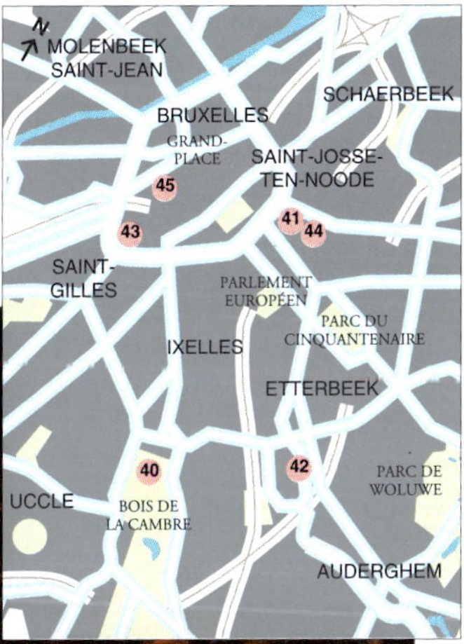
N
MOLENBEEK
SAINT-JEAN
SCHAERBEEK
BRUXELLES
GRAND-
PLACE
SAINT-JOSSE-
TEN-NOODE
45
43
41
44
SAINT-
GILLES
PARLEMENT
EUROPÉEN
PARC DU
CINQUANTENAIRE
IXELLES
ETTERBEEK
40
42
PARC DE
WOLUWE
UCCLE
BOIS DE
LA CAMBRE
AUDERGHEM

40

41

43

45

What to see

Comic-strip capital
Since 1991, the city's historic center and subway stations have been invaded by cartoon characters ➡ 12: Keep your eyes open! There is a statue of Gaston Lagaffe and twenty or so large mural paintings, some of them in less frequented areas. They are gradually taking over the place: to be continued…

Guided tours

Arau
The urban environment of Brussels as seen by its inhabitants.
55, bd Adolphe-Max / 1170
☎ 219 33 45
➡ 219 86 75

Arcadia
Historians take a look at the art of Brussels.
38, rue du Métal / 1060
☎ 534 38 19
➡ 534 60 73

Talking bus
Walks and bus tours with a running commentary.
12, rue des Thuyas / 1170
☎ 673 18 35
➡ 675 19 67

Itineraries
Stroll in the footsteps of famous local figures.
157, rue Hôtel-des-Monnaies / 1060
☎ 539 04 34
➡ 534 02 14

The many faces of Brussels: Musée Album
A lively little museum where you can learn about Brussels and Belgium through newspapers, photographs, movies, music, strip cartoons, etc.
25, rue des Chartreux / 1000 Ⓜ *Bourse* ⏲ *Wed.–Mon. 1–7pm*
• *from 50 to 200 BEF, depending on how long you spend in the museum.*

52 Sights
THE INSIDER'S FAVORITES

Festivals and events

Ommegang
Early July. On the evidence of old documents and pictures, this annual procession in 16th-century costume in honor of Our Lady was instituted in 1549, when the Emperor Charles V presented his heir, Philip II, to the people of Brussels.

Carpet of flowers, Grand-Place
Mid-August, every two years. Thousands of flowers are used to create an immense carpet of vivid color.

Planting the Meyboom
Every year, August 9. To commemorate their victory over the city of Louvain, in 1213, the Bruxellois dig up a tree in the forest of Soignes and, accompanied by giant figures and horsemen, carry it in procession to the corner of Rue des Sables and Rue du Marais. There they plant it (before 5pm), with jubilant shouting and music. The planting of the May tree *(Meyboom)* is then celebrated around a bonfire until late into the night.

INDEX BY TYPE

Greater Brussels (known in french as the Région de Bruxelles-Capitale) is a metropolitan area consisting of 19 municipalities. It has 950,000 inhabitants and covers an area of 63 sq miles. Of the region's 75 elected representatives, 65 are Francophone and 10 are Flemings. The regional government has two ministers who are French speaking and two Flemish speaking, a neutral

What to see

The traditional face of Brussels: the giant figures wheeled out for local festivals.

A cosmopolitan city

Brussels is the only capital city in the world hosting three diplomatic missions from each foreign country: one to the Belgian state, one to the European Union, and one to NATO. As well as all these diplomats and 'Eurocrats', there is a large immigrant population, making Brussels a real Tower of Babel. Fortunately, communication does take place, despite the many different languages. Talking of Babel, in the local dialect '*babbeler*' is the word for having a good natter. The visitor who strays out of the city center toward such districts as Saint-Gilles, Schaerbeek or Saint-Josse might well think he was in Spain, Morocco or Turkey. At least, anyone spending a long period in Brussels does not have to look far in order to find the authentic national cuisine of his or her country of origin.

A city on a human scale

A colorful city, and a city with an abundance of greenery, though you might not think so at first sight. According to one study, Brussels is the second greenest city in the world – after Washington D.C. – with 48 sq yards of parkland per inhabitant (as against 1.79 sq yards in the case of Paris). While joggers from the ministries and banks prefer to work up a midday sweat in the Parc Royal, those from the European Union favor the Parc du Cinquantenaire. With their attractive mix of architecture and greenery, both are places where you can forget the city's building sites and traffic problems. Of course, they might appear very 'provincial' to someone from Athens, Rome, Paris or Cairo. Brussels is still a relatively small city, more or less human in scale, despite the fact that, as capital of the kingdom, it is invaded each morning by over 300,000 commuters, some traveling considerable distances from Wallonia and Flanders to occupy the acres of newly built office space. Unfortunately, these construction projects and the related real-estate frenzy have led to the destruction of streets full of character and historic buildings, leaving ugly scars on the urban fabric. The discerning visitor will tend to hop from one unspoiled island to another.

president and three secretaries of state.

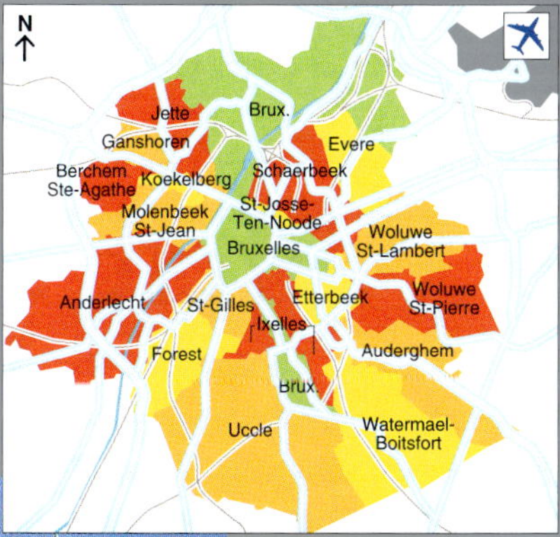

An urban archipelago

From the main 'island', centered on the Grand-Place, narrow streets branch out to some of the most obvious sights, such as Manneken Pis, the Bourse, the Galeries Saint-Hubert, and the good and less good restaurants in the Rue des Bouchers district. A 'bridge' connects it with the cathedral of Saints-Michel-et-Gudule. A few minutes walk up the hill brings you to the Palais des Beaux-Arts, designed by Horta, the Place Royale and the adjacent royal palace, and the art museums where Van der Weyden, Memling, Bosch, Bruegel and Rubens exist in uneasy proximity with Permeke, Ensor, Magritte and Delvaux. Then you are only a short walk from the Sablon, with its abundance of antique shops and restaurants. Other islands in this archipelago are the European district, the Cinquantenaire, Heysel, Laeken, and so on. You can get from one to the other by subway, or on foot.

A long process of urban development

On the whole, thanks are due to the Maréchal de Villeroy who, on the orders of Louis XIV, bombarded Brussels on August 13 and 14, 1695. In the wake of this disaster, the municipal authorities obliged the owners of properties on the Grand-Place to seek approval for their rebuilding plans. The result was the magnificent square we see today. Credit is also due to Leopold II – the king with the big white beard – who was the force behind such building projects as Notre-Dame-de-Laeken, the Bourse, the Palais de Justice, the church of Sainte-Marie, the Cinquantenaire, the Laeken conservatories, the Musée d'Art Ancien and the Tervuren museum, even though his megalomania led to the destruction of many of the – often unhealthy – working-class districts. Three cheers, too, for Horta who, with the intelligence of an enlightened middle-class industrialist, embellished the city with Art-Nouveau architecture, setting the example for the later Art-Deco style of the 1920s. And *fourt!* for all those who have not struggled to preserve the urban fabric from greedy developers. And hats off to those people who are returning to live in the city center, reversing the 'inevitable' exodus toward the more fashionable suburbs. The fact that Brussels is not entirely dead in the evenings is very much due to them.

In the area

The best way to surprise and impress an unsuspecting friend on first visit to Brussels is to for a walk through the narrow streets surrounding the Grand-Place, then suddenly emerge into the open square. This was once the Nedermerct, or lower market, heart of the city when it began

What to see

Grand-Place (1)

Ⓜ *Bourse, Gare-Centrale, De Brouckère* 🚌 *many routes*

After Louis XIV's bombardment in 1695, little of the square was left standing: only the outer walls of the Hôtel de Ville and the Maison du Roi. 3,850 houses in the city center had been destroyed by fire. The magistrate of the day decreed that the owners should submit their plans to him before rebuilding any of the houses overlooking the 'market'. The result of this inspired decision was the splendid square that still casts its spell. The Italian Baroque style, in the hands of Flemish architects, lends it an appearance of unity that can accommodate even the Louis XIV-style façades of Le Renard (the Fox) and Le Cygne (the Swan). Every house is identified by a name, which does not always correspond to the guild that owned it. For example, nos. 1 and 2, now called Le Roi d'Espagne, were formerly owned by the bakers. No. 3, known as La Brouette (the Wheelbarrow), belonged to the tallow-chandlers. No. 4, owned by the cabinet-makers and coopers, is referred to as Le Sac. Then come La Louve (the She-Wolf, archers, no. 5), Le Cornet (boatmen, no. 6), Le Renard (mercers, no. 7), L'Étoile (the Star, no. 8), Le Cygne (butchers, no. 9), where Marx and Engels drafted the *Communist Manifesto*, L'Arbre d'or (the Golden Tree, brewers, no. 10), which of course houses a brewing museum. La Maison des Ducs de Brabant (nos. 13–19) incorporates La Fortune (tanners, no. 15), Le Moulin à vent (the Windmill, millers, no. 16), Le Pot d'étain (the Pewter Pot, carpenters and wheelwrights, no. 17) and La Colline (the Hill, sculptors, masons and stone-cutters, no. 18). The old guildhalls are completed by La Chaloupe d'or (the Golden Galleon, tailors, nos. 24 and 25) and Le Pigeon (painters, nos. 26 and 27), where Victor Hugo stayed in 1851. The other buildings were private dwellings.

Hôtel de ville (2)

Grand-Place / 1000

Ⓜ *Bourse, Gare-Centrale, De Brouckère* 🚌 *many routes* *(in French) Apr.–Sept.: Tues. 10.45am, 2.30pm; Wed. 2.30pm; Sun. 10.45am / Oct.–Mar.: Tues. 10.45am, 2.30pm; Wed. 2.30pm ● 75 BEF* ♿

This is the highest expression of secular Gothic architecture. Work on the left-hand wing and belfry was begun in 1402; the construction of the right-hand wing in 1444. As the original tower seemed crushed by the two wings, it was replaced by the present belfry, erected between 1449 and 1454. It is 317 ft in height, including the gilded copper statue of Saint Michael overcoming the dragon (16 ft 6 in). The interior decoration is impressively rich, including tapestries from Brussels (18th century) and Malines (19th century), sculptures, many portraits of kings and queens and some fascinating views of Brussels, painted by Van Moer between 1872 and 1874.

Not forgetting

■ **Maison du roi (3)** Grand-Place / 1000 ☎ 279 43 58 🕒 Mon.–Thurs. 10am–12.30pm, 1.30–5pm (Oct.–Mar.: closed at 4pm); Sat.–Sun. 10am–1pm
This is probably called the King's House because the Emperor Charles V, also king of Spain, built it on the site of the 12th-century bread market. But no king has ever lived in it. After 1695, it was rebuilt on its original foundations using 17th-century prints for guidance. It is now the city museum, with original statues from the Hôtel de Ville's façade and a collection of costumes for Manneken Pis, from 1747 to the present.

to expand in the 11th century confirmed by the names of the adjacent streets.

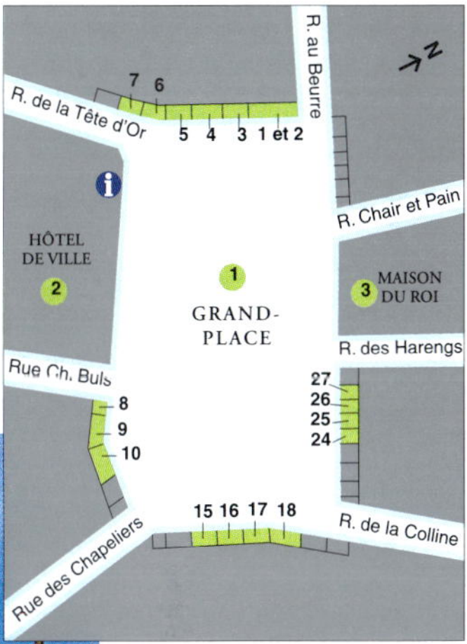

1

1

1

2

3

A refurbishment of the façade of the Hôtel de Ville was completed in 1998, restoring its original whiteness.

In the area

The 'îlot sacré' (sacred island) is the network of small streets surrounding the Grand-Place. ■ Where to stay ➡ 18 ➡ 20 ➡ 22 ➡ 26 ■ Where to eat ➡ 40 ➡ 42 ■ After dark ➡ 62 ➡ 64 ➡ 66 ➡ 68 ➡ 70 ➡ 72 ■ What to see ➡ 80 ■ Where to shop ➡ 126 ➡ 128 ➡ 130 ➡ 138

What to see

Galeries Saint-Hubert (4)
Rue du Marché-aux-Herbes / 1000

M *Gare-Centrale, De Brouckère, Bourse* 🚌 *many routes*

This is the place to see and be seen, and a real pleasure to visit at any time. Built in 1846, the Galeries Saint-Hubert were the first covered arcades of their kind in Europe. There are three in all: one dedicated to the Queen, the second to the Princes, the third to the King. It was at no. 7 of the Galeries du Roi that the brothers Lumière staged the first movie show in Belgium (1896). Restaurants, boutiques and theaters make the arcades a rendezvous of the well-to-do. They were designed by Cluysenaer and decorated in a graceful neoclassical style by Joseph Jacquet.

Musée du Costume et de la Dentelle (5)
6, rue de la Violette / 1000 ☎ 512 77 09 ➡ 279 43 62

M *Bourse, Gare-Centrale, De Brouckère* 🚌 *many routes* 🕑 *Apr.–Sept.: Mon., Tues. and Thurs.–Fri. 10am–12.30pm, 1.30–5pm; Sat., Sun. and public holidays. 2–4.30pm / Oct.–Mar.: closed at 4pm / closed in Jan.* ● *100 BEF*

In a street of uncharacteristically decrepit buildings, this museum houses a collection of women's garments dating from the 18th century to the present day, and also celebrates the art of lace-making, in Brussels and elsewhere, from the 17th to the 20th centuries. Items are displayed in special drawers to protect them from the light. The museum also has a section devoted to contemporary lace, and stages temporary exhibitions.

Manneken Pis (6)
Angle de la rue du Chêne et de la rue de l'Étuve / 1000

M *Ankeessens, Bourse* 🚌 *many routes*

Everyone wants to see him, but his size – a mere 2 ft, tiny compared with the long jet of water he emits – disappoints many visitors. According to legend, the statue commemorates a small boy who used his natural fire-hose to extinguish the fuse of a bomb. In fact, it was simply a fountain, installed in the 16th century, to supply the district with drinking water. The present statue is an 1817 recasting of the original made by Duquesnoy *père* in 1619. Brussels' most famous citizen has been stolen several times, and owns a wardrobe of several hundred costumes, which can be viewed in the Maison du roi ➡ 80.

Not forgetting

■ **Théâtre royal de Toone (7)** 21, Petite-Rue-des-Bouchers / 1000 ☎ 511 71 37 🕑 Performances Tues.–Sat. 8.30pm *At the far end of a cul-de-sac in the restaurant district, this tavern dates from 1696. By day, it is a place to have a drink and admire the marionettes which hang from the beams. In the evenings, it puts on fascinating performances of traditional puppet theater* ➡ *70. Using the local dialect, often adapted to the composition of his audience, José Géal, better known as Toone VII, presents a repertoire which takes in the life of Christ, Dumas, Molière, Shakespeare, Gounod and Bizet.* ■ **La Bourse (8)** 2, rue Henri-Maus / 1000 *Designed by Léon Suys, this eclectic-style temple of commerce was inaugurated in 1873. Auguste Rodin, who lived in Brussels from 1870 to 1877, helped Carrier-Belleuse make the frieze of cupids for the elevation fronting the Rue Henri-Maus, and the caryatids inside the building.*

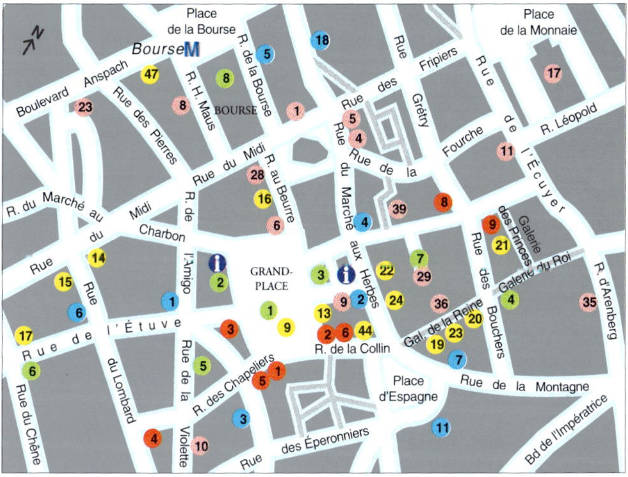

6

4

4

The Galeries Saint-Hubert, with luxury stores, café terraces and places of entertainment, have always been a focus of social life

5

In the area

De Brouckère was burgomaster of Brussels from 1848 to 1860. The square assumed its present form in 1893. Its 19th-century charm is symbolized by the Metropole hotel ➥ 28 built by Bordiaux in 1870 and altered by Chambon in 1894. ■ Where to stay ➥ 26 ➥ 28 ■ Where to

What to see

Église Saint-Jean-Baptiste-au-Béguinage (9)

Place du Béguinage / 1000

M *Sainte-Catherine, De Brouckère* 🚌 *47, 63 ; many tram routes* 🕓 *July–Aug.: Tues.–Sat. 11am–5pm; Sun. 10am–5pm / Sept.–June: Tues 10am–5pm; Wed.–Fri. 9am–5pm; Sun. 9.30am–1.30pm* ♿

Although richly decorated, this church is built in a luminous, sober Baroque style prefiguring a whole series of Italo-Flemish Renaissance edifices. The architect is unknown, but there are some striking similarities with the church of the Riches-Claires, erected by Fayd'herbe in 1665. It has a remarkable pulpit (1757), transferred from a former Dominican church in Malines. It was made by Parent of Namur and features the awesome heretic-hunter, Saint Dominic. On either side of the building are three typical 18th-century confessionals.

Église Sainte-Catherine (10)

Place Sainte-Catherine / 1000

M *Sainte-Catherine, De Brouckère* 🚌 *63 ; tram 18* 🕓 *Mon.–Sat. in summer: 8.30am–6pm, in winter: 8am–5pm; Sun. 8.30am–1pm / closed on public holidays.*

The present church was built by Poeleart in 1854, at the same time as he was engaged on Notre-Dame-de-Laeken. What an appetite for work! It stands on the site of a former dock, heart of the old river port, filled in in 1853 after the River Senne flooded its banks. The covering over of what had become an open sewer (1867–71) totally changed the appearance of old Brussels. A blend of various styles, St Catherine is not particularly harmonious, but in the 19th century represented a bold architectural experiment. On the square itself, the 1664 tower is all that remains of the former church, demolished in 1893.

The old port area (11)

M *Sainte-Catherine* 🚌 *63 ; tram 18*

The decision to fill in the docks of the old port, which connected Brussels with the sea, was taken in 1907. In the 16th century, St Catherine's dock was the hub for all river traffic. All that now remains are the names of the former quays. Here, if you walk along with your nose in the air, you will see some fine old façades. The Quai aux Briques and the Quai du Bois-à- Brûler opposite are separated by two artificial lakes which serve as a reminder of the good old days. Behind the Square des Blindés, there are some fine old houses on the Quai aux Barques and Quai aux Bois-de-Construction (nos. 1–10). From there, the Quai au Foin and Quai aux Pierres-de-Taille will bring you to the Théâtre Royal Flamand.

Not forgetting

■ **Maison de la Bellone (12)** 46, rue de Flandre / 1000 ☎ 513 33 33
This house, entered from a courtyard, is reminiscent of the buildings on the Grand-Place. Its classical façade, with Flemish-style decoration, dates from 1697. It now houses the Maison du Spectacle, headquarters of various cultural organizations.

■ **Théâtre royal flamand (13)** 146, rue de Lacken / 1000 ☎ 219 49 44
This former warehouse, on the dock where hay was unloaded, was converted into a theater by J. Base in 1887 in the Flemish neo-Renaissance style. The rear elevation has remained unaltered since it was built in 1781.

eat ➥ 44 ➥ 48 ■ After dark ➥ 64 ➥ 72 ■ Where to shop ➥ 126 ➥ 132

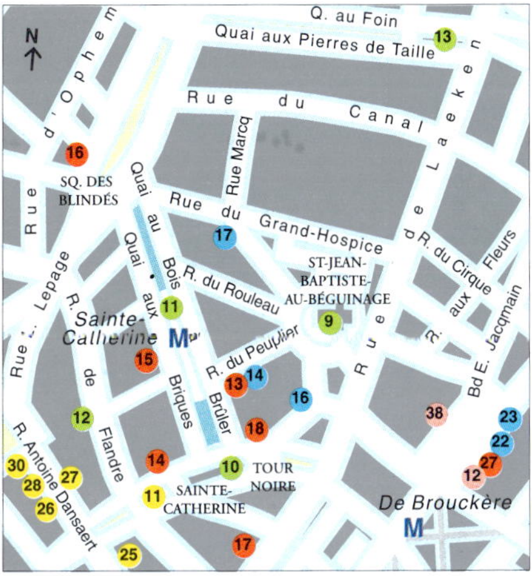

9

10

The church of Saint-Jean-Baptiste with its Flemish triple-gabled façade, is all that remains of a *béguinage* (religious community) founded in the 12th century by a priest from Liège, Lambert le Bègue.

11

In the area

Nothing here is beyond the range of a reasonably fit pedestrian. From the cathedral, go past the austere buildings of the Banque Nationale and follow the rather uninteresting boulevard that leads to the Botanique. A short detour will bring you to the comic-strip museum. A pleasant walk in search

What to see

Cathédrale des Saints-Michel-et-Gudule (14)
Parvis Sainte-Gudule / 1000

Gare-Centrale *many routes* *Daily 8am–6pm*

A chapel dedicated to the archangel Michael stood on this hill as early as 1047. Jean I, Duke of Brabant from 1190 to 1235, also known as Jean Primus or Gambrinus, commissioned the present building. Work began on the apse in 1220 and ended with the north tower in 1480. This French-style cathedral with twin towers (unusual in this part of the world) is one of the finest examples of the Gothic style of architecture. Its stained-glass windows alone deserve a special visit, particularly those of the transept, made between 1537 and 1538 to designs by the painter Van Orley, representing celebrities of the day: Louis II and Mary of Hungary, Charles V and Isabella of Portugal. The windows of the choir, 1522–1525, are also worth seeing. The chapel of Notre-Dame-de-la-Délivrance, planned by Jérôme Duquesnoy *fils*, to the right of the ambulatory, has some remarkable sculptures and windows. If you are in a hurry, at least stop to admire the Baroque pulpit by Verbruggen, completed in 1699. The Rubenesque twelve apostles (1644), again by Duquesnoy *fils*, are works of some merit.

Centre belge de la bande dessinée (15)
20, rue des Sables / 1000 ☎ 219 19 80 ➟ 219 23 76

Botanique, Gare-Centrale, Rogier *38, 58, 61 ; many tram routes* *Tues.–Sun. 10am–6pm* ● *200 BEF (a museum ticket ensures free admission to the reading room)*

Hidden away in a not very attractive street, but still near the bustling Rue Neuve, this building combines two Belgian specialties: Art Nouveau and the comic strip. It was built by Victor Horta in 1903 for the textile wholesaler Charles Waucquez, and is the sole survivor of six warehouses he designed. Long derelict, the premises were saved from total ruin by the comic strip, which goes perfectly with the atmosphere, and above all the lighting, of Art-Nouveau architecture. As well as staging temporary exhibitions, it traces the development of the genre in Belgium, from its beginnings to the latest creations. One room illustrates the genesis of a comic strip; another shows how it is made into an animated cartoon. But, for the connoisseur, the greatest attraction is the 300 or so original plates on display, drawn from the center's collection of over 1,500. With the world's largest library of comic strips, a fabulous shop and a high-class brasserie/restaurant, this is a must for all devotees of the genre.

Le Botanique (16)
236, rue Royale / 1210 ☎ 226 12 11

Botanique *58, 59 ; tram 92, 93, 94* *Daily 10am–6pm, except performances*

The brilliant Pierre Gineste was the architect of the glass structures which crown what was once Brussels' second botanical garden: a rotunda surmounted by a dome and flanked by two graceful wings, in the noble traditions of 18th-century orangeries. Sculptures by Constantin Meunier (*Summer* and *Autumn*) adorn the gardens of this complex, which now houses the cultural center of Belgium's French community ➡ 68. ★ An ideal spot to take a stroll, read a book, or have a 'snack with a view'.

of the Belgian psyche! ■ Where to stay ➡ 22 ➡ 32 ■ Where to eat ➡ 48 ■ After dark ➡ 62 ➡ 68 ➡ 70 ■ Where to shop ➡ 138

14

16

15

16

In the area

The Mont des Arts was a romantic garden laid out in 1909 on the hill between the Place Royale and the Grand-Place. Unfortunately, the area was developed in 1956. ■ Where to stay ➡ 22 ■ Where to eat ➡ 42 ■ After dark ➡ 62 ➡ 68 ■ Where to shop ➡ 124 ➡ 126 ➡ 138

What to see

Palais des Beaux-Arts (17)
23, rue Ravenstein / 1000 ☎ 507 82 20

M Gare-Centrale, Trône, many routes, 10am–7pm, except performances, exhibitions ● depending on the exhibition or concert

Although from the outside this building is not particularly striking, Horta was very skillful in making the best possible use of the available space. Between 1922 and 1928, he created a 9,568 sq yard complex which includes vast exhibition rooms and a concert hall with matchless acoustics seating 2,200 people. The Reine-Élisabeth music competition is held in this auditorium. The palace is also the venue for prestigious exhibitions, particularly those organized as part of the 'Europalia' festival.
★ Since 1967, a movie museum has also been housed here ➡ 72.
It consists of an exhibition illustrating the early history of the industry, with 40 displays, and a library of 35,000 movies. Five historic productions are shown each day: three talkies and two from the days of the silent screen, with piano accompaniment. The museum has its own entrance, at 9 rue Baron-Horta.

Bibliothèque royale Albert-Ier (18)
4, boulevard de l'Empereur / 1000 ☎ 519 53 11 ➡ 519 55 33

M Gare-Centrale, Trône, many routes, Mon.–Fri. 9am–8pm; Sat. 9am–5pm ● 100 BEF / week

Also known as the Albertine, this library is a bookworm's delight. The average tourist will ignore the 4 million volumes, the 17 floors housing the reserve collection and the 62 miles of shelves, to concentrate on the collections of manuscripts and medals. In the engravings department, you can have a print made from any one of 5,000 woodcuts or copper plates. There is also a printing museum that possesses some rare items, such as Félicien Rops's press, but unfortunately the décor is rather unimaginative. Of special interest are reconstructions of the working environments of Max Elskamp and Henry Van de Velde, Michel de Ghelderode and Émile Verhaeren.

Église Notre-Dame-de-la-Chapelle (19)
4, rue des Ursulines / 1000

M Anneessens, 20, 48, June–Sept. : Mon.–Fri. 9am–5pm; Sat. 1.30–5pm; Sun. 1.30–3.30pm

Although the choir and transept date from the early 1400s, the nave was not built until the 15th century. The result is a mixture of Romanesque, early and even flamboyant Gothic, which makes this building one of the most interesting in Belgium. Typical of the Brabant version of Gothic architecture are the capitals of the columns in the nave, with their 'curly-cabbage-leaf' decoration, and, as in the cathedral, the impressive statues carved by Duquesnoy *fils* and Fayd'herbe in the years between 1645 and 1657. After admiring Plumier's pulpit (1720), you must pay your respects to Pieter Bruegel the Elder, or 'Boeren Bruegel' (died 1569), whose marble epitaph can be seen opposite the altar. The epitaph was made by his son, Jan 'Velvet' Bruegel, and refashioned in 1676 by his great-grandson, David Teniers III, son of David Teniers II and Anne Bruegel. Quite a dynasty!

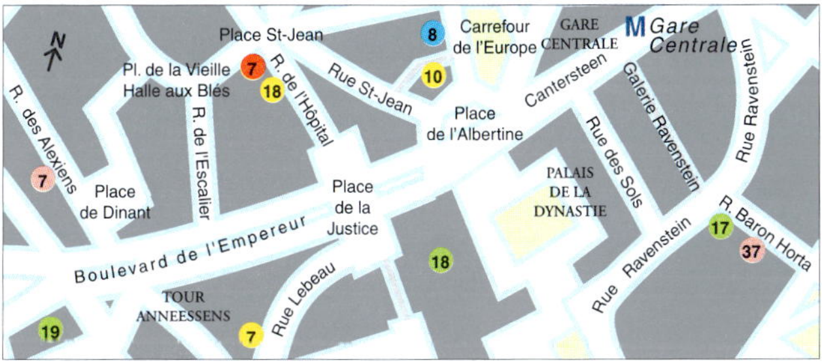

18

18

19

The bell tower of Notre-Dame-de-la-Chapelle, one of Brussels' oldest and most beautiful churches (12th century), is late-17th-century.

In the area

Credit for this fine square is due to Charles of Lorraine, governor general of the Netherlands in the late 18th century, who wanted to make Brussels more like Vienna. In the center, the statue of Godfrey of Bouillon, by Simonis (1848), leads the eye toward the church of Saint Jacques-sur-Coudenberg.

What to see

Musée d'Art ancien (20)

3, rue de la Régence / 1000 ☎ 508 32 11 ➠ 508 32 32

Gare-Centrale, Parc; many routes; tram 92, 93, 94; Tues.–Sun. 10am–5pm ● joint admission to this museum and the Musée d'Art moderne 150 BEF, free for under 12s

The monumental entrance to this museum was designed in 1876 by Balat, Leopold II's favorite architect. Here you can see works by the Flemish 'Primitives' (15th century) – Van der Weyden, Bouts, Memling and Bosch – and also by Lucas Cranach the Elder and Gérard David. These are followed by the Bruegel family, then Rubens, Van Dyck and Jordaens. The 19th century is represented on the ground floor: French painters such as Courbet and Jacques-Louis David, the 'social sculpture' of the Belgian Constantin Meunier, much admired by Rodin, and Impressionist and Neo-Impressionist paintings by the likes of Van Rysselberghe, Evenepoel and Van Gogh. Marvel at the pure Symbolism of Fernand Khnopff, and do not forget Gauguin, Bonnard, Vuillard, Seurat, Signac, Ensor, Rodin, Rops, Renoir, Monet and Sisley. This section is soon to be enlarged to include the Dutch painters, who for the time being remain consigned to the reserves. From here, a corridor conveys you to the world of 20th-century art.

Musée d'Art moderne (21)

3, rue de la Régence / 1000 ☎ 508 32 11 ➠ 508 32 32

Gare-Centrale, Parc; many routes; tram 92, 93, 94; Tues.–Sun. 10am–5pm ● joint admission to this museum and the Musée d'Art ancien 150 BEF, free for under 12s

The museum's collection of 20th-century art is arranged on eight basement levels around a central 'well', designed by the architect Bastin. Belgian artists rub shoulders with their contemporaries from other countries. The Brabant Fauves, represented by Rik Wouters and Spilliaert, are followed in rough chronological order by Matisse, Braque, Picasso, Kokoschka and Chagall. Belgian Expressionism is well represented by Permeke, Van den Berghe and De Smet, while the Surrealists Delvaux and Magritte hang alongside De Chirico and Dalí. The Belgian 'new wave' finds expression in Delahaut, Van Lint and Bertrand. After Alechinsky and the Cobra group, the permanent exhibition ends with some bold examples of contemporary work.

Palais royal (22)

Palais royal / 1000 ☎ 551 20 20 ➠ 502 38 49

Trône; 95, 96; tram 92, 93, 94; end of July–end of Sept.: Tues.–Sun. 10.30am–4.30pm ● admission free

In 1827, William I of the Netherlands commissioned Suys to build a central portico connecting two old town houses. In 1904, Leopold II altered this porch with its five arches and six Corinthian columns, adding a pediment and raising the roofline. Inside, the main staircase and throne room were designed by Balat. The long gallery, reception rooms and hall of mirrors are in a slightly severe Louis XVI manner. It is amazing to think that, at the same time, Horta and his disciples were working in so different a style for the wealthy middle classes. To the far right of the palace is the Hôtel de Bellevue, housing a museum devoted to the Belgian royal dynasty, with special emphasis on the reigns of Leopold I and Albert II.

What to see ➥ 104

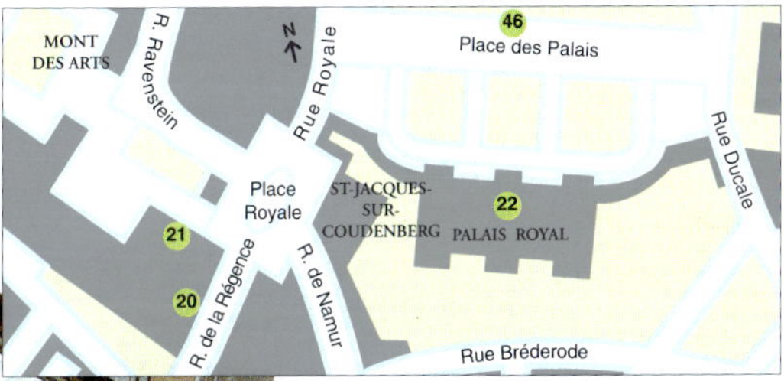

22

21

Rubens figures prominently at the Musée d'Art ancien: portraits, drawings, and compositions e.g. *The Adoration of the Magi.*

20

In the area

A vast plain of marsh and sand, the Sablon was a practice ground for crossbowmen, who in 1304 built a chapel there dedicated to Our Lady. In 1348, a certain Baet Soetkens contributed a miraculous statue, filched from Antwerp, attracting many pilgrims. ■ Where to stay ➥ 34 ➥ 36

What to see

Notre-Dame-du-Sablon (23)

3B, rue de la Régence / 1000 ☎ 511 57 41 ➟ 514 25 26

20, 34, 48, 95, 96; tram 92, 93, 94 Mon.–Fri. 9am–6pm; Sat., Sun. 10am–6pm on request

The culmination of Brussels Gothic (1549), and regarded as the finest example of the flamboyant style in Belgium, this church is more a celebration of the goldsmith's art than of the architect's. The *sacrarium* – enclosing the choir – bears witness to the elaborate richness of the workmanship. In addition to the 'curly cabbage' capitals typical of Brabant Gothic, it features a unique nave with four aisles. It is easy to understand why Paul Claudel, the French ambassador to Belgium, frequently came here to pray. Be sure to visit the two Baroque chapels flanking the choir, given by the princes of Thurn and Taxis. The Renaissance sculptors Fayd'herbe and Duquesnoy *fils* were also employed on the building.

Place du Petit-Sablon (24)

20, 34, 48, 95, 96; tram 92, 93, 94

This wonderful square, inaugurated in 1890, was laid out by the architect H. Beyaert, who also designed the fine station at Tournai. There are 48 statues, each personifying one of the corporations or crafts of Brussels. In the background is the fine sculptural group of Counts Egmont and Horne. These bronzes were modeled by Fraikin in 1864 and originally stood on the Grand-Place. They commemorate the beheading in 1568 of two noblemen who opposed the Spanish occupation under the Duke of Alba. At no. 17 is a musical instrument museum, which will soon be moving to the fine Art-Nouveau 'Old England' building on the Place Royale. It houses a collection of 6,000 instruments, ranging from prehistoric times to the present day. At no. 30 is the royal conservatory of music.

Place du Grand-Sablon (25)

20, 34, 48, 95, 96; tram 92, 93, 94

This square owes its charm to the old houses that surround it, Louis XIV, XV and XVI styles rubbing shoulders with 16th-century crow-step gables. High society is attracted by the café terraces, antique shops and one of Brussels' most famous patisseries, Wittamer ➥ 124. No. 40 houses the Musée des Postes et Télécommunications.

Le palais de justice (26)

Place Poelaert ☎ 508 65 78 ➟ 508 64 54

M Louise 34, 95, 96; tram 91, 92, 93, 94 Mon.–Fri. 8am–3pm ● admission free

Dominating a hill which, in the Middle Ages, was known as the Galgenberg (the sinister 'gallows mountain'), the law courts by the architect Poelaert were inaugurated in 1883. This huge building was the largest edifice erected on the European continent in the 19th century. It covers an area of 31,100 sq yards, has 27 courtrooms and 245 other rooms (chambers, cells, etc.), and a vast waiting area (4,300 sq yards). Some people think it a monstrosity. Poelaert was harshly criticized at the time, for his megalomania, but also because so much of the working-class Marolles district had to be cleared to make way for the building.

Where to eat ➥ 50 ➥ 54 After dark ➥ 70 Where to shop ➥ 124

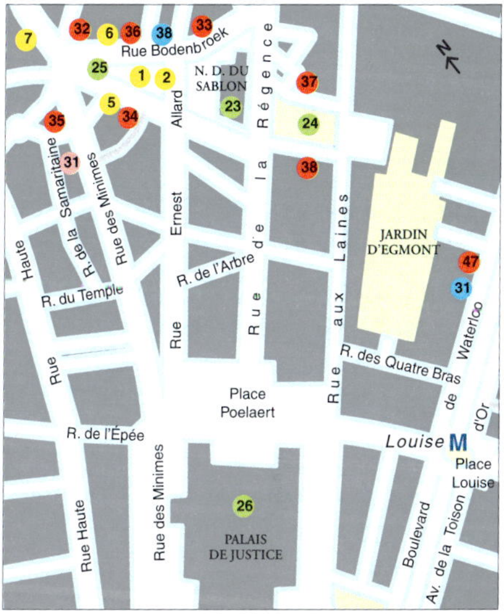

23

24

25

The Grand-Sablon was originally a horse market, and later a fruit and vegetable market. Now it is dominated by antique dealers.

26

In the area

On this former parade ground, Bordiau, a pupil of Poelaert, laid out a park with a pavilion and two semi-circular colonnades to house the 1880 National Exhibition celebrating Belgium's fiftieth anniversary. In 1897, the site was used for a Universal Exhibition. The triple arch

What to see

Musées royaux d'Art et d'Histoire (27)

10, parc du Cinquantenaire / 1000 ☎ 741 72 11 ➠ 733 77 35

M *Mérode, Schuman* *many routes; tram 81, 82* P *Tues.–Fri. 9.30am–5pm; Sat., Sun. and public holidays 10am–5pm* ***Treasure room*** *Tues.–Fri. 10am–noon, 1–4pm* ● *150 BEF; admission free on 1st Wed. of month 1–5pm*

A manifestation of the encyclopedic spirit of the 19th century, the royal museums of art and history are among the largest in Europe, with remarkable exhibits from all parts of the world and every historical period. Including the loot from Belgian excavations in Egypt and the Middle East, the collections are so well stocked that every section really deserves a separate visit. The absolute masterpieces are a reconstruction of the Roman Apamea colonnade and mosaics discovered in Syria; a splendid model of ancient Rome; a bas-relief of Queen Tiy, wife of Amenhotep III; the so-called Montezuma feather cloak (16th century); and a colossal statue from Easter Island. The new treasure room contains masterpieces of goldsmith work from the Meuse area, 12th-century enamels, 16th-century altarpieces, lace and tapestries. The cherry on the cake is room 50, featuring Art Nouveau, with display cabinets designed by Horta himself in 1912.

Autoworld (28)

11, parc du Cinquantenaire / 1000 ☎ 736 41 65 ➠ 736 51 36

M *Mérode, Schuman* *many routes; tram 81, 82* P *Oct.–Mar. 10am–5pm / Apr.–Sept. 10am–6pm* ● *200 BEF*

Housed in one of the dazzling pavilions built for the 1897 exhibition, this is the largest automobile museum in Europe. It consists of some 450 steam, electric and petrol-driven vehicles from the 1,000-strong collection of Ghislain Mahy of Ghent. Three hundred of them are in good working order. Almost all the Belgian car manufacturers are present – Minerva, FN, Imperia, etc. – and the German, American, French, British and Italian car industries are well represented. Further attractions are the limousines owned by International heads of state and celebrities (for example, Albert I, J.F. Kennedy), and the D'Ieteren room, featuring a collection of horse-drawn conveyances.

Not forgetting

■ **Le musée de l'Air (29)** 3, parc du Cinquantenaire ☎ 734 21 57 Tues.–Sun. 9am–noon, 1–4.45pm *Opposite Autoworld, this section of the army museum houses over 90 military and civilian aircraft, including all the great planes of both world wars. Of special interest is the Ouragan, the first French jet fighter, brought into production by Dassault in 1949.*

■ **Musée royal de l'Armée et de l'Histoire militaire (30)** 3, parc du Cinquantenaire ☎ 734 52 52 Tues.–Sun. 9am–noon, 1–4.45pm *Linger in front of the remarkable displays of weapons and armor from the Middle Ages to the 19th century. There are military memorabilia from all periods of Belgian history, sometimes rather unimaginatively presented. Here you can gain an idea of Belgium's experience of occupation, revolution and two world wars. There are some fine items from the Napoleonic wars, and also some armored vehicles.*

symbolizing Brabant was completed by Girault in 1905.

What to see ➥ 104

As well as its fine collections (below), the Musée royal de l'Armée et de l'Histoire militaire has a documentation center and library.

28

30

28

In the area
Who could have anticipated the little old Luxembourg station and 'Leopold district' undergoing such a transformation? Undistinguished exit point for commuters from the south of the country, it has been caught up in one of the century's largest architectural developments.

What to see

Espace Léopold (31)
Place du Luxembourg / 1000

Trône *many routes*

One of the major building projects of the last ten years, the 'Space' was obtained by roofing over the railroad tracks of the Leopold district station. In its new form, the station will be able to handle 25,000 passengers a day. The area now consists of a 5-acre tree-planted esplanade, and the redevelopment of derelict industrial sites will result in the creation of a 'Mall' with 2,600 offices, 16 conference halls and 52 meeting rooms for the members and staff of the European Parliament. It will also include restaurants, bars, a sports center, a meditation room and the Parliament library. Close attention has been paid to the lighting and acoustics, and innovative, environment-friendly techniques have been used.

Hémicycle européen (32)
60, rue Wiertz / 1000 ☎ 284 21 11

Trône, Maalbeek *20*

Behind the new 'Mall', the distinguishing feature of the Leopold building is its 230-ft tower. Though some have nicknamed it 'caprice des dieux' (whim of the gods), it is really more like a good old Wurlitzer juke box – all shiny chrome. When they are not in Strasbourg, the MEPs and their civil servants are here, three weeks out of four. Actually, the building belongs to the Centre international de Congrès, which rents it to the EU. The hemicycle itself has seating for 750 parliamentarians, plus a 500-seat gallery for the public and press. Close by are three further amphitheaters, seating 150, 250 and 350 people. Special care has been lavished on the furniture and light fittings. *Confluences*, the shiny steel sculpture in the atrium by Olivier Strebelle, reaches to the third floor. The large reception area is often used for exhibitions, and the *salon d'honneur*, right at the top under the glass roof, boasts a work by Aligi Sassu, 1,615 sq ft in area, consisting of 583 ceramic tiles: *The Rape of Europe*.

Muséum des sciences naturelles (33)
260, chaussée de Waire / 1000 ☎ 627 42 38 ➡ 627 41 13

Trône, Maalbeek *many routes* *Tues.–Sat. 9.30am–4.45pm; Sun. 9.30am–6pm* ● *150 BEF* *on request*

People come from all over the world to stand in wonder before this herd of 29 fossilized iguanodons. Sixteen feet tall and 32ft long, they make more impression than the automated and very lifelike model dinosaurs nearby. They were discovered in 1878 in a coal mine at Bernissart, in the Hainaut region. Though they steal the show, a close second are the skeletons of Neanderthal 'Spy Man', found near Namur in 1886. If you are short of time, do not miss the fascinating whale room, where the skeletons of these magnificent creatures, like concrete sculptures, brush the heads of visitors. Also beautifully presented are the shell collection, live spiders and scorpions, and a teeming ants' nest.

When work is finished, this district will be truly amazing.
■ Where to eat ➥ 40
■ What to see ➥ 104

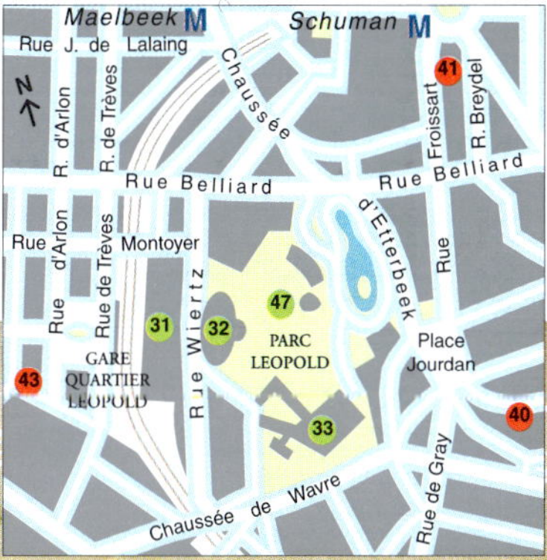

32

33

At the Muséum des sciences naturelles, this magnificent wooden Neanderthal man was reconstructed from a real skull.

33

33

In the area

The area around the Abbaye de la Cambre is a haven of peace, with a 16th-century church and the national school of architecture and decorative art.
■ Where to stay ➥ 34 ■ Where to eat ➥ 46 ➥ 54 ➥ 56 ■ After dark ➥ 64 ➥ 66 ➥ 70 ➥ 74 ■ What to see ➥ 104

What to see

Musée communal d'Ixelles (34)

71, rue J.-Van-Volsem / 1050 ☎ 511 90 84 ➠ 647 66 72

many routes; tram 81, 82 *Tues.–Fri. 1–7pm; Sat., Sun. 10am–5pm* ● *free (except for temporary exhibitions* *on request*

In an out-of-the-way district where car parking is difficult, the museum took over the former municipal slaughterhouse in 1892. It owns more than 13,000 items, including 19th-century posters (in particular 28 by Toulouse-Lautrec) and fine collections of 19th- and 20th-century paintings. All schools are represented, from Berthe Morisot to Pop Art. Permeke, Delvaux and Gaston Bertrand feature prominently, and there is a room devoted to Magritte.

Musée Horta (35)

25, rue Américaine / 1060 ☎ 543 04 90 ➠ 538 76 31

54, 60 ; tram 81, 82, 91, 92 *Tues.–Sun. 2–5.30pm* ● *150 BEF, Sat., Sun. 200 BEF*

Victor Horta had this dual-purpose building erected in the years from 1898 to 1901, one part as a residence, the other as a workshop and laboratory. Behind the unassuming façade, all the techniques developed by the Belgian master of Art Nouveau are in evidence: the use of iron to do away with partition walls and give a greater sense of space; glass and mirrors to introduce more light; and the open stairwell to link and define the different levels. Every detail – from door-handle to radiator to light-fitting – is designed as part of the whole. An object lesson in sensitivity and refinement taken to the nth degree.

Porte de Hal (36)

Boulevard du Midi / 1000 ☎ 534 15 18

M *Porte-de-Hal* *20, 48 ; tram 23, 55, 90, 52, 56, 81*

This gate, built between 1357 and 1383, is all that remains of the city's second circle of walls. It has undergone many modifications over the years, and in 1870 Henri Beyaert added a tower with a spiral staircase, transforming it into a romantic little castle.

Musée David-et-Alice-Van-Buuren (37)

41, avenue L.-Errera / 1180 ☎ 343 48 51

60 ; tram 23, 90 *Sun. 1–5.30pm; Mon. 2–5.30pm* ***Gardens*** *daily 2–5pm* ● *300 BEF* ***Gardens*** *100 BEF* *on request*

David Van Buuren, a Dutch banker (1886–1955), and his wife first laid out the gardens, not adding the house until 1929. An extension, in spirit if not in form, of the 'total art' concept of Art Nouveau, their creation is remarkably consistent and harmonious. Of the interior features, the furniture and mosaics were designed by the Parisian studio of Dominique, while the staircase and office were based on Van Buuren's own designs. The couple built up an eclectic collection which includes cushions by Sonia Delaunay, a version of *The Fall of Icarus* by Bruegel, 32 paintings by Van de Woestijne, a close family friend, and works by Fantin-Latour, Van Gogh, Ensor, Braque, Evenepoel, Wouters and others. The 3-acre garden was the province of Alice Van Buuren, who died in 1973.

■ Where to shop ➥ 134 ➥ 136 ➥ 138

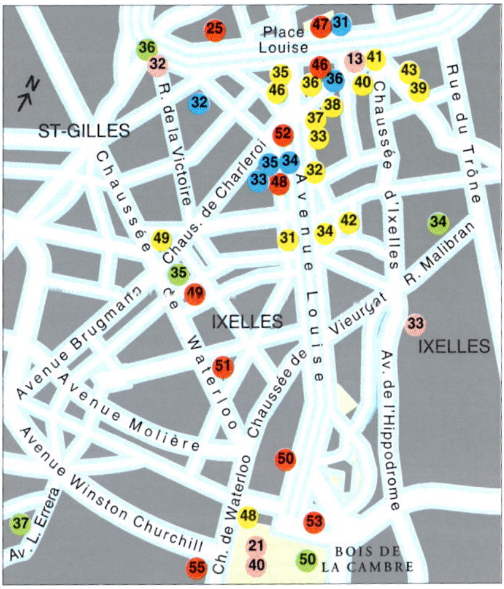

37

36

South of the city center, where the main boulevard crosses the inner ring road, stands the medieval Porte de Hal.

34

In the area
Anderlecht? Yes, it is a football club financed by an industrial brewing dynasty. No, it is not one of the most attractive parts of Brussels. But that is no reason to give it a miss, especially if its associations with Humanism and the traditional brewing of *gueuze* beer are considered.

What to see

Maison d'Érasme (38)
31, rue du Chapitre / 1070 ☎ 521 13 83 ➟ 527 12 69

M *Saint-Guidon* 🚌 *47, 49; tram 56* 🕓 *Wed., Thur. 10am–noon, 2–5pm; Sat.–Mon. 10am–noon; 2–5pm* ● *50 BEF* *on request*

Dating from the 16th century, this is one of the last surviving examples of Gothic domestic architecture in the region. It was restored in 1986 with a grant from the Belgian Petrofina corporation. Erasmus (1469–1536), originally from Rotterdam, taught at the universities of Oxford, Cambridge and Bologna. Pacifist, priest, and a friend of Thomas More, to whom he dedicated his *Praise of Folly*, he lived in this house from May to October 1521. It contains some impressive late-Gothic and Renaissance furniture, and a collection of 15th- and 16th-century paintings: Van der Goes, Van der Weyden, a splendid *Adoration of the Magi* by Hieronymus Bosch, David, Bouts, Dürer and Metys. Do not miss the collection of censored books. An astonishing oasis in the surrounding urban wilderness.

Musée bruxellois de la Gueuze (39)
Brasserie Cantillon, 56, rue Gheude / 1070 ☎ 521 49 28 ➟ 520 28 91

M *Clemenceau, Gare-du-Midi* 🚌 *20, 47, 49, 50; many tram routes* 🕓 *Mon.–Fri. 8.30am–5pm; Sat. 10am–5pm* ● *100 BEF* *on request*

This is very much a living museum: the last *gueuze* brewery active in the Brussels built-up area. Before 1914, there were 50 of them. Amazingly, it is impossible to make *gueuze* other than in the valley of the River Senne, which has a monopoly of the micro-organisms essential to the fermentation process. Because this happens spontaneously, and the temperature must be right, *gueuze* is only brewed from the end of October to the end of March. A mixture of water, uncooked wheat and malt is brought to boiling point, then hops are added. The wort obtained in this way is left to cool in a tank under the eaves. This is when the *Brettanomyces lambicus* and *bruxellensis* yeasts get to work on the tasty liquid and cause it to ferment. The flat beer which results – *lambic* – is then put in bottles to undergo a secondary fermentation. The final result is the frothy, sourish beer known as *gueuze*. ★ Twice a year, it is possible to watch the brewing process from 6.00am. Call to inquire about the dates.

Basilique du Sacré-Cœur (40)
1, parvis de la Basilique / 1083

M *Simonis* 🚌 *13, 14, 20, 87; tram 17* 🕓 ***Church** summer: daily 8am–6pm / winter: daily 8am–5pm **Panorama** daily 9am–5.15pm / winter: 10am–4.15pm* ● ***Panorama, cupola, exhibition** 100 BEF* *on request*

Instead of 'basilique de Koekelberg', its detractors call this church the 'koekelik de baselberg' — a reference to its cake-and-bun appearance. The foundation stone of a seven-towered Gothic edifice, intended to soar to a height of 492 ft, was laid by Leopold II in 1905. But the original project proved too expensive and was never finished. In 1926, Van Huffel took up the challenge and the work ended in 1969 with the completion of the 295-ft cupola. The basilica has some fine windows by Anto Carte and a statue of the Sacred Heart by Georges Minne, who died while working on it in 1941. He also sculpted the poignant crucifix, located on the outside wall of the apse. ★ From the top, there is a magnificent view over the city.

Where to stay ➥ 36
Where to eat ➥ 46 ➥ 58
Where to shop ➥ 126

38

39

40

In the area

The football stadium, now named after King Baudouin, is not the only attraction of the Heysel plateau. All year round, the pavilions of the Centenaire are used for trade exhibitions of all kinds. And as well as all the commercial bustle, there are some genuine tourist attractions, and the

What to see

L'Atomium (41)

Boulevard du Centenaire / 1020 ☎ 474 89 77 ➟ 474 83 98

Heysel 84, 89; tram 23, 81 Apr.–Aug. Daily 9am–8pm / Sept.–Mar.: daily 10am–6pm ● 200 BEF if booked in advance

Designed by Waterkeyn and built by A. and J. Pollak, this is one of the few vestiges of the 1958 Universal Exhibition. It represents a crystalline iron molecule enlarged 165 billion times. The nine spheres, each 59 ft in diameter, represented Belgium's nine provinces. The elevator travels from the ground to the summit (335 ft) in 23 seconds. And if you are having a meal at the Adrienne restaurant (closed on Sundays), in the highest of the spheres, the elevator ride is free. Major refurbishment work is due to begin soon.

Mini Europe and Brupark (42)

1 et 20, avenue du Football / 1020 ☎ 478 05 50 ➟ 478 26 75

Heysel, Houba, Brugman 84, 89; tram 23, 81 ***Mini Europe*** *July–Aug.: daily 9.30am–8pm / Sept: daily 9.30am–6pm / Oct.–Jan.: daily 10am–6pm / Apr.–June: daily 9.30am–6pm ● 395 BEF*

Around the Atomium is a recreational complex known as the Brupark. It includes Kinépolis ➥ 72, with its 30 movie theaters and 682-sq-ft Imax screen, a tropical environment and aquarium known as Océade, cafés and restaurants – an attempt to recapture the fun-centered atmosphere of Expo '58. The main attraction is Mini Europe, a 5-acre development owned by the Walibi group. It consists of 300 models, the 1:25 scale of which gives Big Ben a height of 13 ft. All the EU's major sights and monuments are there.

Crypte royale de Notre-Dame-de-Laeken (43)

Avenue du Parc-Royal ☎ 0900 10 000 (code 11 077)

Bockstael 49, 53, 89; tram 81, 94 Sun. 2pm–5pm

This church was built as a memorial to Louise-Marie, first Queen of the Belgians. The architect was J. Poelaert (see Palais de Justice ➥ 92) Begun in 1854, it was consecrated in 1872, though not really finished. Unusually, the choir is not at the east end, but faces northwest, so that the main frontage provides a backdrop for the new avenue honoring the queen. In its unfinished state, the church leaves much to be desired: the pillars are made of brick rendered with concrete and the capitals are molded rather than carved. A 13th-century Virgin and Child, repainted in bright colors in 1872, has its devotees. The main reason for visiting the building is the crypt, last resting place of Belgium's kings and queens.

Not forgetting

■ **La Tour japonaise (44)** 44, avenue Van-Praet / 1020 ☎ 268 16 08 Tues.–Sun. 10am–4.45pm *Impressed by the Parisian architect Alexandre Marcel's 'Tour du Monde', built for the 1900 Paris Exhibition, Leopold II asked him to design this Buddhist pagoda (1901–1904). It is used for exhibiting items of 19th- and 20th-century Japanese decorative art.* ■ **Le Pavillon chinois (45)** 44, avenue Van-Praet / 1020 ☎ 268 16 08 Tues.–Sun. 10am–4.45pm *By the same architect as the Japanese Tower above, and originally designed to house a restaurant, this pavilion is now used for exhibiting the Chinese porcelain collections of the royal art and history museums. Its fine wooden paneling was made in Shanghai.*

region's largest movie theater complex. ■ Where to eat ➥ 58 ■ After dark ➥ 58 ■ What to see ➥ 104

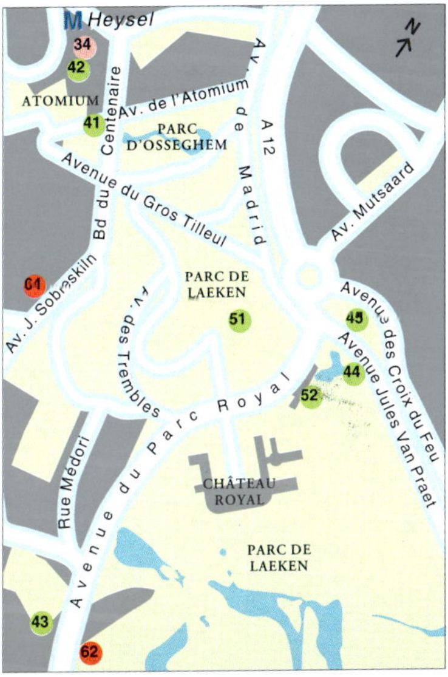

44

41

43

42

Brussels can rightly congratulate itself on the fact that 13.8 percent of its ground area is covered in greenery. It is impossible to mention all the capital's parks and gardens, but pride of place must go to the Forêt de Soignes, a 'green lung' where the beech rules supreme. Also significant are the parks of Duden, Forest, Josaphat, Baudouin, Woluve and

What to see

47

50

46

48

Parc de Bruxelles (46)

Parc, Trône
95, 96; tram 92, 93, 94

This garden, dating from 1774, is often referred to as the 'royal park', or simply 'the park'. It was here that the Belgian volunteers besieged the Dutch in the 1830 Revolution that led to the founding of the Belgian state. Extending 500 by 350 yards, it lies between the Palais Royal and the Palais de la Nation, which houses the Chamber of Representatives and the Senate. Geometrical in layout, the park is a delightful place to sit on a bench at lunchtime and have a sandwich. It is surrounded by Louis XVI-style buildings.

Parc Léopold (47)

Rue Belliard
Maelbeek
20

The entrance is at the bottom of the Rue Belliard, just past the European Parliament building. Laid out in 1851, it is now in the heart of the European district. Ernest Solvay wanted to turn it into a science complex and you can still admire the Solvay library, built by Bosmans and Henri Vandeveld in 1901, which is miraculously preserved. Formerly the Institute of Sociology, the building is regularly used for staging exhibitions.

Square Ambiorix (48)

Maelbeek, Schuman
54, 63

It was Leopold II (again) who, in 1875, commissioned Gédéon Bordiau, a colleague of Poelaert to create this attractive series of open spaces, named after Marguerite, Ambiorix and Marie-Louise. They are the last remnants of the old Maelbeek valley. The Marguerite and Ambiorix sections are laid out in the French style, with waterfalls, while the Square Marie-Louise is an English-style garden with grottoes. The adjacent streets contain some fine Art-Nouveau buildings, in particular Horta's Hôtel Van Eetvelde (no. 4 Avenue Palmerston).

Wolvendael, of Tintin fame.

52

Parc du Cinquantenaire (49)

Schuman, Mérode *20*

Laid out in 1880, to mark the fiftieth anniversary of the Revolution, this 93-acre complex features a number of interesting statues, including Constantin Meunier's *Reaper*. There is also a pavilion designed by Horta in his youth. For the 1880 National Exhibition, a Moorish-style building with a minaret was built to house a panorama of Cairo. In 1978, it was converted into the city's main mosque and Islamic cultural center.

★ Close by, at no. 5 Rue des Francs, is the Maison Cauchie (1905), one of the best examples of an Art-Nouveau residence. It is open to visitors the first weekend of each month, from 11am to 6pm (☎ 673 15 06).

Bois de la Cambre (50)

tram 23, 90, 93, 94

At the end of the Avenue Louise, which was laid out with access in mind, this wood covers 304 acres. It was planned by Edouard Keilig, who adopted the style of 18th-century English landscaped gardens. Closed to motor vehicles on weekends, it is very popular with hikers, cyclists, riders, skaters and canoeists.

Parc de Laeken (51)

53 ; tram 19, 23, 52, 92

Located to the north of the city center, this 395-acre park was also the brainchild of Leopold II. It contains the king's palace, in the Louis XVI style, which was rebuilt by Girault following a fire on January 1, 1890. Not far away is the Belvedere (1788), which in 1958 was adopted by the then Prince Albert (the present king) and Princess Paola as their official residence. For bird watchers: the park is home to a large colony of herons.

Serres royales (52)

Avenue du Parc-Royal / 1020

53 ; tram 19, 23, 52, 92

Built in the years from 1870 to 1879, this complex of 11 glass pavilions and vaulted galleries was designed by Balat, a teacher of Victor Horta. The large rotunda is 197 ft in diameter and 98 ft high. The buildings house an extraordinary collection of tropical and subtropical plants: tree ferns, palm trees, camellias, azaleas, fuchsias, etc. The complex is open to the general public for two weeks each year, in April/May, and is well worth waiting in line to see.

Further afield

Other towns

Brussels is a good base for visiting other Belgian towns, all interesting places to explore, and less than an hour's train journey away:

Louvain (Leuven), 16 miles
Malines (Mechelen), 17 miles
Antwerp (Anvers/Antwerpen), 30 miles
Ghent (Gand/Gent), 34 miles
Namur (Namen), 39 miles
Mons (Bergen), 42 miles
Tournai (Doornik), 53 miles
Liège (Luik), 59 miles
Bruges (Brugge), 61 miles

Brussels and Belgium

The metropolitan area of Bruxelles-Capitale is one of the three regions of Belgium. The other two are Flanders (to the north) and Wallonia (to the south), each of which is divided into five provinces. Flanders consists of West- and East-Flanders, Brabant (Flemish part), Antwerp and Limburg; Wallonia of Hainaut, Brabant (Walloon part), Namur, Liège and Luxemburg.

21 Days out

THE INSIDER'S FAVORITES

Seeing the country by bicycle

ProVélo

Guided bicycle tours (one day) taking in the forests, valleys, castles and villages of Brabant. This organization also runs group excursions lasting several days.

32 a, rue Ernest-Solvay / 1050

☎ 502 73 55 ➠ 502 86 41

Mon.–Fri. 9am–6pm

• guided tours: half-day 500 BEF; full day 700 BEF; hire of bicycles: 1 hour 100 BEF, 4 hours 300 BEF, whole day 400 BEF.

SNCB (Belgian railroads)

Bicycles can be hired at 35 stations.

☎ 224 88 61 Bruxelles-Midi station

• combined train + bicycle ticket: 335 to 615 BEF, depending on length of journey.

Seeing the country by boat

Brussels by Water

Seven guided cruises on the canals of Brussels and Brabant (Brussels/Scheldt sea-going canal and Brussels/Charleroi canal). Sights include the inclined plane at Ronquières ➥ 116, the impressive hydraulic lifts at La Louvière ➥ 116, the port of Brussels, and the town of Halle.

2 bis, quai des Péniches / 1000

☎ 420 59 20 ➠ 420 59 21

May–Sept. Mon.–Fri. 9am–6pm

• guided cruises: Brussels–Ronquières, Scheldt country 650 BEF, hydraulic lift route 550 BEF, port of Brussels 200 BEF, Halle 150 BEF.

INDEX BY TYPE

The metropolitan area of Bruxelles-Capitale is surrounded by the Flemish and Walloon parts of Brabant and, a little further to the west, the province of Hainaut. You can get an idea of these prosperous regions by venturing out twenty or thirty miles into the local countryside, characterized by forests, castles, canals, farms and small towns.

Further afield

9

5

3

Palais Stoclet (1)

Montgomery, Josephine-Charlotte *20, 61, 80; tram 39, 44*

Bibliotheca Wittockiana (2)

Boileau *36*

Musée du transport urbain bruxellois (3)

36, 42; tram 39, 44

Musée royal de l'Afrique centrale (4)

NL; tram 44 *Avenue de Tervuren / Ring Est, Tervuren exit*

Château de Rixensart (5)

(35 mins) From central station, trains to Namur stop at Rixensart (every 30 mins) ● *270 BEF (round trip)* *(17 miles) E411 (Brussels-Namur), exit 5*

Walibi (6)

(45 mins) From central station, trains to Ottignies and Wavre stop at Bierges-Walibi (every 25 mins) ● *270 BEF (round trip)* *(18 miles) E411, (Brussels–Namur), exit 6 (Wavre)*

Louvain-la-Neuve (7)

(50 mins) From central station, take a train to Ottignies, then Ottignies–Louvain-la-Neuve (every 20 mins) ● *280 BEF (round trip)* *(21 miles) E411 (Brussels–Namur), exit 9*

Abbaye de Villers-la-Ville (8)

(1 hr 18 mins) From central station, take a train to Ottignies, then Ottignies–Charleroi sud, and get off at Villers-la-Ville (every 35 mins) ● *320 BEF (round trip)* *(22 miles) N5 (Brussels–Charleroi), exit Baisy-Thy*

Visitors' center and Butte du Lion (9)

(14 miles) Ring-road east, exit 21

Wellington museum (10)

(27 mins) From central station, trains to Charleroi stop at Waterloo (every hour) ● *190 BEF (round trip)* *(12 miles) Ring-road east, exit 24*

Napoleon's last head-quarters (11)

(15 miles) Ring-road east, exit 23, then N5, exit Genappe

Panorama de la bataille (12)

(14 miles) Ring-road east, exit 21

Collégiale de Nivelles (13)

(27 mins) From central station, trains to Charleroi stop at Nivelles (every 30 mins) ● *300 BEF (round trip)* *(21 miles) A7–E19, exit 19*

Ronquières inclined plane (14)

(31 miles) A7–E19 (Brussels–Mons), exit 20

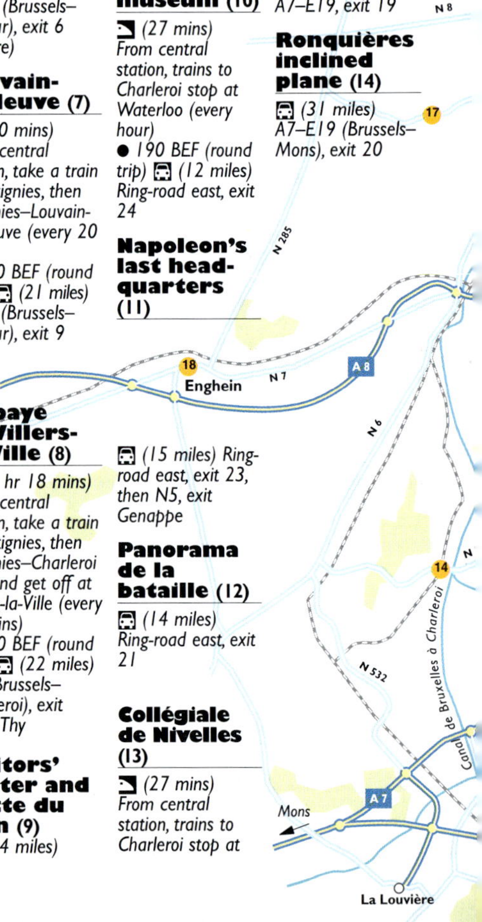

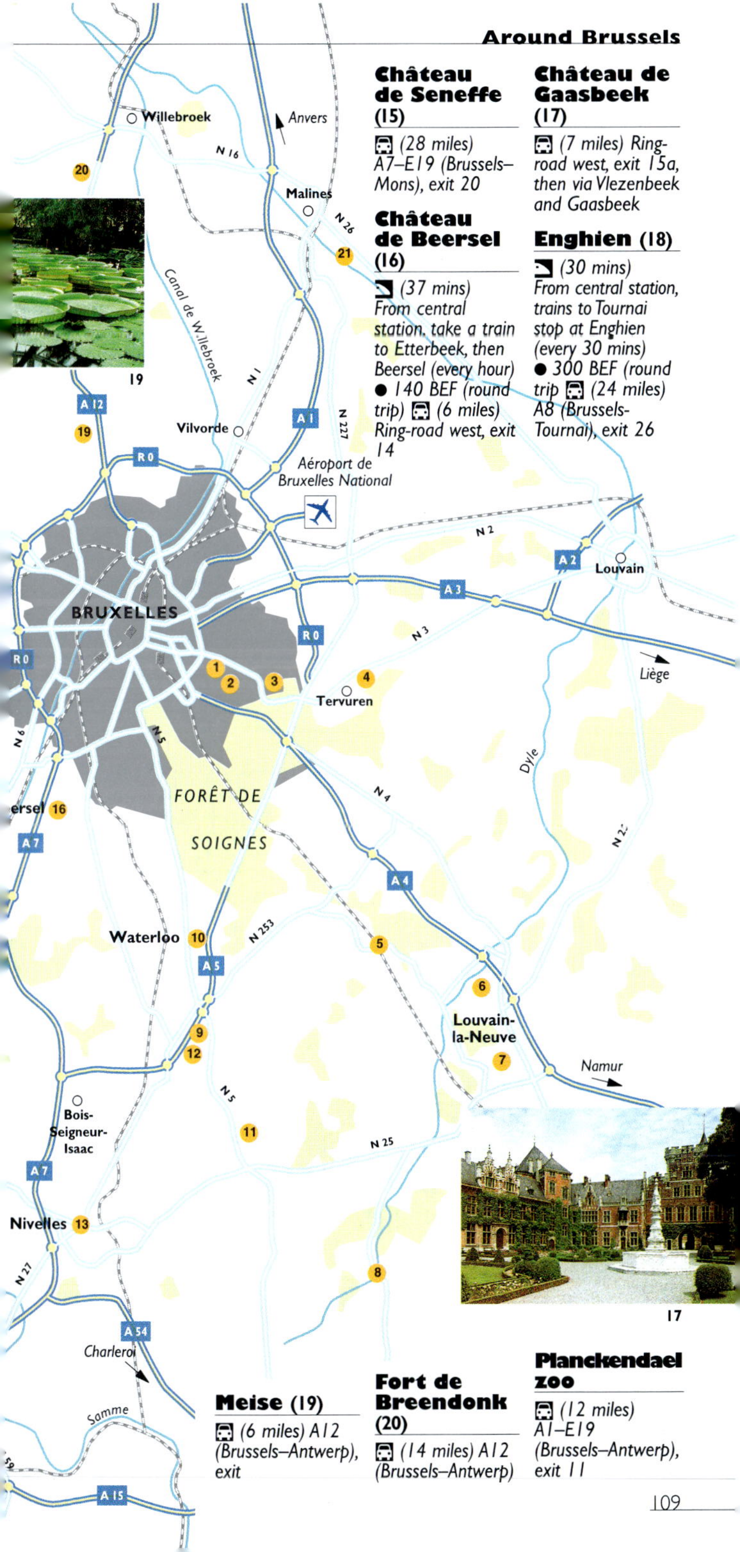

19

Château de Seneffe (15)

(28 miles) A7–E19 (Brussels–Mons), exit 20

Château de Beersel (16)

(37 mins) From central station, take a train to Etterbeek, then Beersel (every hour) ● 140 BEF (round trip) (6 miles) Ring-road west, exit 14

Château de Gaasbeek (17)

(7 miles) Ring-road west, exit 15a, then via Vlezenbeek and Gaasbeek

Enghien (18)

(30 mins) From central station, trains to Tournai stop at Enghien (every 30 mins) ● 300 BEF (round trip (24 miles) A8 (Brussels-Tournai), exit 26

17

Meise (19)

(6 miles) A12 (Brussels–Antwerp), exit

Fort de Breendonk (20)

(14 miles) A12 (Brussels–Antwerp)

Planckendael zoo

(12 miles) A1–E19 (Brussels–Antwerp), exit 11

The long Avenue de Tervuren was laid out to connect the Cinquantenaire, where the 1897 Universal Exhibition was held, with the site of the Colonial Exhibition at Tervuren – another of Leopold II's bright ideas. It is one of the city's most attractive drives, passing through the area of the Mellaert lakes.

Further afield

Palais Stoclet (1)

281, avenue de Tervuren / 1150

Adolphe Stoclet, railroad engineer, collector, and son of a rich banker, had this residence built in the years 1905–11 by the Austrian architect Joseph Hoffman, a leader of the movement known as the 'Viennese Secession'. Following the principles of Victor Horta, it has one of the finest early 20th-century interiors to be found anywhere in Europe, including magnificent mosaics by Gustav Klimt. But when will the Stoclet family decide to open this masterpiece to the general public?

Bibliotheca Wittockiana (2)

21-23 rue de Bemel / 1150 ☎ (02) 770 53 33 ➟ (02) 762 21 39

Tues.–Sat. 10am–5pm • 100 BEF on request

This building (1983) was designed by Emmanuel de Callataÿ to house a collection of rare books and bindings owned by the industrialist Michel Wittock. The exhibits include gilded volumes dating from the 16th century and some remarkable contemporary creations. Of special interest are Diderot's *Encyclopedia* and a 23-volume edition of the *Description of Egypt*.

Musée du Transport urbain bruxellois (3)

364b, avenue de Tervuren / 1150 ☎ (02) 515 31 08 ➟ (02) 515 31 09

Apr. 4–Oct. 4: Sat., Sun. and public holidays 1.30—7pm • 150 BEF (including a tram ride)

This former depot of the STIB (Société des Transports Intercommunaux Bruxellois) was constructed in 1896–97 for the Brussels–Ixelles-Boendael narrow-gauge railroad company. In 1897, this company built the tramway connecting the Cinquantenaire Universal Exhibition with the Colonial Exhibition at Tervuren. The buildings now house a collection of 60 carriages and tractor units dating from 1868 to the present day. The admission charge includes a ride in one of these old vehicles, with a 'Wattman' driver and ticket collector in turn-of-the-century costume, either toward Tervuren or into the cathedral-like greenery of the Forêt de Soignes. ★ Every Sunday at 10am, from April through September, the volunteers of the 'Brussels Tourist Tramway' organize a guided tour to the Heysel (returning around 1.15pm). It is popular, so book ahead.

Musée royal de l'Afrique centrale (4)

13, Leuvensesteenweg / 3080 Tervuren ☎ (02) 769 52 11

Tues.–Fri. 10am–5pm; Sat., Sun. 10am–6pm • 80 BEF P

In 1897, while the Universal Exhibition was being held to mark the Cinquantenaire, Tervuren was preoccupied with Belgium's Colonial Exhibition. In view of its success, Leopold II (again!) asked the architect Charles Girault (creator of the Petit Palais museum in Paris) to design a neoclassical complex to house a permanent Congo museum. It is a repository of African culture and wildlife. There is a remarkable display of tribal masks, a superb collection of sculptures, a collection of the woods of 50,000 different tree species, and the world's largest collection of African insects. The museum is fascinating, even if the rather static displays sometimes seem to belong to a long-forgotten era.

4

1

4

The façade is all that now remains of the Palais des Colonies, built to promote Leopold's economic interests in the Congo.

3

Leaving Brussels via the Bois de la Cambre, you immediately find yourself in the Forêt de Soignes, the city's great green lung. If you then carry on toward Rixensart without taking the motorway, you pass La Hulpe and the Solvay estate. Nearby is Genval with its lake, attractive setting, the Water and Fountain museum and many restaurants.

Further afield

5

Château de Rixensart (5)

40, rue de l'Église / 1330 Rixensart ☎ (02) 653 65 05

Easter–Sep.: Sun. and public holidays 2–6pm ● *150 BEF* *every 30 mins*

In Wallonia, the term *'sart'* means 'clearing', but there is still plenty of woodland in this region. Charming rather than impressive, this fine castle has been somewhat neglected by tour operators in recent years, but is well worth visiting. It is built of brick and stone in the Spanish Renaissance style favored by its creator, De Spinola, who was an adviser to Archduke Albert and Archduchess Isabelle. Erected in the mid-17th century, it was acquired in the 18th century by the Mérode family, who still live there. Features of the second courtyard are the reinforcing bars spelling out the dates 1631 and 1662 above the upper windows and the cool arcades. The attractively furnished interior features Gobelins tapestries and wooden paneling.

Walibi (6)

B / 1300 Wavre ☎ (010) 42 15 00 ➟ (010) 41 10 66

Apr. 4–June: daily 10am–6pm / July, Aug.: daily 10am–7pm / Sep.–18 Oct.: Sat., Sun. 10am–6pm ● *760 BEF, children 680 BEF* ***Aqualibi*** *☎ (010) 42 16 00* ● *495 BEF, children 420 BEF*

This theme park gets its name from the first two letters of the three local *communes*: Wavre, Limal and Bierges – nothing to do with the Australian marsupial, though the logo does feature a kangaroo. There is something here for every age group, from attractive flower beds to stomach-churning rides. Fans of Tintin, Ali Baba, Lucky Luke and the Daltons will not be disappointed. The park draws over a million visitors a year, the most popular attractions being the Tornado and Sirocco roller-coasters and the Dalton Terror (which includes a free fall of 250 ft reaching 60 mph). There is also the Aqualibi slide-and-splash complex (kept at a temperature of 84°F) with its two chutes (460 ft).

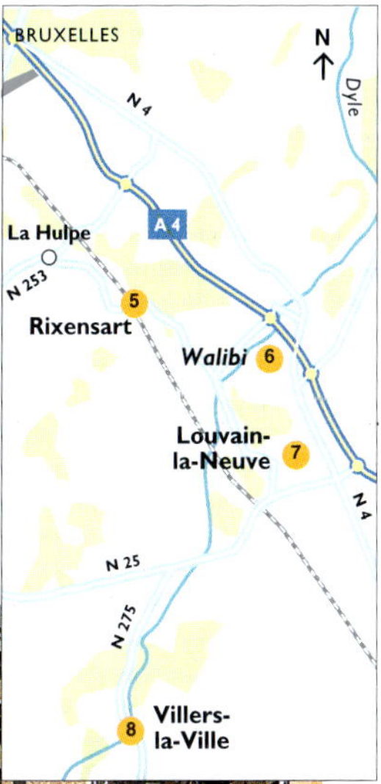

8

6

7

Louvain-la-Neuve (7)

This is Belgium's most recent 'new' town, the only one to have been created from scratch since Charleroi in 1666. Previously, the Catholic university was based solely at Leuven, on Flemish territory. Following anti-Walloon demonstrations in 1968, it was decided to establish a new university campus in the municipal district of Ottignies to house the Francophone faculties and their students, who were transferred there between 1972 and 1979. Louvain-la-Neuve now has 16,000 inhabitants, 9,000 of them students. The whole town is pedestrianized, with an entire road and railroad system functioning underground. The attractive features of this university town are its narrow streets, numerous works of art including tremendous murals, and ever-expanding museum. The most popular pastimes are taking a stroll and enjoying a glass of beer.

Abbaye de Villers-la-Ville (8)

53, rue de l'Abbaye / 1495 Villers-la-Ville ☎ 071/87 88 62

Apr.–Oct.: daily 10am–6pm / Nov.–Mar.: daily 10am–5pm / Oct.–May: closed on Tue. ● *150 BEF* *Mar.–Oct.: Sun. 3pm* P

In 1146, Cistercian monks from Clairvaux settled in this delightful spot on the banks of the Thyle. St Bernard himself laid the foundation stone in 1147. In the 13th century, Villers was one of the most important monastic communities in the Western world. Visitors marvel at its size (37 acres) and are immediately captivated by its romantic ruins. Its later history was turbulent. It was sacked by the Spanish and the Gueux (Calvinist Dutch guerrillas) in the 16th century, the Austrians in 1798, and the French revolutionaries in 1796, when it finally closed. In this region, stone was a common building material in earlier times. You can visit the *chauffoir* (warming-room), cellars and kitchen, refectory (13th century), cloister (16th century), abbey church (295 ft long and 75 ft high), built during the first three quarters of the 13th century, and the fine Romanesque brew-house dating from the same period.

It was here that on June 18, 1815, Napoleon fought and lost his last battle against a coalition of European nations: England, Holland and Prussia. Interestingly, 'Belgians' fought on both sides. The battlefield, now flatter than in the past, takes in the *communes* of Braine-l'Alleud, Genappe (Vieux-Genappe), Lasne (Plancenoit) and Waterloo. Several farms played a

Further afield

Visitors' Center and Butte du Lion (9)

252-254, route du Lion / 1420 Braine-l'Alleud ☎ (02) 385 19 12

Apr.–Sep.: daily 9.30am–6.30pm / Oct.: 9.30am–5.30pm / Nov.–Feb.: daily 10.30am–4pm / Mar.: daily 10am–5pm ● 200 BEF ***Butte du Lion*** *40 BEF for video presentations*

The Center has two audio-visual presentations. The first illustrates the progress of the battle, using a 108-sq ft model and electronics. This makes the visit to the battlefield much more meaningful. It is followed by a short movie, intended mainly for children, using footage from the Russian director Bondartchouk's *Waterloo*. There is then a long climb (226 steps) to the summit of the mound raised on the spot where William of Orange was wounded. Between 1823 and 1826, the builders moved over 10 million cubic ft of soil. From the top (133 ft), there is a view over the whole battlefield. The lion, weighing 30 tons, stands 147 ft above the fray. Sculpted by Van Geel, it looks toward France in an attitude of eternal vigilance.

Wellington Museum (10)

147, chaussée de Bruxelles / 1410 Waterloo ☎ (02) 354 78 06

Apr.–Sep.: daily 9.30am–6.30pm / Oct.–Mar.: daily 10.30am–5pm ● 100 BEF

The museum is housed in a former post-house, the final stopping place on the road to Brussels, which was used as a headquarters by the Duke of Wellington, commander of the allied armies, on June 17 and 18, 1815. Weapons, engravings, furniture and items of clothing give the battle a more human dimension. The newer exhibition rooms at the rear illustrate the progress of the battle hour by hour. There is also a small museum devoted to the history of Waterloo itself, with a room covering more than 90 localities throughout the world, from the USA to Australia, which bear the same name. Incidentally, it was Wellington who, as British Prime Minister, called the London conference of Great Powers which led to the establishment of an independent Belgian nation in 1830.

Napoleon's last headquarters (11)

66, chaussée de Bruxelles / 1472 Vieux-Genappe ☎ (02) 384 24 24

Apr.–Oct.: daily 10am–6.30pm / Nov.–Mar.: daily 1–5pm ● 60 BEF

It was at the Ferme du Caillou, on the territory of Vieux-Genappe, that Napoleon spent the night of June 17/18, 1815. This small museum has memorabilia associated with the imperial staff and, more interestingly, with the Emperor himself: camp bed, hat, death mask, and so on. The ossuary at the rear gives pause for thought, and there is a new room devoted to the Belgian campaign. It is organized by the Belgian Society for Napoleonic Studies and gives a rather 'French' version of events.

Not forgetting

■ **Panorama of the battle (12)** 252-254, route du Lion / 1420 Braine-l'Alleud ☎ (02) 385 19 12 Apr.–Sep.: 9.30am–6.30pm / Oct.–Mar.: 10.30am–4pm. *At the foot of the mound stands a cylindrical building, inaugurated in 1912. It contains a panorama of the battle by the French painter Charles Dumoulin (on canvas 360 ft in circumference, 40 ft high). Clever perspective effects give the visitor the impression of being in the thick of the fighting.*

prominent part in the struggle: Hougoumont; la Haie-Sainte, where the English were heavily engaged; and la Belle-Alliance, where Blücher and Wellington met in the moment of victory.

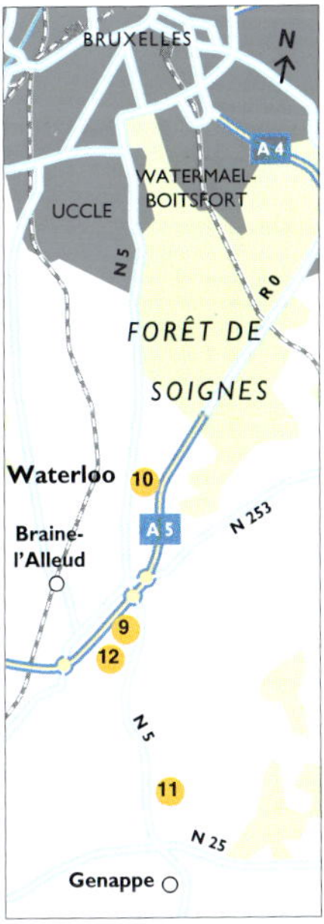

9

9

10

9

When venturing into Hainaut (the Walloon province where Seneffe is located), you must visit the Collégiale de Nivelles – one of the architectural pearls of Walloon Brabant – and also try and find time for a short detour to Bois-Seigneur-Isaac. This village has two interesting architectural complexes: a 15th-century Augustinian abbey with a fine chapel, and a

Further afield

Collégiale de Nivelles (13)

Oct.–Easter: daily 9am–5pm / Easter–Oct.: 9am–6pm (no visiting during Sunday morning service *150 BEF (daily 2pm; Sat., Sun. 2pm and 3.30pm)* ☎ *(067) 21 54 13*

Here, in the 7th century, Gertrude, daughter of the mayor of the palace Pepin the Elder, founded a mixed Benedictine abbey run by a woman. The abbess continued to be mayor and magistrate of Nivelles until 1798. Nowadays, Nivelles is a lively commercial center and the abbey still attracts tourists. Built in the 11th and 12th centuries, it is about 330 ft in length. The choir and west end have a rather new appearance – the result of a long-term restoration project completed in 1984. As part of the restoration, the local people were asked to decide between a Gothic spire, like the one destroyed by the German bombardment in 1940, and a more original Romanesque tower. The latter solution was adopted, and the impression created is one of solid simplicity, inside and out. There is a shrine containing the relics of Saint Gertrude by the contemporary artist Félix Roulin, and a replica of the original 13th-century shrine, destroyed by fire in May 1940. Archeological excavations have uncovered vestiges of five earlier churches on the site, including the 7th-century Merovingian structure. The church also contains the tombs of Hilmeltrude, first wife of Charlemagne, and of Saint Gertrude.

The Ronquières' inclined plane (14)

☎ (065) 36 04 64

Mar.–Nov.: daily 10am–7pm ● 330 BEF (including audio presentation) P

This impressive piece of engineering is designed to lift boats navigating the Brussels–Charleroi canal the 223 ft from one level to another. The inclined plane, in operation since 1968, is almost a mile in length. Two 300-ft caissons, which can accommodate a 1,350-tonne barge or several smaller boats, are drawn over metal rollers by a 5,732-ton counterweight. The 500-ft tower dominating the complex provides an excellent viewing platform. It also houses an outstanding exhibition of life on a canal. Equipped with headphones, the visitor is introduced to the way of life of bargees past and present, through impressionistic displays accompanied by a very realistic soundtrack.

Château de Seneffe (15)

6, rue Lucien-Plasman / 7180 Seneffe ☎ (064) 55 69 13

Tue.–Sun. 10am–6.30pm ● ***Château*** *150 BEF* ***Park and gardens*** *admission free* P

This fine residence is set in the depths of a 54-acre park. Constructed of brick and local blue-stone in the neoclassical style (Louis XVI), it was built to plans by Laurent Dewez between 1763 and 1768. Following a long period of restoration, it has a rather shiny-new look, particularly where the gilding is concerned. But it is well worth visiting, if only for the restored parquet floors. Not surprisingly, visitors are required to wear cloth pads on their feet. By an inspired decision, the château also houses a museum of goldsmiths' work owned by Belgium's French community. As well as temporary exhibitions, it displays some of the finest pieces from Claude and Juliette d'Allemagne's collection of European jewelry.

magnificent classical-style château (1720–40), built of stone, slate and whitened brick. A little further on are the museum and park of Mariemont. Also well worth visiting are the hydraulic lifts of the Brussels–Charleroi canal.

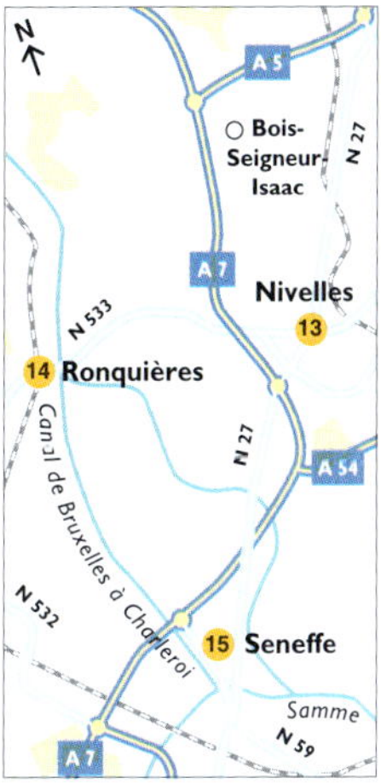

13

14

At Ronquières, discover the joys and frustrations of the barge people's daily lives.

15

You need not go far from Brussels to discover some real architectural jewels. Just west of the capital, in Flemish Brabant and Hainaut are Beersel, Gaasbeek and Enghien (Edingen in Flemish). And do not forget that even Ghent and Antwerp are only half an hour's drive away.

Further afield

Château de Beersel (16)

65, Lotsestraat / 1650 Beersel ☎ (02) 331 00 24

Tues.–Sun. 10am–noon, 2–6pm

Only just outside the city ring-road, this castle, built around 1300, is one of the best-preserved examples of a medieval stronghold in a lowland area. Built entirely of brick and surrounded by a moat, it consist of three imposing towers linked by curtain walls. It once belonged to the lords of Witthem, then passed to the Duke of Arenberg and the princes of Mérode, but fell into disuse in the 19th century. Restoration work began in 1948, based on a 17th-century engraving, which explains the attractive little roofs crowning the towers. Unfortunately, it is unfurnished. ★ This is the ideal place to try the regional specialty of a *demi-gueuze* accompanied by a slice of bread and white cheese (*plattekees*), radishes and green onions. Not far away is the 220-acre provincial leisure area of Huizingen.

Château de Gaasbeek (17)

40, Kasteelstraat / 1750 Gaasbeek ☎ (02) 531 01 30

Apr.–Oct.: Sat.–Thu. 10am–5pm (the park is also open in winter) ● 150 BEF P

This is the part of Flemish Brabant associated with the painter Bruegel. Unlike Beersel, Gaasbeek is more of a museum. The 13th-century feudal castle was destroyed in 1388, and the present 16th-century residence was built for the Count of Hoorne. It was acquired by the Count of Egmont in 1565, three years before these two heroes of the resistance to Spanish rule were beheaded. Further changes were made in the 19th century, and the complex has belonged to the Belgian state since 1921. It is remarkably harmonious in design, and the formal, French-style gardens stand in piquant contrast to the surrounding countryside. The château houses the collections of the last private owner, Marchioness Arconati: Brussels and Tournai tapestries (15th century), Persian carpets, 16th-century paintings and alabaster sculptures, 16th-century Italian porcelain and earthenware, antique furniture and silverware, Limoges enamels and a remarkable 'fitted' kitchen.

Enghien (18)

Tourist information ☎ (02) 395 84 48

A town of 10,000 inhabitants on the border of Flemish Brabant and Hainaut province, to which it belongs, Enghien is sure to please. Its principal attraction is the **Arenberg Park**, all that remains (apart from a 16th-century chapel) of a château that was demolished in 1806 after suffering serious damage during the Revolution. The park is surprisingly large (845 acres) and harmonious. Laid out by the Arenberg family in the 17th century, its wide avenues radiate from the Pavillon des Sept Étoiles, offering prospects of lakes and fountains. As well as the chapel, the stables and Chinese Pavilion are worth visiting. In the town of Enghien, the **church of St-Nicolas** has a 51-bell carillon and interesting baptismal fonts. It was restored in 1964 in the Hennuyer Gothic style. Not far away is the **Capuchin convent church**, established by Charles d'Arenberg and Anne de Croÿ in 1614. It contains a superb mausoleum to another of the De Croÿs, who was archbishop of Toledo. In the crypt lie 60 members of this illustrious family. Finally, the **Maison Jonathas**, a 16th-century building with a 12th-century tower, houses a charming museum of locally made tapestries.

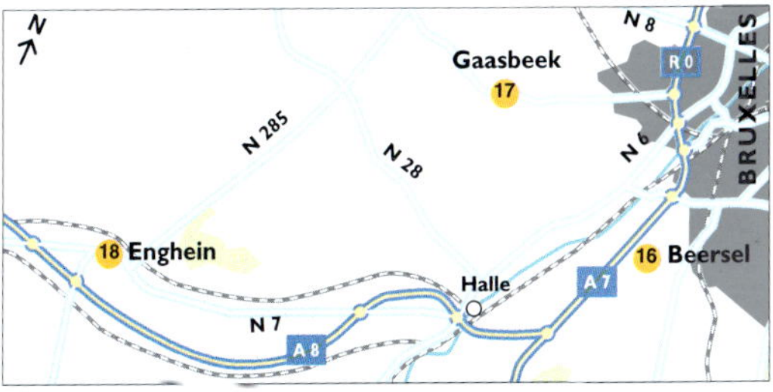

16

As in the Middle Ages, you enter Beersel castle over a drawbridge.

17

17

You can, of course, push on as far as Louvain (16 miles) or Malines (18 miles), but these towns are more than just a day's outing. You need to spend some time in Belgium to explore its wealth of 'small' provincial towns. If you do go there, Louvain's town hall, a masterpiece of Brabant flamboyant Gothic, and St Rombaut's cathedral in Malines are the two

Further afield

Meise (19)

Domaine de Bouchout / 1860 Meise ☎ (02) 269 39 05

🕐 ***Park*** *Apr.–Oct.: 9am–6.30pm / Nov.–Mar.: 9am–5pm* ***Palais des Plantes*** *Easter–Oct.: Mon.–Thu. and Sat. 1–4pm / Nov.–Thu. before Easter: Mon.–Thu. 1–3.30pm* ● ***Park*** *admission free* ***Palais des Plantes*** *120 BEF*

The national botanical garden *(Nationale Plantenuin)* occupies a 227-acre site around the Château de Bouchout. From 1879 to 1927, this was the residence of the Empress Charlotte, widow of Emperor Maximilian of Mexico and sister of Leopold II. Purchased by the state in 1938, the property was eventually converted to its present use in 1958. Most of the park is given over to trees, including such exotic and evocative species as the Virginia tulip-tree, the giant sequoia and the Louisiana cypress. But by far the most popular attraction is the Palais des Plantes: a complex of 13 large and 22 smaller greenhouses covering over two acres. In all, the garden is home to 18,000 plant species (from America, Africa, Asia, Australia and New Zealand), 10,000 of which are kept under glass. It is a surprise to see tea, cotton, rubber and cocoa growing. But the star of the show must be Victoria *amazonica*, a giant water lily, the leaves of which reach 6 ft in diameter and can support the weight of a small child.

Fort de Breendonk (20)

☎ (03) 886 62 09

🕐 *Apr.–Sep.: daily 9am–5pm / Oct.–Mar.: 10am–4pm* ● *75 BEF*

In the municipal district of Willebroek, this former fort was built in the years from 1906 to 1914. A key point in the defenses of Antwerp, it was the position that held out longest against the Germans in 1914, but between 1940 and 1944, the Nazis used it as a concentration camp. It is reckoned that 4,000 prisoners passed through here on their way to the main death camps. Some 200 of them were executed on the spot. Having visited this silent hell with a survivor, José Cornet, alias 'Nicolas', author of the book *Il fera jour demain* (Day will dawn tomorrow), we would urge you to go and see it. Everything is preserved just as it was: dormitories, cells, 'interrogation rooms'... A moving experience for later generations. The Fort de Breendonk is now classified as a national monument to World War II.

Planckendael zoo (21)

582, Leuvensesteenweg / 2812 Muizen/Mechelen
☎ (015) 41 49 21 ➟ (015) 42 29 35

🕐 *Apr.–Oct.: daily 9am–6.15pm / Nov.–Mar.: daily 9am–4.30pm* ● *420 BEF*

This estate with its 16th-century castle once belonged to the painter Coxie. It was purchased in 1956 by Antwerp zoo as a center for breeding endangered species. Today, more than 1,000 animals live here in considerable freedom on its 100 acres of lakes and greenery. Its attractions include a monkey island, a bee trail, a children's farm, a treetop walk (45 ft above the ground in places), a games area, and an African village.

outstanding features around which to organize your visits.

19

20

21

Where to shop

What to buy in Brussels
Pralines (the celebrated Belgian chocolates) ➡ 124 ➡ 130 ➡ 136, *spéculoos* (spicy cookies cut into shapes) and other cakes ➡ 124 ➡ 128, bottled beer (seasonal, *lambic* or trappist) ➡ 130, lace ➡ 128, antiques from the Sablon district ➡ 124 and comic strip books ➡ 138 ➡ 139.

Shopping districts

The best places to shop are in the streets around the Place de la Monnaie, the Rue A.-Dansaert and the Grand-Place. The high-class stores are concentrated around the Place Louise and the Porte de Namur. There are also some attractive boutiques around the Place Brugmann. The Sablon and Marolles districts are renowned for their antiques dealers.

50 Stores

THE INSIDER'S FAVORITES

INDEX BY TYPE

In the area

Interesting furniture, works of art old and new, items to beautify the home – the Sablon is famous beyond the frontiers of Belgium as a place to come and hunt for antiques. It owes its dynamism largely to the ASBL association (see below).

Where to shop

Sablon Quartier des Arts et du Commerce (ASBL)(1)

1, rue des Minimes / 1000 ☎ 512 98 41 ➟ 512 82 70

20, 34, 48, 95, 96; tram 92, 93, 94 ***Antiques, art galleries, jewelers, carpets, interior design*** *duty-free facilities and shipment abroad*

Concerned to safeguard the authenticity of the Sablon area, this association of 130 traders seeks to preserve and promote its heritage. ★ It organizes two very interesting events: **Les Nocturnes du Sablon**: an evening exhibition, staged every year on the last Thursday, Friday and Saturday of November, featuring the finest items in the collections of Sablon antique dealers and art galleries. Determined not to do things by halves, the ASBL arranges transport by horse-drawn carriage. Class and sophistication of the purest kind. **Le Printemps baroque du Sablon:** concerts and recitals in some of the Sablon's most attractive venues to celebrate the arrival of spring. The festival is organized by Marion Lemesre, councilor with special responsibility for the arts Brussels city.

Marché des antiquités et du livre du Sablon (2)

Place du Grand-Sablon / 1000 ☎ 279 40 20 ➟ 279 40 44

20, 34, 48, 95, 96; tram 92, 93, 94 ***Market selling antiques and old books*** *Sat. 9am–6pm; Sun 9am–2pm ● 100 BEF*

A series of red-and-green tents (the city colors), pitched along the side of Notre-Dame-du-Sablon, display the wares of a hundred or so antiques dealers: curios, small items of furniture, jewelry, engravings, old books, silverware, vases… A magnetic attraction, summer and winter.

Nuhr Nebi (3)

23, rue Blaes / 1000 ☎ 514 07 17 ➟ 514 07 17

20, 34, 48, 95, 96; tram 92, 93, 94 ***Interior design and Middle-Eastern furniture*** *Thu.–Sun. 11am–6pm* *duty-free facilities and shipment abroad*

Africa, Asia, India and the Orient… Nuhr Nebi ('light of the poet' in Arabic) sends its scouts to the four corners of the earth in search of furniture, rugs, lamps and other exotica. You can be sure of finding a good selection of ancient and modern items, and a friendly welcome.

Not forgetting

■ **New de Wolf (4)** 91-93, rue Haute and 40-42, rue Blaes / 1000 ☎ 511 10 18 Mon.–Sat. 10am–6.30pm; Sun. 10am–3pm *A vast area entirely devoted to interior design, featuring decorative ideas and color schemes (seaside, country, British, white, and many more).* ■ **Pierre Marcolini (5)** 39, place du Grand-Sablon / 1000 ☎ 514 12 06 Tue.–Sun. 10am–6.30pm *World confectionery champion at Lyon in 1995, Pierre Marcolini is highly inventive. His pralines are made in subtle jasmine, tea and lemon-tea flavors, as well as thyme and ginger. Irresistible.* ■ **Wittamer (6)** 6-12 & 13, place du Grand-Sablon / 1000 ☎ 512 37 42 Mon. 10am–6pm; Tue.–Sun. 7am–7pm *The Sablon's top pâtissier-confiseur has been selling quality products for several generations. * If footsore, try the Salons du Sablon, on the first floor.* ■ **Rosalie Pompon (7)** 65, rue Lebeau / 1000 ☎ 512 35 93 Tue.–Sun. 10.30am–6.30pm *This boutique is a one-off, stocking outrageous creations by young artists. Jewelry, furniture, picture frames, bath mats, clocks, puppets… bound to make you smile.*

- Where to stay ➥ 36
- Where to eat ➥ 46 ➥ 50
- After dark ➥ 70
- What to see ➥ 88 ➥ 92

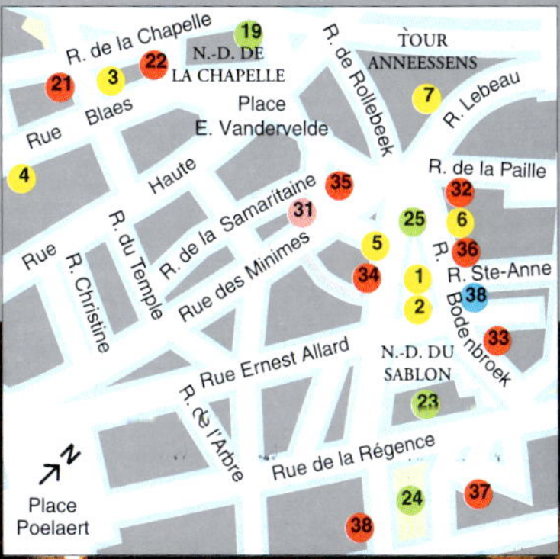

1

1

A Sunday stroll in the Sablon district is a Brussels institution. You sense a general atmosphere of optimism and creativity in this area.

4

6

One of the flea markets most popular with the locals is held on the first Sunday of each month on the Place Saint-Lambert, in the leafy district of Wolume-Saint-Lambert (7am–1pm). Families and friends wander round the stalls before having a drink – or a bowl of soup, when the weather gets cold – at one of the cafés around the square.

Where to shop

Vieux Marché (8)

Place du Jeu-de-Balle / 1000 ☎ 279 40 29 ➡ 279 40 44

20, 48 ***Flea market*** *Daily 7am–2pm*

Right at the heart of the Marolles district, the Place du Jeu-de-Balle is the realm of scrap metal dealers and other secondhand merchants. Tools, old clothes, postage stamps, pictures, furniture… a paradise of jumble and bric-à-brac: *brol* as it is called here. On Fridays, there is a fruit and vegetable market (4–9pm). ★ At any time of year, you can buy winkles *(bulots)* from a handcart, or a bag of French fries. It was in 1873 that the Old Market (Vieux Marché) forsook the Place Anneesens and moved to the Place du Jeu-de-Balle, named after an old street game – *pelota* – the city version of *jeu de paume* (real tennis).

Marchés de la Grand-Place (9)

Grand-Place / 1000 ☎ 279 40 00 ➡ 279 40 44

M *Gare-Centrale* *many routes* ***Bird market, flower market*** ***Bird market*** *Sun. 7am–2pm* ***Flower market*** *Tue.–Sun. 8am–6pm*

The most picturesque of the markets held on the Grand-Place is still the Sunday bird market, or *Vogelmet*. Come before ten o'clock if you want to avoid the crowds. On weekdays, the most beautiful square in the world, surrounded by Gothic and Baroque buildings in the purest Flemish style, is adorned with the bright splashes of flowers and plants. No wonder Jean Cocteau referred to it as a glorious outdoor theater.

Galerie Bortier (10)

55, rue de la Madeleine / 1000

Of the seven arcades built between 1820 and 1880 to embellish the city, only three remain: the Passage du Nord, the Galeries Saint-Hubert and the Galerie Bortier, also designed by Cluysenaer (1848). The Baroque façade conceals its own little world of bookshops. As well as new and secondhand books (Genicot), engravings and old photographs (Schwilden), feminist literature, more than 60,000 postcards, and all sorts of accessories (Artemys), there is the Van Der Elst store, which alone takes up half of the arcade. This is the place to buy and sell books. The arcade is heated in wintertime.

Not forgetting

■ **Marché aux fruits et légumes (11)** Place Sainte-Catherine / 1000 ☎ 279 40 20 *Near the Bourse, in a district that formed the heart of the old medieval town, this attractive market is the place to buy fresh vegetables, flowers and plants, daily from 7am to 5pm.* ■ **Brocantes aux abattoirs (12)** 4, rue Rospy-Chaudron / 1070 ☎ 521 54 19 *Hi-fi equipment, crockery, clothes… on Fridays and Saturdays, from 7am to 1pm, all sorts of items are sold here, at bargain prices, in the Grande Halle, the 108,000 sq ft canopy of which is supported at 30-ft intervals by fluted cast-iron columns. Not far away, the covered meat market is visited at weekends by housewives from all parts of the city, variously dressed in jeans or smart outfits. A fine example of industrial-age architecture, the Grande Halle and the two pavilions at the main entrance have been listed buildings since 1988.*

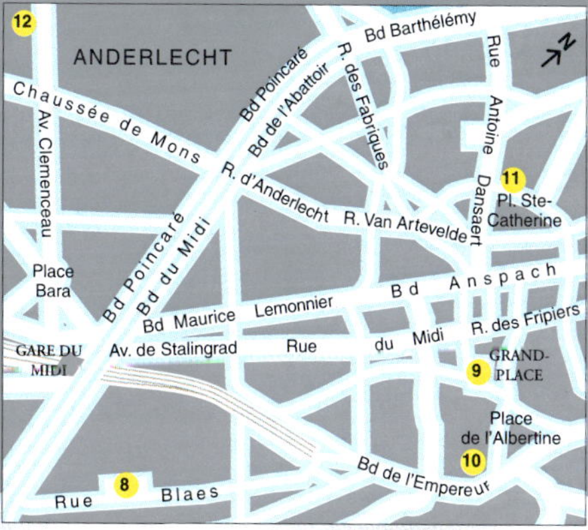

9

8

10

From dawn to 1pm, you can scour the Place du Jeu-de-Balle in search of hidden treasures.

9

8

In the area

In the Rue au Beurre, Galler products form a tempting window display. ★ Try their *langues de chat* (cats' tongues), by a chocolate maker and Philippe Geluck, creator of *The Cat* comic strip. ■ Where to stay ➥ 18 ➥ 20 ➥ 24 ■ Where to eat ➥ 40 ➥ 42 ■ After dark ➥ 62 ➥ 64 ➥ 70

Where to shop

F. Rubbrecht (13)

23, Grand-Place / 1000 ☎ 512 02 18 ➡ 502 06 81

M *De Brouckère* 🚌 *many routes* ***Period and contemporary lace*** 🕓 *Mon.–Sat. 9am–7pm; Sun. 10am–6pm* ▭

Embroidered in 'vieux Bruxelles' style (17–18th century), featuring a rose point with detached petals, or '*luxeuil de Bruxelles*', a technique using braid invented in 1900, Rubbrecht's lace is a throw-back to an industry for which the city was famed. The less heavy 'princess' stitch is used for handkerchiefs, doilies and blouses. ★ They can also restore antique items.

Elvis Pompilio (14)

18, rue du Lombard / 1000 ☎ 511 11 88 ➡ 502 75 20

M *De Brouckère* 🚌 *many routes* ***Hats*** 🕓 *Mon.–Sat. 10.30am–6.30pm* ▭

In the last fifteen years, Elvis Pompilio has revolutionized the world of hat-making with models that can be adapted to suit the weather and the mood of the moment. A real character, Pompilio sees it as his mission to find the right hat for everyone who crosses his threshold!

Dans la presse ce jour-là... (15)

23, rue du Lombard / 1000 ☎ 511 43 89 ➡ 511 78 73

M *De Brouckère* 🚌 *many routes* ***Unusual gifts*** 🕓 *Mon.–Fri. 11.30am–6.30pm, Sat. 11.30am–5pm* ▭

A simple but brilliant idea: instead of a bunch of flowers, why not give a friend a newspaper published on the day he or she was born, presented in a special folder? Stéphane Maroy and Christian Cauchie also have some ideas for wine buffs, with a good selection of ports, armagnacs and vintage wines. Their Family History scrapbooks combine old newspaper clippings and blank pages, for you to decorate with souvenirs of special events.

Dandoy (16)

31, rue au Beurre / 1000 ☎ 511 03 26 ➡ 511 81 79

M *De Brouckère* 🚌 *many routes* ***Cookie makers*** 🕓 *Mon.–Sat. 8.30am–6.30pm; Sun. and public holidays 10.30am–6.30pm* ▭ ◆ *Tea-room 14, rue Charles-Buls / 1000*

Dandoy *spéculoos*, Greek bread and marzipan are much appreciated by those with a sweet tooth. Founded in 1829 in one of Brussels' oldest streets, proud possessors of the royal license, the Dandoys have lost nothing of their traditional skills over the generations. ★ In summer, try their delicious ice creams and sorbets – homemade, of course.

Not forgetting

■ **Le Ket de Bruxelles (17)** 28, rue des Grands-Carmes / 1000 ☎ 512 32 97 *A stone's throw from Manneken Pis, this craftsman enamelist makes plaques based on old Brussels street signs. He can fulfil any (reasonable) order within 24 hours.* ■ **Au Grand Rasoir (18)** 7, rue de l'Hôpital (place Saint-Jean) / 1000 ☎ 512 49 62 *Founded in 1821, and still supplying the royal family, this store is a magnet for lovers of high-quality knives. Jean Gielem learned his skills from his grandmother and is equally at home with a collector's item or a pen-knife. He will restore and sharpen anything with a blade.*

What to see ➥ 80 ➥ 82 Where to shop ➥ 126 ➥ 138

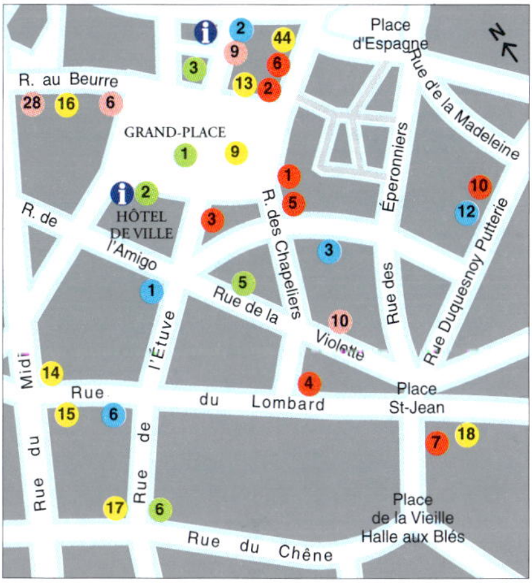

13

14

15

16

18

In the area

The Galeries Saint-Hubert form a monumental covered street, some 220 yards in length. The façades of the stores are Italian Renaissance in style. Right in the heart of the city, these shopping arcades soon became the center of the city's social life. ■ Where to stay ➡ 20 ➡ 22

Where to shop

Patrick Anciaux (19)

7-9, galerie de la Reine / 1000 ☎ 511 52 15 ➡ 512 19 93

M *De Brouckère* 🚌 *many routes* ***Antique and contemporary jewelry*** 🕐 *Mon. 2–6pm; Tue.–Sat. 11am–6pm* 💳

Located in the superb Galeries Saint-Hubert, Patrick Anciaux offers a fine selection of antique jewelry, dating from the 18th century to the 1930s. Rings, necklaces, strings of pearls and bracelets are chosen for their rarity value or originality. The same is true of the Schiaparelli theater jewelry and Josef of Hollywood's creations for the cinema. On a contemporary note, the store displays and sells Irène de Groot's Galalithe artifacts and the Baroque pearls of Myriam Haskenn.

Delvaux (20)

31, galerie de la Reine / 1000 ☎ 512 71 98

M *De Brouckère* 🚌 *many routes* ***De luxe leather goods*** 🕐 *Mon.–Sat. 10am–6.30pm* 💳 *27, bd de Waterloo / 1000 ☎ 513 05 02*

Delvaux has been in business since 1829, constantly refining the skills that have earned it a place among the great brands. In the early days, the firm made trunks and other items of baggage; then, in 1935, it launched its famous collection of leather goods, designed by Franz Schwennicke. Its reputation now rests on its women's handbags, and it also produces the more youthful, more affordable DEUX line of accessories. Perfection is the watchword.

Tropismes (21)

11, galerie des Princes / 1000 ☎ 512 88 52 ➡ 514 48 24

M *De Brouckère* 🚌 *many routes* ***General-interest bookstore*** 🕐 *Tue.–Thu. 10am–6.30pm; Fri. 10am–8pm; Sat. 10.30am–6.30pm; Sun., Mon. 1.30–6.30pm* 💳

The setting is extraordinary – a former dance hall once frequented by the daughters of the rich – but the regulars are barely aware of it, so focused are they on the titles in the sociology, philosophy and fine-art departments. You are bound to be parted from some of your cash! ★ The ideal place to end up on a Sunday afternoon, in the heart of the Galeries Saint-Hubert, one of Brussels' finest shopping arcades.

Not forgetting

■ **Bier Tempel (22)** 56B, rue du Marché-aux-Herbes / 1000 ☎ 502 19 06 *Glasses, gift packs and virtually everything associated with traditional Belgian beer, just a short walk from the Galeries Saint-Hubert.* ■ **Neuhaus (23)** 25–27, galerie de la Reine / 1000 ☎ 512 53 59 *Founder of one of the country's oldest businesses, in 1857, Jean Neuhaus invented the praline chocolate in 1912 and the* ballotin, *a new form of packaging. Rather than the traditional cornet, he came up with a rectangular box shape, for which Mme Neuhaus chose the colors green and gold, and the initial letter 'N'. ★ Before buying anything, sample the Neuhaus Caprice: fresh cream covered in dark-chocolate nougatine, and the Tentation: a coffee-flavored praline filled with fresh cream and similarly smothered in nougatine. Heavenly!* ■ **Maison Brand (24)** 60, rue du Marché-aux-Herbes / 1000 Bruxelles ☎ 512 48 93 *Electric trains, replica cars and models of old sailing ships. The Brand company has been in the business of scale modeling since 1825. You can be sure of good advice, and virtually anything can be ordered.*

■ Where to eat ➥ 42
■ After dark ➥ 62
➥ 64 ➥ 66 ➥ 70 ➥ 72
■ What to see ➥ 82

24

19

21

20

20

In the area

Looking for a central location and affordable rents, in the early 1980s young Flemish designers set up shop in the immense ground-floor rooms of 19th-century buildings in the Rue Dansaert. The concept of minimalist boutiques was soon adopted by other creative artists.

Where to shop

Nathalie R (25)

71, rue Antoine-Dansaert / 1000 ☎ 511 60 17 ➠ 514 41 73

M *Sainte-Catherine* 🚌 *63* ***Shoes*** 🕒 *Tue.–Sat. 10.30am–6.30pm* 💳

Young and talented, Nathalie R switched roles: unable to find shoes which suited her as a consumer, she decided to become a designer. The consequence? A complete new line in shoes in interesting shapes, materials and predominantly neutral colors.

Stijl Men & Woman (26)

74, rue Antoine-Dansaert / 1000 ☎ 512 03 12

M *Bourse, Sainte-Catherine* 🚌 *63* ***Belgian fashion designers*** 🕒 *Mon.–Sat. 10.30am–6.30pm* 💳 ◆ ***Kat & Muis*** *(children's wear) 32, rue Antoine-Dansaert*

Sonia Noël, founder member of the 'Dansaert village', now a crucible of Belgian fashion, moved in here thirteen years ago. Visit her boutique to discover such legendary Antwerp designers as Dries Van Noten, Dirk Bikkembergs, Walter Van Beirendock, Raf Simons and Ann Demeulemeester, who present their collections alongside Helmut Lang, and Jan & Carlos. Sonia Noël's strength is her matchless flair and the attention she pays to young designers. Just down the road is Stijl Underwear, for lingerie by some of the great names of the fashion industry.

Les Précieuses (27)

83, rue Antoine-Dansaert / 1000 ☎ 503 28 98

M *Sainte-Catherine* 🚌 *63* ***Accessories*** 🕒 *Fri.–Sat. 11am–6.30pm* 💳

Creator of the Kan label, in conjunction with Jean-Philippe Da Franca, Pilli Collado has established her own boutique in the Rue Dansaert to show off her highly prized accessories: rings, earrings, necklaces, chokers, in imaginative combinations of cut-glass pearls, velvet and silver. These handmade items are designed to go with Jamin Puech handbags.

Idiz Bogam II (28)

76, rue Antoine-Dansaert / 1000 ☎ 512 10 32 ➠ 512 98 64

M *Sainte-Catherine* 🚌 *63* ***secondhand clothing and accessories*** 🕒 *Mon.–Sat. 10.30am–6.30pm* 💳 ◆ *Idiz Bogam I, 162, rue Blaes*

Hollywood-style cocktail dresses, designer items, shoes, spectacles, scarves: Jacqueline Ezman presents the best of the years 1940 through 1970 in an area decorated in the style of a fin-de-siècle drawing-room. A good place to work on your personal image, with helpful advice from Bernard. Everything is on sale, including the furniture.

Not forgetting

■ **Espace Bizarre (29)** 19, rue des Chartreux / 1000 ☎ 514 52 56 *Specialists in futons. They also have a catalog,* Collection privée, *featuring state-of-the-art furniture, accessories and gifts.* ■ **Johanne Riss (30)** 35, place du Nouveau-Marché-aux-Grains / 1000 ☎ 513 09 00 *This boutique, in an old banana ripening warehouse, sells a unique line in black-and-white clothing. The peaceful atmosphere is symbolized by the Japanese winter garden separating the two showrooms: wedding and ball gowns at the rear; comfortable, crease-resistant women's clothing in the salon facing the street.*

Where to stay ➥ 26
Where to eat ➥ 44
What to see ➥ 84
Where to shop ➥ 126

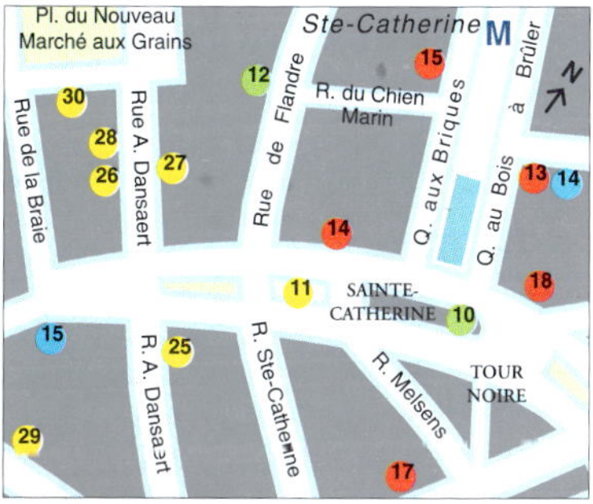

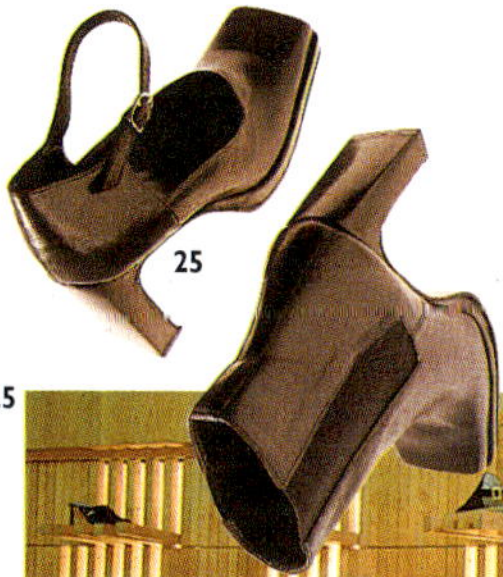

25

25

30

28

27

26

26

In the area

Just a stone's throw from the Carrefour Louise, ★ take a stroll in the Parc d'Egmont, a pleasantly uncrowded garden, where you can rest in the shade of an American walnut. Managed by the State since 1964, the park is open daily, from sunrise to sunset. There are two monumental

Where to shop

Dod (31)

64, rue du Bailli / 1050 ☎ 640 38 98

54; tram 92, 93, 94, 81 ***Secondhand and new clothing*** *Mon.–Sat. 10am–6.30pm* *Dod Enfants (children's wear) ☎ 640 60 40; Dod Hommes (menswear) ☎ 538 02 47*

Dod runs several stores, catering for men, women and children. He continues to delight bargain-hunters but is also now launching his own labels: Debuto (ladies' suits and overcoats) and BJ (sportswear and clothing for girls and young children). Great names at affordable prices.

Senteurs d'ailleurs (32)

100, avenue Louise / 1050 ☎ 511 69 69 ➡ 513 87 70

Louise *tram 92, 93, 94* ***Perfumes*** *Mon. noon–7pm; Tue.–Sat. 10am–7pm; Sun. and public holidays 1–6pm*

A basic principle of this boutique is to present the full range of each brand, or nothing at all. Having begun with L'Occitane, it now stocks Comptoir Sud Pacifique body-care products, Esteban Japanese incense, Dyptique candles, Rosine perfumes, Coudray skin-care products, and the fragrances of Jean-François Laporte – *maître parfumeur et gantier*. Perfumery at its most refined.

Olivier Strelli (33)

72, avenue Louise / 1050 ☎ 512 56 07

Louise *tram 92, 93, 94* ***Ready-to-wear clothing*** *Mon.–Sat. 10am–6.30pm* *Strelli Hommes (menswear), galerie Louise / 1000 ☎ 511 43 83*

Based on straightforward design, Olivier Strelli's contemporary collection appeals to men and women looking for relaxed, easy-to-wear clothing in crease-resistant stretch, viscose and cool-wool materials, plus an attractive range of colors. Of special interest is the 22 Octobre line, designed for younger wearers but irresistible to trendies of all ages.

Gerald Watelet (34)

268, avenue Louise / 1050 ☎ 647 35 50

Louise *tram 92, 93, 94* ***Haute couture*** *Mon.–Fri. 10am–noon, 12.30–6.30pm; Sat. 10am–noon, 12.30–6.30pm*

Gerald Watelet is the personification of Belgian haute couture. His unfussy creations, typified by asymmetrical panels of different colors and reversible fabrics, are exported to Italy, New York, London and Paris. He also markets a more basic Almost Couture line, available in all his usual fabrics; although more ready-to-wear in style, it is still on the expensive side.

Not forgetting

■ **Dille & Kamille (35)** 16, rue Jean-Stas / 1060 ☎ 538 81 25 *A one-off in the context of Brussels, Dille & Kamille will appeal to environmentalists. A wide range of kitchen accessories, organic products and teas.* ■ **La Librairie de Rome (36)** 50b, avenue Louise / 1050 ☎ 511 79 37 *The best place for foreign newspapers; open until late at night.* ■ **La Compagnie de la Chine et de l'Orient (37)** 1A, place Stéphanie / 1000 ☎ 511 43 82 *Crafts and clothing from the Far East. You will be captivated by the silks from China, India and Burma.*

entrances, in the Rue du Cerf and the Boulevard de Waterloo, beside the Hilton hotel. ■ Where to stay ➥ 34 ■ Where to eat ➥ 54 ■ Where to shop ➥ 138

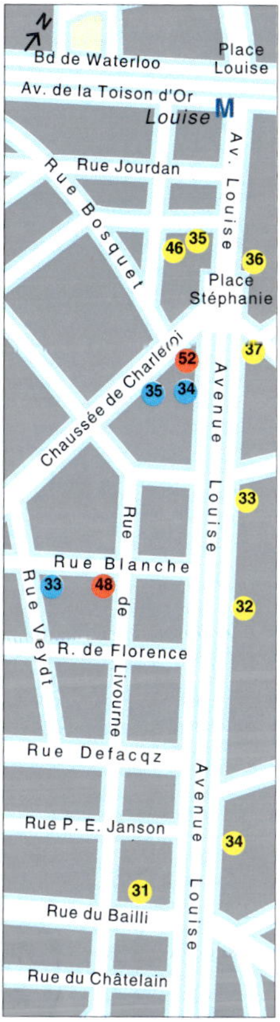

32

34

33

In the area
At the bottom of the Chaussé d'Ixelles is a series of lakes leading toward the Abbaye de la Cambre. One was filled in to form the Place Flagey. The others – the Plennebroeck and the Ghevaert – are the haunt of swans and ducks, Egyptian geese and naturalized green parrots. ■ Where to

Where to shop

Baltazar (38)
100, rue de Stassaert / 1050 ☎ 512 85 13

Ⓜ *Porte-Louise* 🚌 *71* ***Art, decoration and books*** 🕓 *Tue.–Sat. 10am–7pm; Sun. 11am–5pm* 💳

Just a few minutes from the Place Stéphanie, this former mansion has become a showcase for art. One of its specialties is plaster casts of sculptures and antique jewelry from some of the world's greatest museums. The catalog is the stuff of dreams. Baltazar also extends an invitation to discover contemporary art, displaying original works and magnificent *livres d'artiste* – limited editions combining the skills of artist-illustrators, printers and bookbinders. For adults, exhibitions and talks on art are a further attraction. ★ Children's needs are also catered for: Baltazar has a carefully chosen range of works to arouse the interest of the young. You will enjoy the peace and quiet of the spacious rear courtyard.

The Matonge district (39)
Porte de Namur

Ⓜ *Porte-de-Namur* 🚌 *71* ***African specialties*** *District lying between the Porte de Namur and the Place de Londres, the Porte-de-Namur and Ixelles shopping arcades.*

A corner of Africa in the heart of Ixelles, Matonge was created by Congolese exiles escaping from Mobuto's regime in the former Zaïre. And because the northern skies are often gray, they have tried to recreate the atmosphere of their native land. Named Matonge after the commercial district of Kinshasa, it vibrates with life. This is the place to stock up on *saka saka*, palm oil, chile peppers, plantains, sweet potatoes and cassava. ★ In the middle of the Ixelles shopping arcade, Musica Nova is well worth a visit. Run by an Italian couple, it specializes in ethnic music. If they do not stock the African, Caribbean, Afro-Cuban or South American recording you are looking for, they will be happy to order it for you (Musica Nova ☎ 511 66 94).

Côté Vaisselle (40)
46, rue de Stassaert / 1050 ☎ 513 76 08 ➠ 512 03 27

Ⓜ *Porte-de-Namur* 🚌 *71* ***Gifts, crockery, decorative items*** 🕓 *Mon.–Sat. 10am–7pm* 💳 *30, galerie de la Toison-d'Or / 1050 ☎ 513 76 08; 1384a, chaussée de Waterloo / 1180 ☎ 375 52 76*

Faced with dinner services retailing at unbeatable prices, you are sorely tempted to buy, if only for the pleasure of giving your table a new look. The store is truly a showcase for its wares, defined by the owner as 'attractive, practical and inexpensive'. What more could you ask?

Not forgetting
■ **Léonidas (41)** 5, chaussée d'Ixelles / 1050 ☎ 511 11 51 *Belgium's most popular brand of pralines. An interesting sales concept, the store has a counter giving onto the pavement, where you can pick and mix. Great if you want to eat chocolates as you stroll along window shopping.* ■ **La Fondation pour l'architecture (42)** 55, rue de l'Ermitage / 1050 ☎ 649 02 59 *A venue for exhibitions of urban art, landscape painting, architecture and the decorative arts. It also has a specialized library.*

stay ➥ 34 ■ Where to eat ➥ 54 ■ After dark ➥ 64 ■ What to see ➥ 98 ■ Where to shop ➥ 138

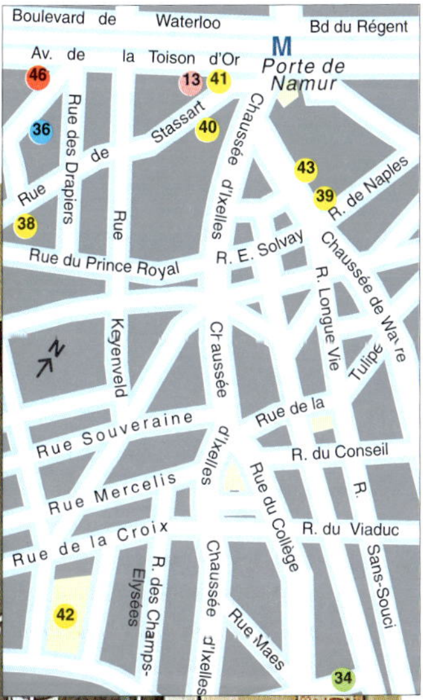

38

42

Hergé's style of cartoon drawing quickly attracted a huge following, and Belgian comic-strip creations have become famous world-wide. They are an art in their own right, well documented at the Centre belge de la bande dessinée (BD = comic strip) ➡ 86. There is even a BD trail through the streets of Brussels, with many familiar comic-strip heroes painted on walls

Where to shop

50 SLUMBERLAND

48

49

46

La Bande des Six Nez (43)

179, chaussée de Wavre / 1050
☎ 513 72 58
Ⓜ Trône
🚌 95, 96, 34
🕒 Mon.–Sat. 10.30am–7pm 💳

This was the first specialized BD bookstore to launch into silkscreen printing and 3D artifacts. The owner is regarded as Brussels' greatest connoisseur of the genre. It is a friendly, welcoming place, and alterations are being made so that exhibitions can be staged on the premises. You can buy BDs, portfolios and first editions, and there is a secondhand corner. A paradise, where you can spend many hours happily hunting around.

La Boutique de Tintin (44)

13, rue de la Colline / 1000
☎ 514 51 52
➡ 502 32 57
Ⓜ De Brouckère
🚌 34, 48, 95, 96, 71 🕒 Mon. 11am–6pm; Tue.–Sat. 10am–6pm; Sun. 11am–5pm 💳
Tintin Stockel
☎ 779 38 58

Everything the Hergé fan could desire: Tintin, of course, but also Quick and Flupke, the adventures of Jo, Zette and Joko, and the complete Men, Women and Children's range. The tribulations of Tintin and Milou are available in 26 languages, including Bengali and Tibetan. The Spanish versions are especially popular. Here you can rediscover your parents' favorite albums, and enthuse over the collection of figurines.

Sans Titre (45)

8, avenue de Stalingrad / 1000
☎ 514 25 12
Ⓜ Anneessens 🚌 34, 48, 95, 96 🕒 Mon.–Sat. 11am–6.30pm 💳

An integral feature of this bookstore is its art gallery. It stocks a vast range of comic-strip books, paying special attention to the quality of the story-lines, and making space for smaller publishers. There is also a well-stocked children's department. As well as leafing through your latest discoveries, be sure to enjoy the regular exhibitions which are held on the premises.

Ziggourat (46)

34, rue Dejoncker / 1060
☎ 538 40 37
Ⓜ Louise 🚌 tram 92, 93, 94
🕒 Tue.–Sat. 11am–6.30pm 💳

A gallery and bookstore specializing in comic-strip books and graphic art, Ziggourat occupies a special niche in Brussels life. Its monthly exhibitions are well attended by a knowledgeable crowd of *aficionados*. You will also find limited editions of silkscreen prints, bookplates and collectors' items. In 1997, the firm launched its own publishing house, Pyramides.

by the original draftsmen, for instance Roba's Boule et Bill (Rue du Chevreuil), Schuiten's Le Passage (Rue du Marché-au-Charbon) and Morris's Lucky Luke (Rue de la Buanderie)

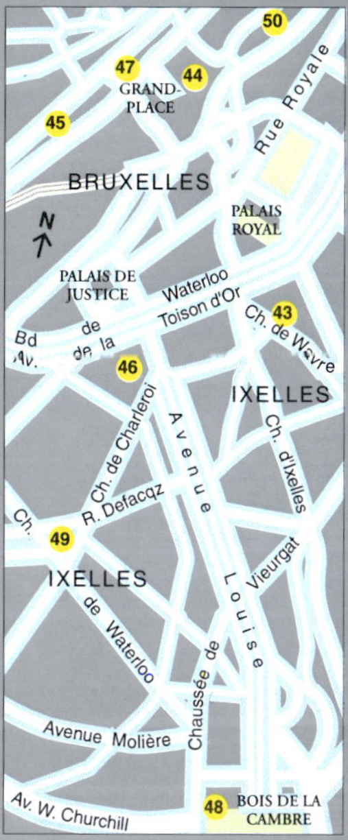

Brüsel (47)

100, boulevard Anspach / 1000
☎ *511 08 09*
➡ *502 35 52*
M *De Brouckère*
⏲ *Mon.–Sat. 10.30am–6.30pm; Sun. noon–6.30pm*

This store stocks almost 5,500 new and cut-price books. Its stated ambition is to cover the whole BD field, including independent publishers and collectives. When you make a purchase, you also receive the quarterly house magazine, with the latest news of the '9th art'. Opened in 1944, Brüsel's *décor* was inspired by Schuiten, and given his blessing. Permanent exhibitions of plates and silkscreen prints are displayed on the metal mezzanine floor.

Schlirf Book (48)

752, chaussée de Waterloo / 1180
☎ *648 04 40*
➡ *640 55 85*
🚌 *38 ; tram 23, 90*
⏲ *Mon.–Sat. 10.30am–7.30pm; Sun. 10.30am–6.30pm*

A short walk from the Bois de Cambre, Schlirf is another magnet for comic-strip buffs. Regarded as the specialist in American BDs, it has spent almost 20 years diversifying its stock. As well as American comics, you will find Japanese *mangas*, traditional classics, a children's section, and some art books. The firm also publishes its own silkscreen prints.

The Skull (49)

336, chaussée de Waterloo / 1060
☎ *538 36 99*
➡ *534 19 39*
M *Horta* 🚌 *54; tram 81, 82, 55 90*
⏲ *Mon.–Sat. 10.30am–7.30pm*

Twenty years ago, Mina launched the first comic-strip bookstore in Brussels. The business is now run by her son, Erik Coune, a walking encyclopedia. From science fiction, the firm has branched out into all types of BD, including a selection of the best *mangas*. The Skull's second attraction is its gallery, which runs talent contests and provides annual grants to collectors of cinema posters.

Slumberland (50)

20, rue des Sables / 1000
☎ *219 58 01*
M *Rogier* 🚌 *38, 61* ⏲ *Tue.–Sun. 10am–6pm*

Housed in the holy of holies, the Centre belge de la bande dessinée ➡ 86, this bookstore stocks all the new publications listed in the catalog, a large number of 3D artifacts, books of a humorous nature, and art books devoted to the architect of the building, Victor Horta himself. The name of the store is a reference to Little Nemo, the character created by Winsor McCay. First published in 1905 in the *New York Herald*, this is revered as the first ever strip cartoon.

Finding your way

Street vocabulary (Flemish)

Gang : cul-de-sac
Hof (or Tuin) : garden
Kaai : quay
Laan : avenue, boulevard
Park : park
Plein : square
Straat : street
Steenweg : causeway, embankment
Weg : path, lane

City layout

The historic center of Brussels, referred to as the Pentagon because of its shape, is enclosed by an inner circle of boulevards, known as the Petite Ceinture. The Ring, an outer ring-road 4 miles in radius, also includes the surrounding municipal districts.

6 Maps

Bruxelles-Capitale

The Bruxelles-Capitale region consists of 19 municipal districts (see map below): Anderlecht, Auderghem, Berchem-Sainte-Agathe, Bruxelles, Etterbeek, Evere, Forest, Ganshoren, Ixelles, Jette, Koekelberg, Molenbeek-Saint-Jean, Saint-Gilles, Saint-Josse-ten-Noode, Schaerbeek, Uccle, Watermael-Boitsfort, Woluwe-Saint-Lambert, and Woluwe-Saint-Pierre.

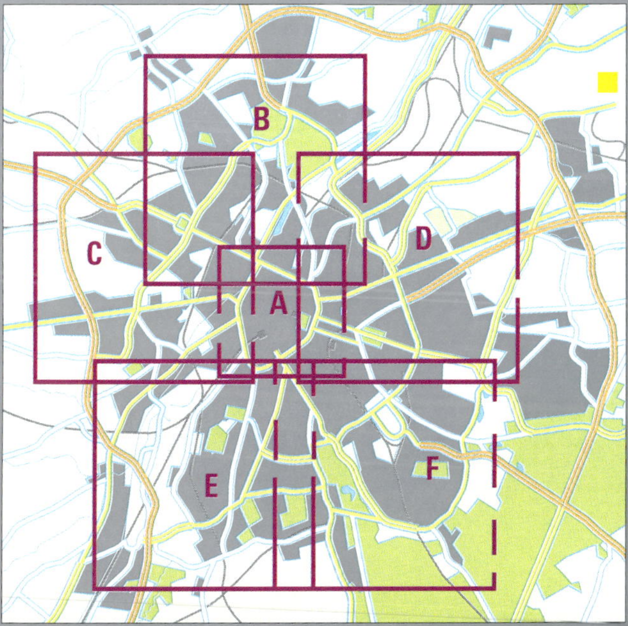

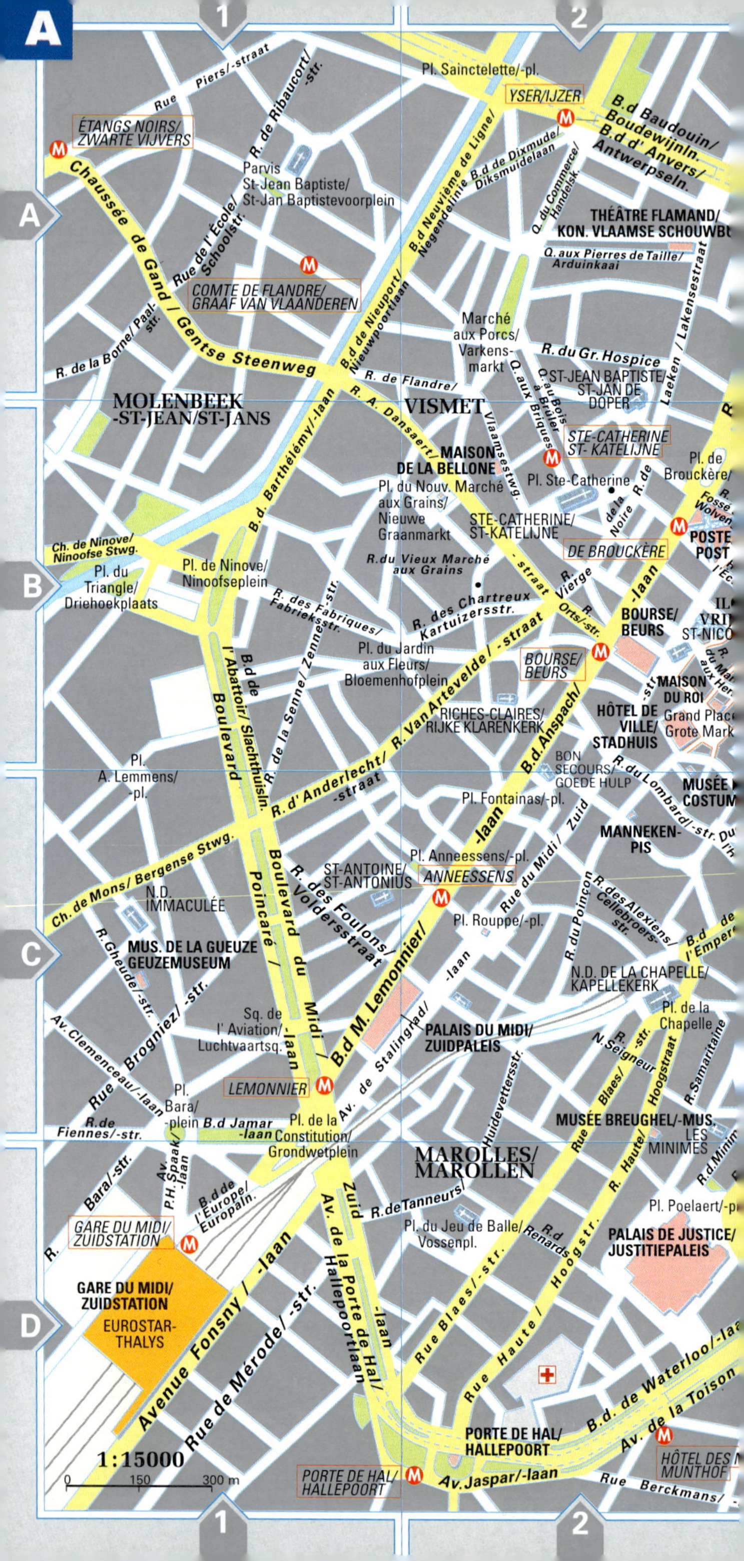

A
1
2
Piers/-straat
R. de Ribaucort/-str.
Pl. Saintctelette/-pl.
YSER/IJZER
B.d Baudouin/ Boudewijnln.
B.d d' Anvers/ Antwerpseln.
ÉTANGS NOIRS/ ZWARTE VIJVERS
Parvis St-Jean Baptiste/ St-Jan Baptistevoorplein
B.d Neuvième de Ligne/ Negendelinie
B.d de Dixmude/ Diksmuidelaan
Q. du Commerce/ Handelsk.
THÉATRE FLAMAND/ KON. VLAAMSE SCHOUWBU
Chaussée de Gand / Gentse Steenweg
Rue de l'École/ Schoolstr.
Q. aux Pierres de Taille/ Arduinkaai
COMTE DE FLANDRE/ GRAAF VAN VLAANDEREN
B.d de Nieuport/ Nieuwpoortlaan
Marché aux Porcs/ Varkens-markt
R. de la Borne/ Paal-str.
R. du Gr. Hospice
ST-JEAN BAPTISTE/ ST-JAN DE DOPER
R. de Flandre/
Laeken/ Lakensestraat
MOLENBEEK -ST-JEAN/ST-JANS
VISMET
B.d Barthélémy/-laan
R. A. Dansaert/
Q. aux Briques
Q. au Bois à Brûler
STE-CATHERINE/ ST- KATELIJNE
MAISON DE LA BELLONE
Vlaamsesteenwg.
Pl. de Brouckère/
Pl. du Nouv. Marché aux Grains/ Nieuwe Graanmarkt
Pl. Ste-Catherine
R. de la Noire
STE-CATHERINE/ ST-KATELIJNE
POSTE POST
Ch. de Ninove/ Ninoofse Stwg.
DE BROUCKÈRE
R. du Vieux Marché aux Grains
Pl. du Triangle/ Driehoekplaats
Pl. de Ninove/ Ninoofseplein
R. des Fabriques/ Fabrieksstr.
R. des Chartreux Kartuizersstr.
R. Vierge
R. Orts/-str.
BOURSE/ BEURS
Pl. du Jardin aux Fleurs/ Bloemenhofplein
R. Van Artevelde/ -straat
BOURSE/ BEURS
B.d de l'Abattoir/ Slachthuisln.
Boulevard
R. de la Senne/ Zenne-str.
MAISON DU ROI
Grand Place
Grote Mark
B.d Anspach/ -laan
RICHES-CLAIRES/ RIJKE KLARENKERK
HÔTEL DE VILLE/ STADHUIS
BON SECOURS/ GOEDE HULP
Pl. A. Lemmens/ -pl.
R. d' Anderlecht/ -straat
R. du Lombard/-str.
MUSÉE COSTUM
Pl. Fontainas/-pl.
MANNEKEN-PIS
Ch. de Mons/ Bergense Stwg.
Boulevard Poincaré /
Boulevard du Midi / -laan
R. Voldersstraat
Pl. Anneessens/-pl.
ST-ANTOINE/ ST-ANTONIUS
ANNEESSENS
Rue du Midi / Zuid
N.D. IMMACULÉE
R. des Foulons/
R. des Alexiens/ Cellebroers-str.
R. du Poinçon
Pl. Rouppe/-pl.
B.d de l'Empereur
MUS. DE LA GUEUZE GEUZEMUSEUM
R. Gheude/-str.
B.d M. Lemonnier/ -laan
N.D. DE LA CHAPELLE/ KAPELLEKERK
Sq. de l' Aviation/ Luchtvaartsq.
Rue Brogniez/ -str.
Av. Clemenceau/-laan
Av. de Stalingrad/
PALAIS DU MIDI/ ZUIDPALEIS
Pl. de la Chapelle
R. N. Seigneur
Hoogstraat
R. Samaritaine
Huidevettersstr.
LEMONNIER
Pl. Bara/ -plein
B.d Jamar -laan
Pl. de la Constitution/ Grondwetplein
MUSÉE BREUGHEL/-MUS.
LES MINIMES
Rue Blaes/-str.
R. de Fiennes/-str.
MAROLLES/ MAROLLEN
Av. P.H. Spaak/ -laan
Bara/-str.
B.d de l'Europe/ Europaln.
R. de Tanneurs/
Pl. Poelaert/-pl
GARE DU MIDI/ ZUIDSTATION
Av. de la Porte de Hal/ Halleportlaan
Pl. du Jeu de Balle/ Vossenpl.
R. d Renards
PALAIS DE JUSTICE/ JUSTITIEPALEIS
GARE DU MIDI/ ZUIDSTATION
EUROSTAR-THALYS
Avenue Fonsny / -laan
Rue de Mérode/ -str.
Rue Blaes/-str.
Rue Haute / Hoogstr.
R. Haute/
B.d de Waterloo/-laan
Av. de la Toison
PORTE DE HAL/ HALLEPOORT
1:15000
0
150
300 m
PORTE DE HAL/ HALLEPOORT
Av. Jaspar/-laan
HÔTEL DES MUNTHOF
Rue Berckmans/
B
C
D

3
4
A
B
C
D
GARE DU NORD/
NOORDSTATION
STE-MARIE/
ST-MARIA
B.d E. Jacqmain/-laan
R. du Progrès/
Vooruitgangstraat
Rue de Brabant/-straat
Rue Verte/ Groenstr.
Rue Royale / Koningsstraat
Ch. de Haecht / Haachtse -stwg.
Josaphat/ -str.
ROGIER
Pl. Rogier/
-plein
B.d du Jardin Botanique/Kruidtuin -laan
B.d St-Lazare / St-Lazarus -laan
R. Gineste
Parc du
Jardin Botanique/
Plantentuinpark
Rue Botanique / Kruidtuinstr.
Av. Victoria Regina/-laan
Rue Grensstr.
du Méridien
ST-JOSSE-TEN-NOODE/
ST-JOOST-TEN-NODE
Adolphe Max/-laan
Nieuwstraat
CITY 2
Broekstr.
BOTANIQUE/
KRUIDTUIN
Av. Galilée/-laan
R. de la Limite/
R. Traversière/
Dwarsstr.
ÉGLISE DE
FINISTÈRE/
FINISTERRAE KERK
Pl. des Martyrs/
Martelaarspl.
Neuve/
CENTRE
BELGE DE
LA BANDE
DESSINÉE/
STRIPVER-
MAA
MUS.
R. du Marais
R. des Sables/
Zandstr.
B.d Pacheco /-laan
Boulevard
Pl. Quetelet/
-plein
CITÉ ADMINISTRATIVE/
ADMINISTRATIEF
CENTRUM
Bischoffsheim/-laan
Av. Astronomie
R. de la Commune/
Gemeentestr.
Pl. du Congress/
-plein
R. du Congres/-str.
THÉATRE DE LA MONNAIE/
MUNTSCHOUWBURG
Chaussée de Louvain / Leuvense - stwg.
B.d de Berlaimont/-laan
R. Assaut
R. Arenberg
R. de l' Enseignement
Pl. de Madou/
-plein
MADOU
BANQUE NATIONALE/
NATIONALE BANK
R. de la
Croix de Fer/ Ijzerenkruis-
straat
Pl. Ste-Gudule
MUSÉE
CHARLIER/-MUS.
R. des Deux Eglise/ Tweekerken-straat
R. de la Montagne
ST-MICHEL-ET-GUDULE/
ST-MICHIEL
GARE CENTRALE/
CENTRAAL STATION
PALAIS DE LA NATION/
PALEIS DER NATIE
Rue de la Loi / Wetstr.
Rue Royale/ Konings -straat
MADELEINE/
PARC/PARK
ARTS-LOI/
KUNST-WET
GARE CENTRALE/
CENTRAALSTATION
Parc de Bruxelles/
Park van Brussel
Rue Ducale/ Hertogs -str.
Av. des Arts/ Kunst -laan
Rue de la Loi / Wetstraat
Pl. de l' Albertine/
Albertinaplein
R. Ravenstein/-straat
MONT D. ARTS/
KUNSTBERG
PALAIS DES BEAUX-ARTS/
PALEIS VOOR SCHONE
KUNSTEN
Handelsstraat
Wetenschapsstr.
MAELBEEK/
MAALBEEK
R. de Trèves/Trierstr.
MUS. D' ART
ANCIENT ET
MODERNE/
Pl. d. Palais/
Paleizen-
plein
MUS.
BELLEVUE
Pl. Royale/
Koningsplein
MUS. VOOR
OUDE EN MODERNE
KUNST
Rue Belliard/-straat
PAL. DES ACADÉMIES/
PAL. DER ACADEMIËN
ST-JACQUES/
ST-JACOB
Regentschapsstr.
Pl.
Gr. Sablon/
Grote
Zavel
PALAIS ROYAL/
KONINKLIJK PALEIS
Pl. du Trône/
Troonplein
R. du Commerce/
R. de la Science
N. DAME
DU SABLON/
ZAVELKERK
CONSERVATOIRE/KONSERVAT.
MUS. DE
LA DYNASTIE/
MUS. V. DE DYNASTIE
TRÔNE/TROON
R. du Luxembourg/
Luxemburgstr.
PARLEMENT EUROPÉEN/
EUROPEES PARL.
Pl. du Petit
Sablon/Kleine Zavel
Pl. du
Luxembourg
Luxemburgpl.
Porte de Namur/
Naamsepoort
SYNAGOGUE/
SYNAGOGE
PORTE DE NAMUR/
NAAMSEPOORT
R.Parnasse
GARE DU
QUARTIER LÉOPOLD/
LEOPOLDSWIJK
PALAIS D' EGMONT/-
-PALEIS
B.d. de Waterloo/-laan
Gulden Vlieslaan
Stassart/-str.
Chaussée de Wavre/ Waverse Steenweg
Rue du Trône / Troon - straat
R. Wiertz/-str.
Louise/
LOUISE/LOUIZA
R. Cap. Crespel
Rue de
Chaussée d' Ixelles/ Elsene Stwg.
R. Keyenveld/ Keienveldstr.
R. Goffart/-str.
Viaductstr.
ST-BONIFACE/
ST-BONIFAAS
Av.Louise/ Louizalaan
Pl.
Stéphanie/
Stephaniapl.
Rue du Viaduc/
Pl. F. Cocq/
-plein
IXELLES/
ELSENE
Ch. de Charleroi

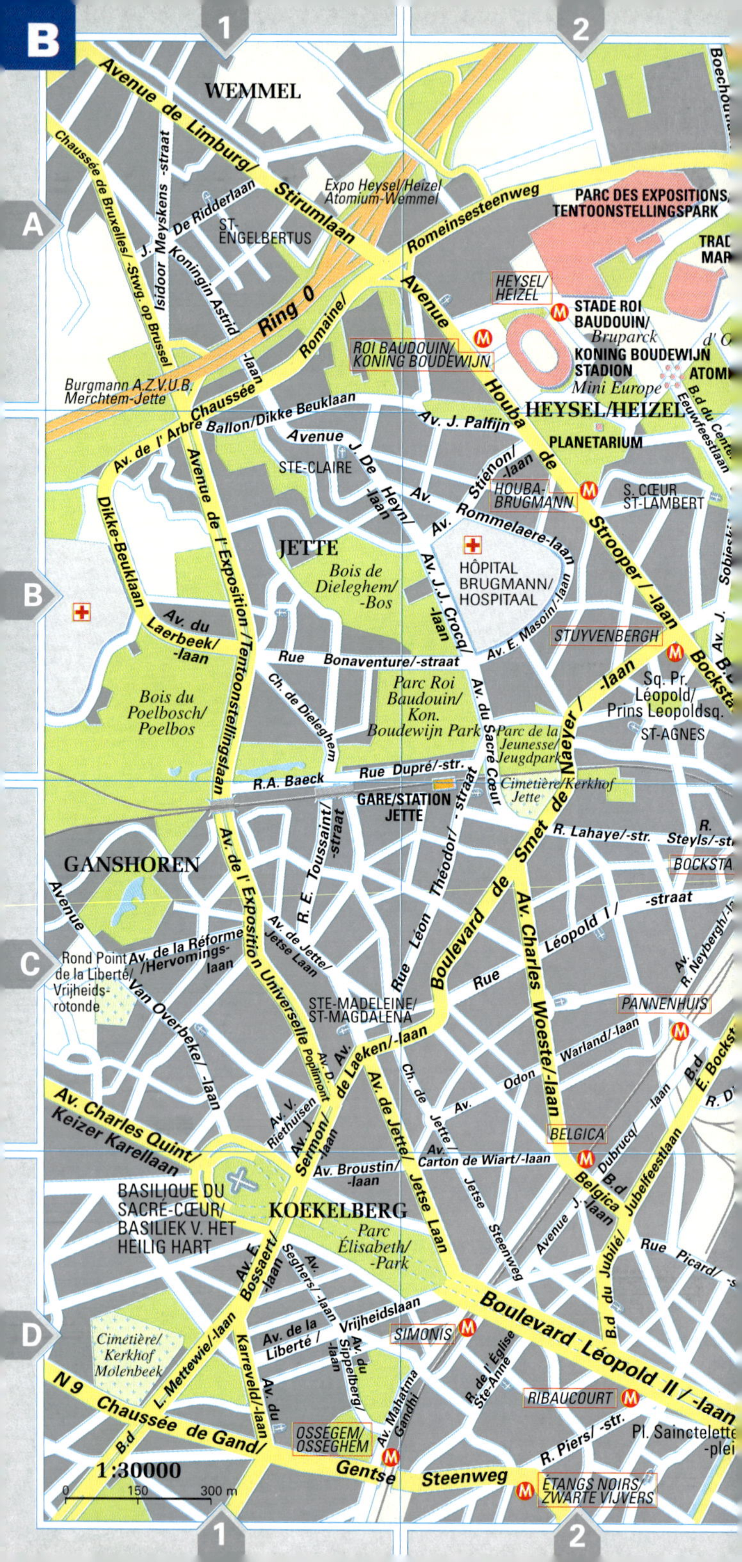

B
1
2
WEMMEL
Avenue de Limburg/
Stirumlaan
Chaussée de Bruxelles/-Stwg. op Brussel
J. Isidoor Meyskens -straat
De Ridderlaan
Koningin Astrid -laan
ST-ENGELBERTUS
Expo Heysel/Heizel
Atomium-Wemmel
Romeinsesteenweg
PARC DES EXPOSITIONS/
TENTOONSTELLINGSPARK
Ring 0
Romaine/
Chaussée
Avenue Houba de Strooper/-laan
HEYSEL/HEIZEL
STADE ROI BAUDOUIN/
Bruparck
KONING BOUDEWIJN STADION
Mini Europe
ROI BAUDOUIN/
KONING BOUDEWIJN
Burgmann A.Z.V.U.B.
Merchtem-Jette
Av. de l' Arbre Ballon/Dikke Beuklaan
Av. J. Palfijn
HEYSEL/HEIZEL
PLANETARIUM
Avenue J. De Heyn/-laan
STE-CLAIRE
Av. Stiénon/-laan
HOUBA-BRUGMANN
S. CŒUR
ST-LAMBERT
Av. Rommelaere-laan
JETTE
Bois de Dieleghem/-Bos
Av. J.J. Crocq/-laan
HÔPITAL BRUGMANN/
HOSPITAAL
Dikke-Beuklaan
Avenue de l' Exposition /Tentoonstellingslaan
Av. du Laerbeek/-laan
Av. E. Masoin/-laan
STUYVENBERGH
Rue Bonaventure/-straat
Bois du Poelbosch/
Poelbos
Ch. de Dieleghem
Parc Roi Baudouin/
Kon. Boudewijn Park
Av. du Sacré Cœur
Parc de la Jeunesse/
Jeugdpark
Sq. Pr. Léopold/
Prins Leopoldsq.
ST-AGNES
R.A. Baeck
Rue Dupré/-str.
GARE/STATION
JETTE
Cimetière/Kerkhof
Jette
Rue Léon Théodor/-straat
R. E. Toussaint/-straat
Boulevard de Smet de Naeyer / -laan
R. Lahaye/-str.
R. Steyls/-str.
GANSHOREN
Avenue
Av. de l' Exposition Universelle
Av. de Jette/
Jetse Laan
Av. Charles Woeste/-laan
Rue Léopold I / -straat
Av. de la Réforme
/Hervomingslaan
Rond Point de la Liberté/
Vrijheidsrotonde
Van Overbeke/ -laan
STE-MADELEINE/
ST-MAGDALENA
PANNENHUIS
Av. de Laeken/-laan
Av. D. Poplimont
Warland/-laan
Av. Odon
Ch. de Jette Jetse Steenweg
Av. Charles Quint/
Keizer Karellaan
Av. V. Riethuisen
Av. J. Sermon/-laan
Av. de Jette/ Jetse Laan
Av. Carton de Wiart/-laan
BELGICA
Dubrucq/-laan
Bd Belgica -laan
Bd E. Bockstael
Jubelfeestlaan
Av. Broustin/-laan
BASILIQUE DU SACRÉ-CŒUR/
BASILIEK V. HET
HEILIG HART
KOEKELBERG
Parc Élisabeth/
-Park
Avenue J.
Rue Picard/
Av. E. Bossaert/-laan
Av. Seghers/-laan
Boulevard Léopold II / -laan
B.d du Jubilé/
Cimetière/
Kerkhof
Molenbeek
Av. de la Liberté / Vrijheidslaan
Av. du Sippelberg/-laan
SIMONIS
R. de l' Église Ste-Anne
B.d L. Mettewie/-laan
Karreveld/-laan
Av. du
Av. Mahatma Gandhi
RIBAUCOURT
N 9 Chaussée de Gand/
Gentse Steenweg
OSSEGEM/
OSSEGHEM
R. Piers/-str.
Pl. Sainctelette -plein
ÉTANGS NOIRS/
ZWARTE VIJVERS
A
B
C
D
1:30000
0
150
300 m

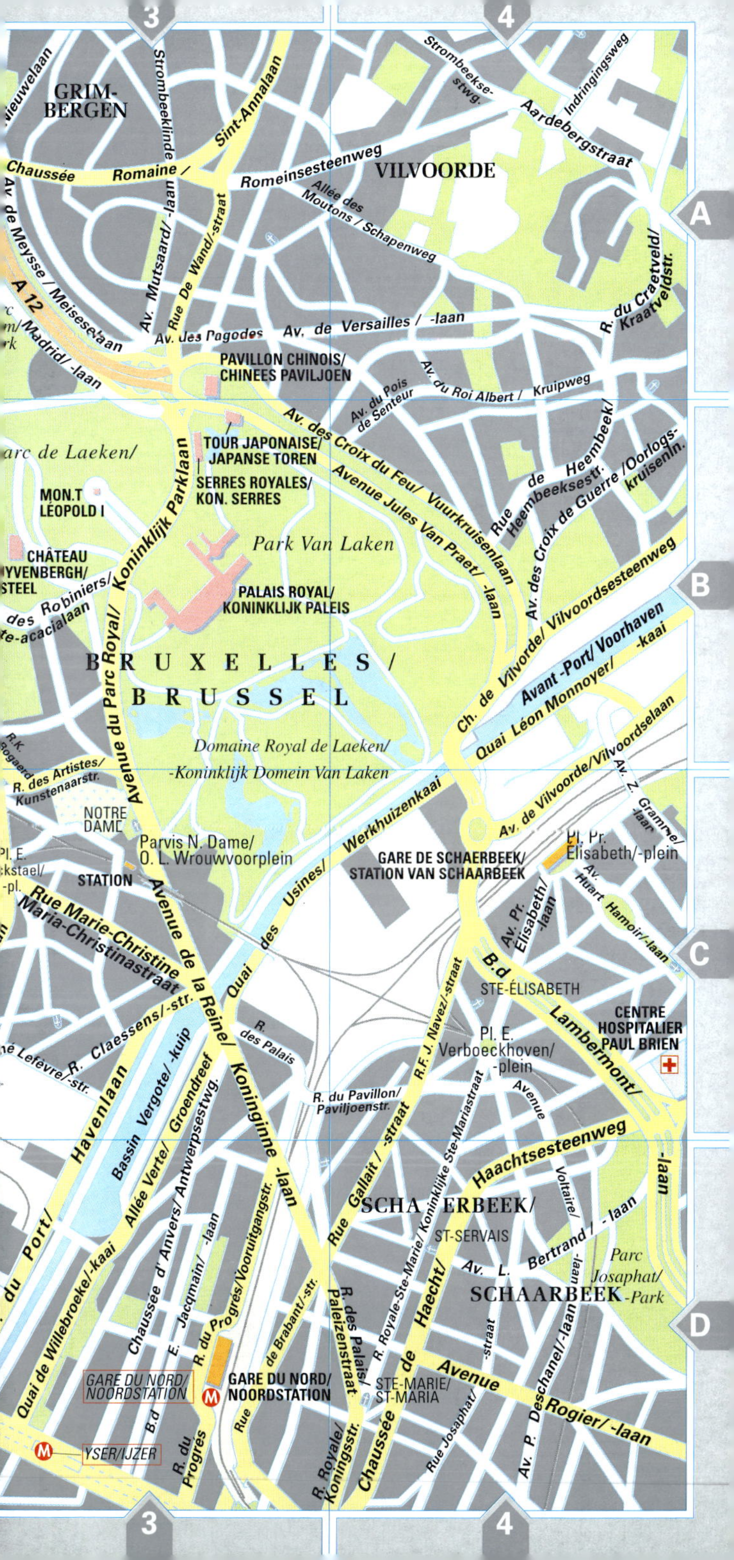
3
4
A
B
C
D
GRIM-BERGEN
VILVOORDE
BRUXELLES / BRUSSEL
SCHAERBEEK/
SCHAARBEEK
Chaussée Romaine / Romeinsesteenweg
Strombeeklinde
Sint-Annalaan
Strombeekse-stwg.
Aardebergstraat
Indringingsweg
Allée des Moutons / Schapenweg
Av. de Meysse / Meiseselaan
A 12
Madrid/ -laan
Av. Mutsaard/ -laan
Rue De Wand/-straat
Av. des Pagodes
Av. de Versailles / -laan
R. du Craetveld/ Kraatveldstr.
PAVILLON CHINOIS/ CHINEES PAVILJOEN
Av. du Pois de Senteur
Av. du Roi Albert / Kruipweg
Av. des Croix du Feu/ Vuurkruisenlaan
Avenue Jules Van Praet/ -laan
Rue de Heembeek/ Heembeeksestr.
Av. des Croix de Guerre /Oorlogs-kruisenln.
TOUR JAPONAISE/ JAPANSE TOREN
SERRES ROYALES/ KON. SERRES
MON.T LÉOPOLD I
Parc de Laeken/
Park Van Laken
CHÂTEAU STUYVENBERGH/ KASTEEL
PALAIS ROYAL/ KONINKLIJK PALEIS
Avenue du Parc Royal/ Koninklijk Parklaan
des Robiniers/ Robiniacacialaan
Ch. de Vilvorde/ Vilvoordsesteenweg
Avant -Port/ Voorhaven
Quai Léon Monnoyer/ -kaai
Domaine Royal de Laeken/ -Koninklijk Domein Van Laken
R. des Artistes/ Kunstenaarstr.
NOTRE DAME
Parvis N. Dame/ O. L. Wrouwvoorplein
STATION
Av. de Vilvorde/Vilvoordselaan
Av. Z. Gramme/ -laan
Pl. Pr. Elisabeth/-plein
Quai des Usines/ Werkhuizenkaai
GARE DE SCHAERBEEK/ STATION VAN SCHAARBEEK
Rue Marie-Christine Maria-Christinastraat
Avenue de la Reine/ Koninginne -laan
Av. Pr. Elisabeth/ -laan
Av. Huart Hamoir/-laan
B.d Lambermont/ -laan
STE-ÉLISABETH
CENTRE HOSPITALIER PAUL BRIEN
R. Claessens/-str.
R. des Palais
R.F. J. Navez/-straat
Pl. E. Verboeckhoven/ -plein
Avenue
Bassin Vergote/ -kuip
Havenlaan
Allée Verte/ Groendreef
R. du Pavillon/ Paviljoenstr.
Haachtsesteenweg
Voltaire/
Rue Gallait / -straat
R. Royale-Ste-Marie/ Koninklijke Ste-Mariastraat
ST-SERVAIS
Av. L. Bertrand / -laan
Parc Josaphat/ -Park
Quai du Port/
Quai de Willebroeke/-kaai
Chaussée d'Anvers/ Antwerpsestwg.
B.d E. Jacqmain/ -laan
R. du Progrès/Vooruitgangstr.
Rue de Brabant/-str.
R. des Palais/ Paleizenstraat
Chaussée de Haecht/
Avenue Rogier/ -laan
Av. P. Deschanel/-laan
Rue Josaphat/ -straat
GARE DU NORD/ NOORDSTATION
STE-MARIE/ ST-MARIA
YSER/IJZER
R. du Progrès
R. Royale/ Koningsstr.

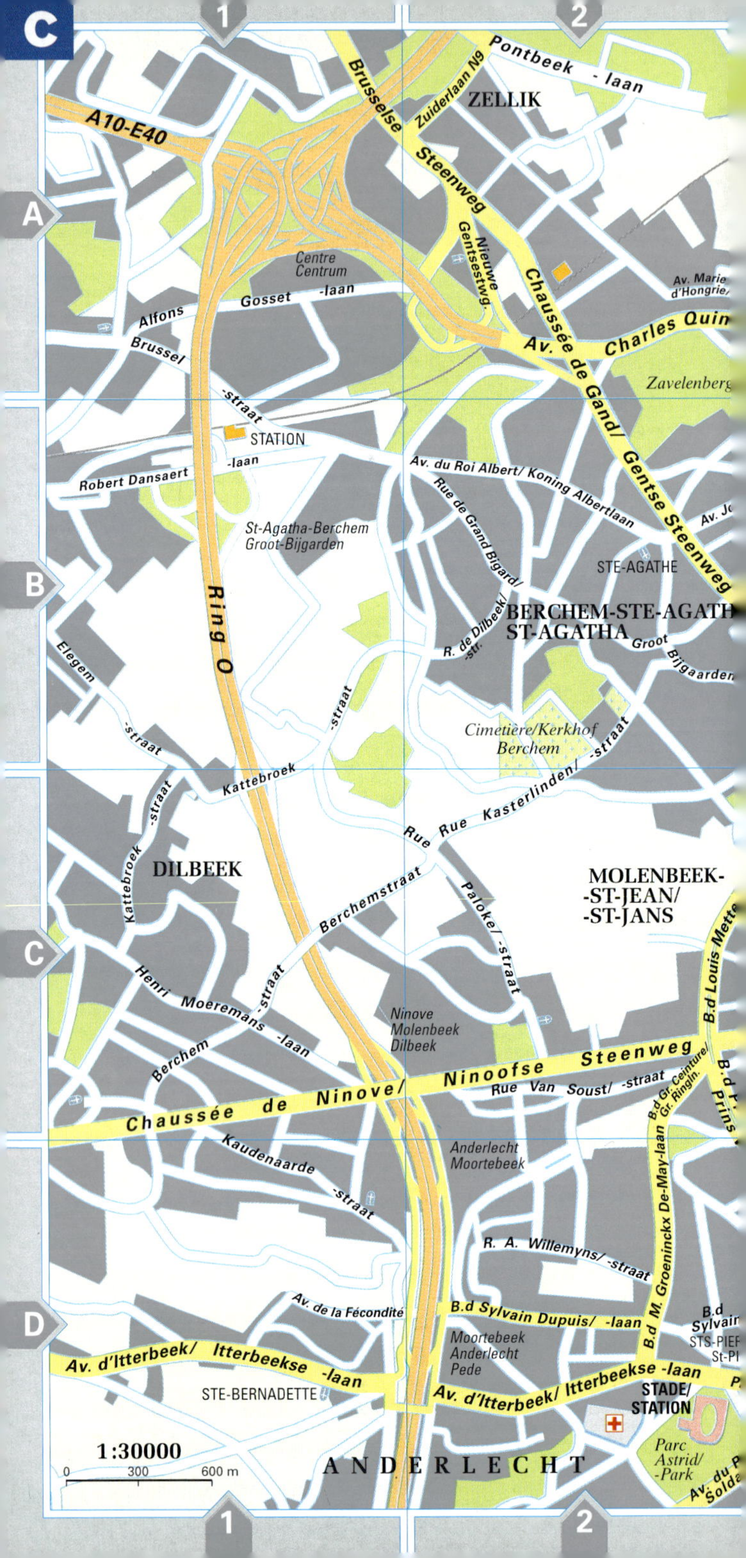

C
1
2
A
B
C
D
A10-E40
Brusselse Steenweg
Zuiderlaan N9
Pontbeek -laan
ZELLIK
Nieuwe Gentsestwg.
Centre Centrum
Alfons Gosset -laan
Brussel -straat
Chaussée de Gand/ Gentse Steenweg
Av. Charles Quin
Av. Marie d'Hongrie/
Zavelenberg
STATION
Robert Dansaert -laan
Av. du Roi Albert/ Koning Albertlaan
Rue de Grand Bigard/
St-Agatha-Berchem Groot-Bijgarden
Av. Jo
STE-AGATHE
BERCHEM-STE-AGATH
ST-AGATHA
R. de Dilbeek/ -str.
Groot Bijgaarden
Ring O
Elegem -straat
-straat
Cimetière/Kerkhof Berchem
Rue Kasterlinden/ -straat
Kattebroek
Kattebroek -straat
Rue
DILBEEK
MOLENBEEK- -ST-JEAN/ -ST-JANS
Berchemstraat
Paloke/ -straat
B.d Louis Mette
Henri Moeremans -laan
-straat
Ninove Molenbeek Dilbeek
Berchem
Chaussée de Ninove/ Ninoofse Steenweg
Rue Van Soust/ -straat
B.d Gr. Ceinture/ Gr. Ringln.
B.d P. Prins
Kaudenaarde -straat
Anderlecht Moortebeek
R. A. Willemyns/ -straat
B.d M. Groeninckx De-May-laan
Av. de la Fécondité
B.d Sylvain Dupuis/ -laan
B.d Sylvain
STS-PIEF St-PI
Moortebeek Anderlecht Pede
Av. d'Itterbeek/ Itterbeekse -laan
STE-BERNADETTE
Av. d'Itterbeek/ Itterbeekse -laan
STADE/ STATION
Parc Astrid/ -Park
Av. du P Solda
1:30000
0
300
600 m
ANDERLECHT

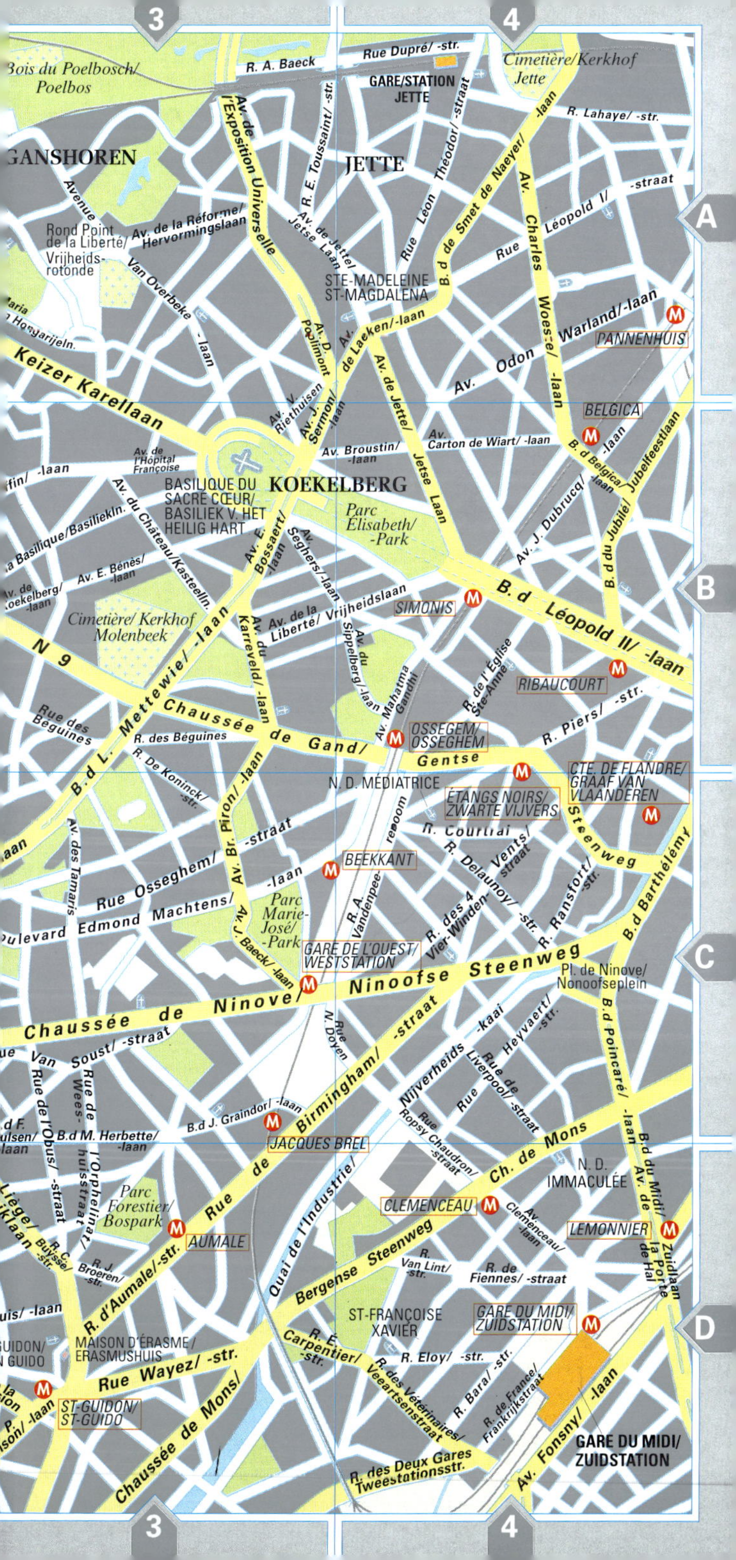
3
4
A
B
C
D
Bois du Poelbosch/ Poelbos
R. A. Baeck
Rue Dupré/ -str.
GARE/STATION JETTE
Cimetière/Kerkhof Jette
R. Lahaye/ -str.
GANSHOREN
JETTE
Av. de l'Exposition Universelle
R. E. Toussaint/ -str.
Rue Léon Théodor/ -straat
B.d de Smet de Naeyer/ -laan
Av. Charles Woeste/ -laan
Rue Léopold I/ -straat
Avenue Van Overbeke -laan
Rond Point de la Liberté/ Vrijheids-rotonde
Av. de la Réforme/ Hervormingslaan
Av. de Jette/ Jetse Laan
STE-MADELEINE ST-MAGDALENA
Av. D. Poplimont
Av. de Laeken/-laan
Av. Odon Warland/-laan
PANNENHUIS
Keizer Karellaan
Av. V. Riethuisen
Av. J. Sermon/ -laan
Av. de Jette/ Jetse Laan
BELGICA
Av. Carton de Wiart/ -laan
B.d Belgica/ -laan
Av. Broustin/ -laan
Av. de l'Hôpital Française
BASILIQUE DU SACRE CŒUR/ BASILIEK V. HET HEILIG HART
KOEKELBERG
Parc Elisabeth/ -Park
Av. J. Dubrucq/
Jubelfeestlaan
B.d du Jubilé/
Av. du Château/Kasteelln.
Basilique/Basiliekln.
Av. E. Bossaert/ -laan
Av. Seghers/ -laan
Av. E. Bénès/ -laan
Av. de Koekelberg/ -laan
Av. de la Liberté/ Vrijheidslaan
SIMONIS
B.d Léopold II/ -laan
Cimetière/ Kerkhof Molenbeek
Av. du Karreveld/ -laan
Av. du Sippelberg/ -laan
N 9
B.d L. Mettewie/ -laan
Av. Mahatma Gandhi
R. de l'Eglise Ste-Anne
RIBAUCOURT
Chaussée de Gand/ Gentse Steenweg
Rue des Beguines
R. des Béguines
R. De Koninck/ -str.
OSSEGEM/ OSSEGHEM
R. Piers/ -str.
N. D. MÉDIATRICE
CTE. DE FLANDRE/ GRAAF VAN VLAANDEREN
ETANGS NOIRS/ ZWARTE VIJVERS
R. Courtrai
Av. des Tamaris
Av. Br. Piron/ -laan
Rue Osseghem/ -straat
BEEKKANT
R. Delaunoy/ -str.
Vents straat
Boulevard Edmond Machtens/ -laan
Parc Marie-José/ -Park
R. A. Vandenpeereboom
R. des 4 Vents/ Vier-Winden-
R. Ransfort/ -str.
B.d Barthélémy
Av. J. Baeck/ -laan
GARE DE L'OUEST/ WESTSTATION
Ninoofse Steenweg
Chaussée de Ninove/
Pl. de Ninove/ Nonoofseplein
Rue N. Doyen
Van Soust/ -straat
Heyvaert/ -str.
Nijverheids -kaai
Rue de Liverpool/ -straat
B.d Poincaré/ -laan
Rue de l'Obus/ -straat
Rue de Wees-huisstraat
B.d J. Graindor/ -laan
B.d M. Herbette/ -laan
Rue de Birmingham/ -straat
JACQUES BREL
Rue Ropsy Chaudron/ -straat
Ch. de Mons
N. D. IMMACULÉE
Av. de la Porte de Hal
B.d du Midi/ Zuidlaan
Parc Forestier/ Bospark
l'Orphelinat/
Quai de l'Industrie/
CLEMENCEAU
Av. Clemenceau/ -laan
LEMONNIER
AUMALE
R. C. Buysse/ -str.
R. J. Broeren/ -str.
R. d'Aumale/-str.
Bergense Steenweg
R. Van Lint/ -str.
R. de Fiennes/ -straat
ST-FRANÇOISE XAVIER
GARE DU MIDI/ ZUIDSTATION
MAISON D'ÉRASME/ ERASMUSHUIS
R. E. Carpentier/ -str.
R. Eloy/ -str.
Rue Wayez/ -str.
R. des Vétérinaires/ Veeartsenstraat
R. Bara/ -str.
R. de France/ Frankrijkstraat
ST-GUIDON/ ST-GUIDO
Chaussée de Mons/
R. des Deux Gares Tweestationsstr.
Av. Fonsny/ -laan
GARE DU MIDI/ ZUIDSTATION

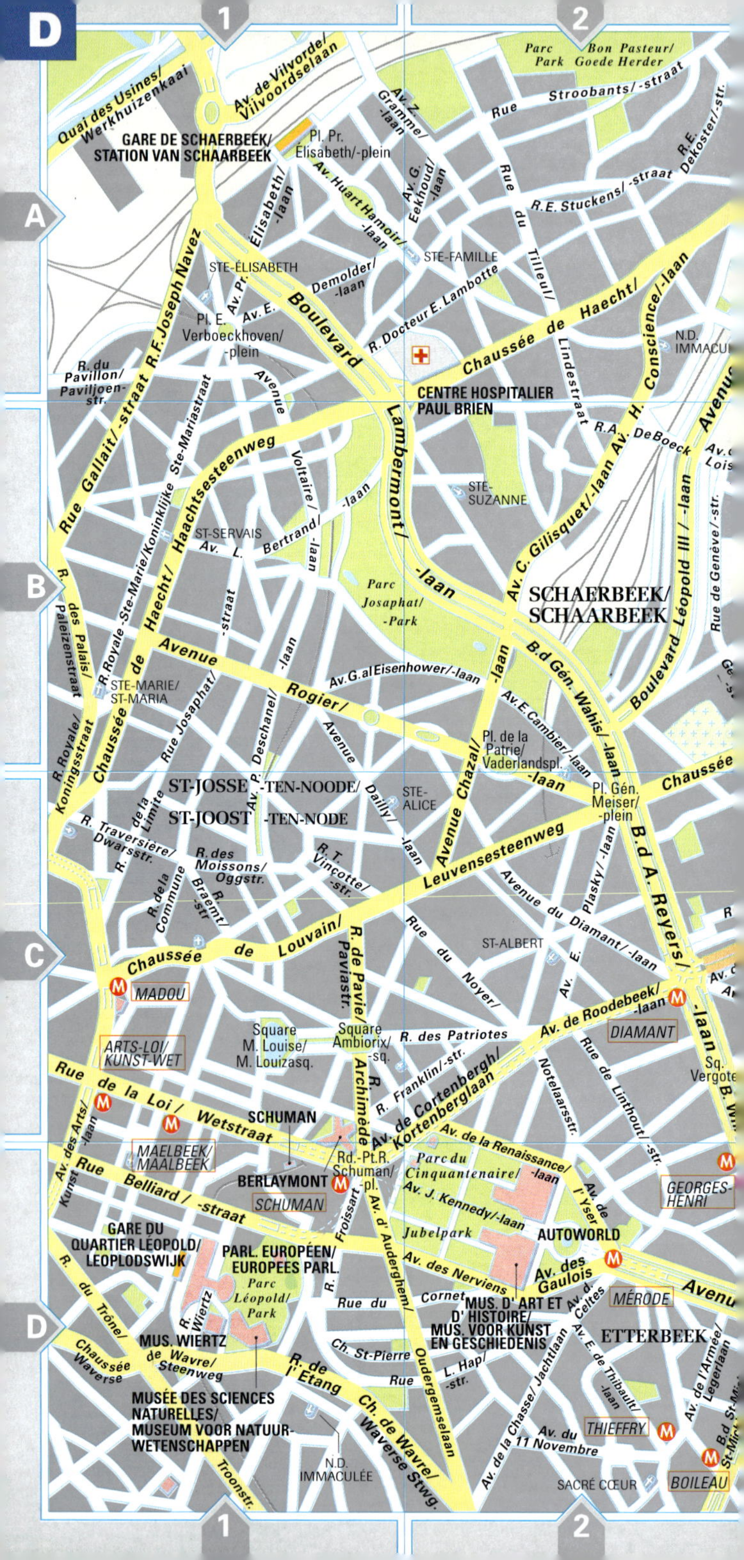

D
GARE DE SCHAERBEEK/
STATION VAN SCHAARBEEK
Quai des Usines/ Werkhuizenkaai
Av. de Vilvorde/ Vilvoordselaan
Pl. Pr. Élisabeth/-plein
Av. Z. Gramme/-laan
Parc Bon Pasteur/ Park Goede Herder
Stroobants/-straat
R.E. Dekoster/-str.
R.E. Stuckens/-straat
Rue du Tilleul/
Av. G. Eekhoud/-laan
Av. Huart Hamoir/-laan
STE-FAMILLE
Demolder/-laan
STE-ÉLISABETH
Av. Pr. Élisabeth/-laan
R.F. Joseph Navez
Boulevard Lambermont/-laan
R. Docteur E. Lambotte
Chaussée de Haecht/
Conscience/-laan
N.D. IMMACU
Pl. E. Verboeckhoven/-plein
Av. E.
R. du Pavillon/ Paviljoen-str.
CENTRE HOSPITALIER
PAUL BRIEN
Lindestraat
R.A. De Boeck
Avenue
Rue Gallait/-straat
Ste-Mariastraat
Haachtsesteenweg
Voltaire/-laan
STE-SUZANNE
Av. C. Gilisquet/-laan
Av. H.
Boulevard Léopold III/-laan
Rue de Genève/-str.
ST-SERVAIS
Av. L. Bertrand/-laan
Parc Josaphat/-Park
SCHAERBEEK/
SCHAARBEEK
R. des Palais/ Paleizenstraat
R. Royale Ste-Marie/Koninklijke Ste-Mariastraat
Chaussée de Haecht/
Avenue Rogier/-laan
Av. G. al Eisenhower/-laan
B.d Gén. Wahis/-laan
STE-MARIE/ ST-MARIA
Rue Josaphat/-straat
Av. P. Deschanel/-laan
Avenue Dailly/-laan
Av. E. Cambier/-laan
Pl. de la Patrie/ Vaderlandspl.
R. Royale/ Koningsstraat
ST-JOSSE -TEN-NOODE/
ST-JOOST -TEN-NODE
STE-ALICE
Avenue Chazal/-laan
Pl. Gén. Meiser/-plein
Chaussée
R. de la Limite
R. Traversière/ Dwarsstr.
R. des Moissons/ Oogstr.
R. T. Vincotte/-str.
Leuvensesteenweg
Plasky/-laan
B.d A. Reyers/-laan
R. de la Commune
R. Braemt/-str.
Avenue du Diamant/-laan
Rue du Noyer/
ST-ALBERT
Chaussée de Louvain/
R. de Pavie/ Paviastr.
MADOU
Av. de Roodebeek/-laan
DIAMANT
Square M. Louise/ M. Louizasq.
Square Ambiorix/-sq.
R. des Patriotes
ARTS-LOI/ KUNST-WET
Sq. Vergote
R. Franklin/-str.
Av. de Cortenbergh/ Kortenberglaan
Notelaarsstr.
Rue de Linthout/-str.
Rue de la Loi/ Wetstraat
R. Archimède
SCHUMAN
Av. des Arts/-laan
Kunst
MAELBEEK/ MAALBEEK
Av. de la Renaissance/-laan
Rd.-Pt.R. Schuman/-pl.
BERLAYMONT
Parc du Cinquantenaire/ Jubelpark
Av. de l'Yser
GEORGES-HENRI
Rue Belliard/-straat
SCHUMAN
Av. J. Kennedy/-laan
Froissart
Av. d'Auderghem/ Oudergemselaan
GARE DU QUARTIER LÉOPOLD/ LEOPOLDSWIJK
PARL. EUROPÉEN/ EUROPEES PARL.
AUTOWORLD
Av. des Nerviens
Av. des Gaulois
Avenu
R. du Trône/ Troonstr.
Parc Léopold/ Park
R. Wiertz
Rue du Cornet
MUS. D' ART ET D' HISTOIRE/ MUS. VOOR KUNST EN GESCHIEDENIS
Av. d. Celtes
MÉRODE
ETTERBEEK
MUS. WIERTZ
Chaussée de Wavre/ Steenweg
Chaussée Waverse
R. de l'Etang
Ch. St-Pierre
L. Hap/-str.
Av. E. de Thibault/-laan
Av. de l'Armée/ Legerlaan
MUSÉE DES SCIENCES NATURELLES/ MUSEUM VOOR NATUUR-WETENSCHAPPEN
Ch. de Wavre/ Waverse Stwg.
Av. de la Chasse/ Jachtlaan
Av. du 11 Novembre
THIEFFRY
B.d St-Mic
N.D. IMMACULÉE
SACRÉ CŒUR
BOILEAU
A
B
C
D
1
2

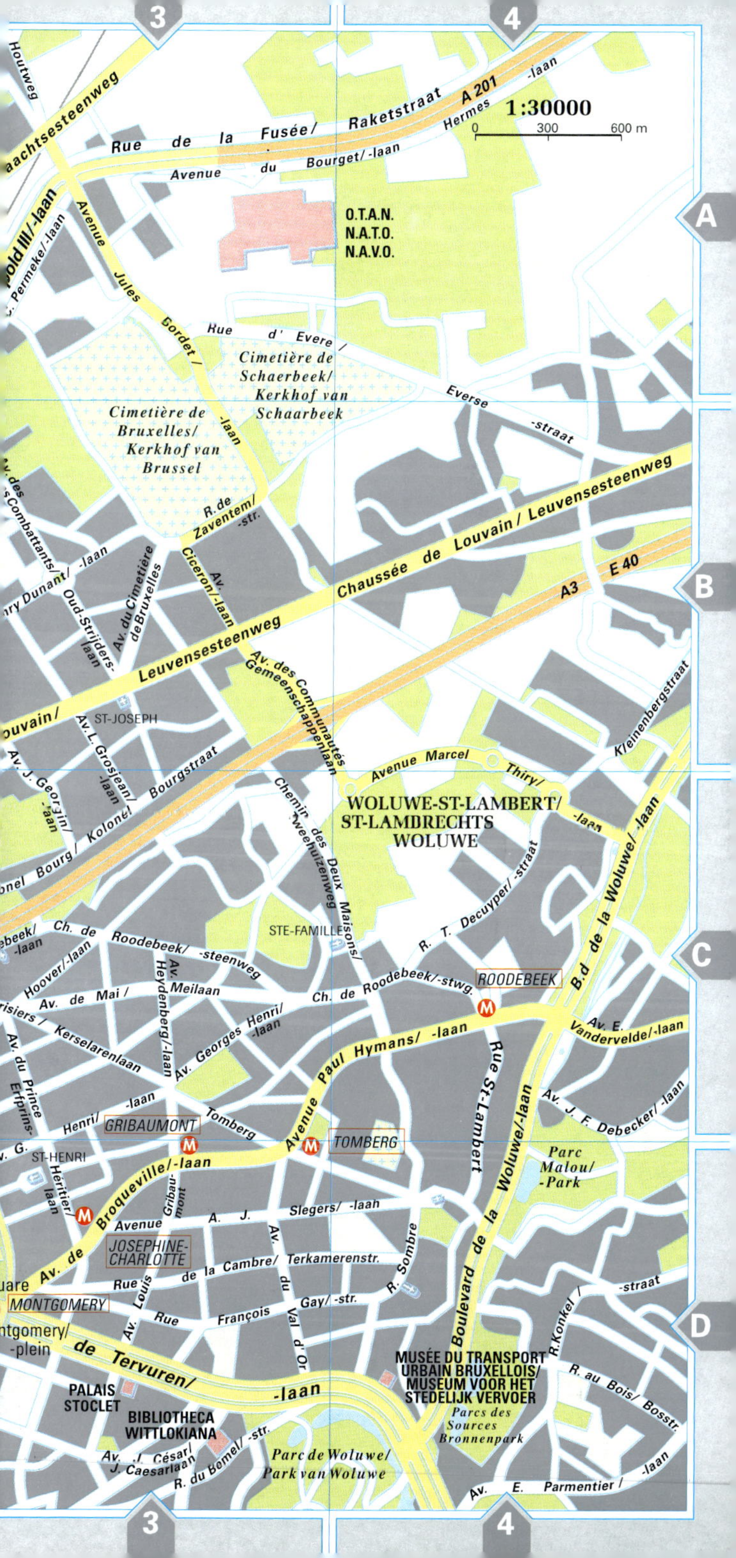
1:30000
0 300 600 m
O.T.A.N.
N.A.T.O.
N.A.V.O.
Rue de la Fusée/ Raketstraat
A 201
Avenue du Bourget/-laan
Hermes -laan
Avenue Jules Bordet/-laan
Rue d' Evere/ Everse -straat
Cimetière de Schaerbeek/ Kerkhof van Schaarbeek
Cimetière de Bruxelles/ Kerkhof van Brussel
R. de Zaventem/ -str.
Av. Cicéron/-laan
Chaussée de Louvain/ Leuvensesteenweg
A3 E 40
Av. des Communautés/ Gemeenschappenlaan
Av. du Cimetière de Bruxelles
Oud-Strijders-laan
ST-JOSEPH
Av. L. Grosjean/-laan
Bourgstraat
Kolonel Bourg
Av. J. Georgin/-laan
Kleinenbergstraat
Avenue Marcel Thiry/ -laan
WOLUWE-ST-LAMBERT/
ST-LAMBRECHTS WOLUWE
Chemin des Deux Maisons/ Tweehuizenweg
R. T. Decuyper/-straat
B.d de la Woluwe/-laan
STE-FAMILLE
Ch. de Roodebeek/-steenweg
Ch. de Roodebeek/-stwg.
ROODEBEEK
Hoover/-laan
Av. de Mai / Meilaan
Av. Heydenberg/-laan
Av. Georges Henri/ -laan
Kerselarenlaan
Av. du Prince Erfprins-
Avenue Paul Hymans/ -laan
Av. E. Vandervelde/-laan
Rue St-Lambert
Av. J. F. Debecker/ -laan
Henri/ -laan
Tomberg
GRIBAUMONT
TOMBERG
ST-HENRI
Av. de Broqueville/-laan
Av. G. Héritier/ laan
Gribau-mont
Avenue A. J. Slegers/ -laan
Parc Malou/ -Park
JOSEPHINE-CHARLOTTE
Rue de la Cambre/ Terkamerenstr.
Av. du Val d'Or
R. Sombre
Boulevard de la Woluwe/-laan
Rue François Gay/ -str.
Av. Louis
MONTGOMERY
R. Konkel / -straat
de Tervuren/ -laan
PALAIS STOCLET
BIBLIOTHECA WITTLOKIANA
MUSÉE DU TRANSPORT URBAIN BRUXELLOIS/ MUSEUM VOOR HET STEDELIJK VERVOER
Parcs des Sources Bronnenpark
R. au Bois/ Bosstr.
Parc de Woluwe/ Park van Woluwe
Av. J. César/ J. Caesarlaan
R. du Bemel/ -str.
Av. E. Parmentier / -laan
3
4
A
B
C
D

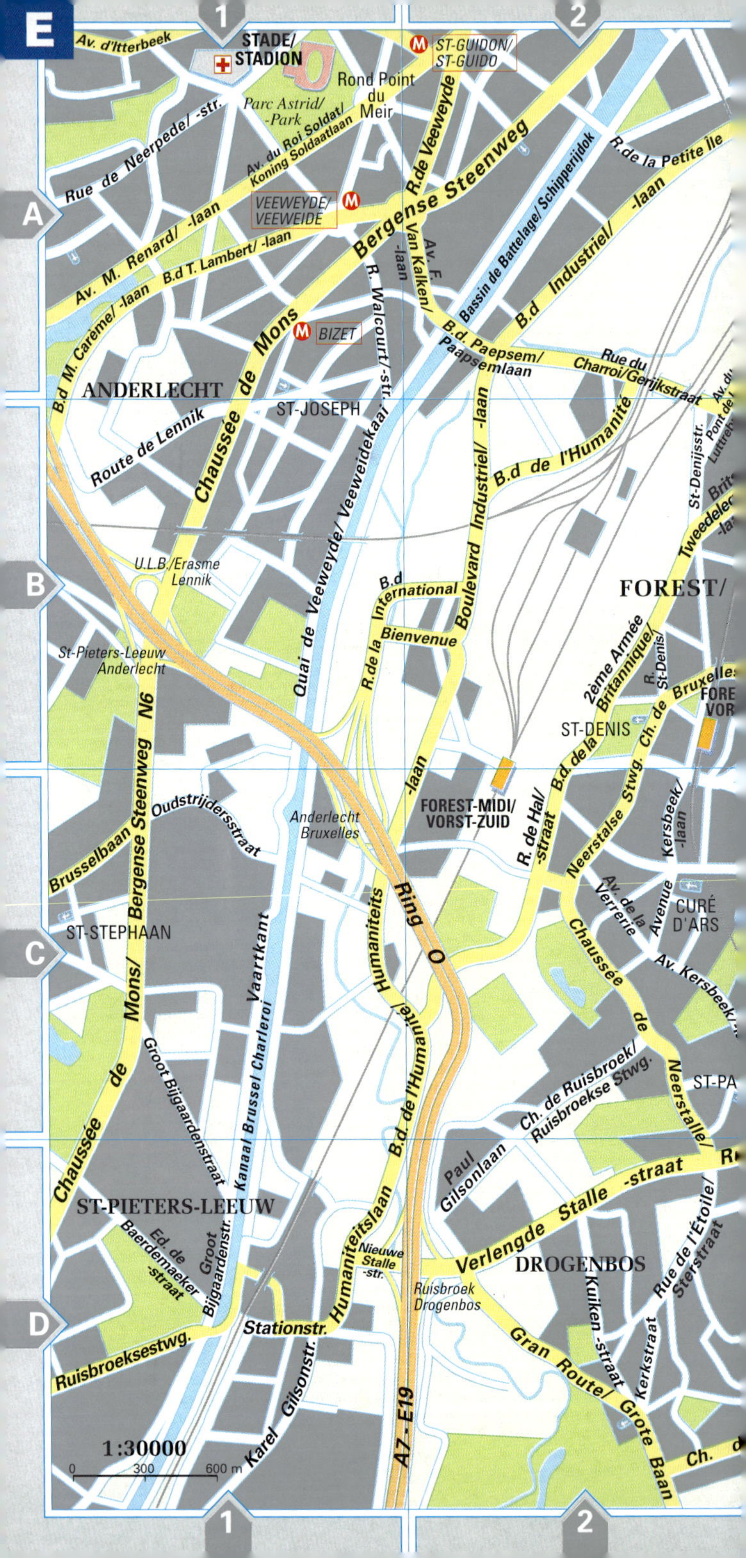

E
1
2
A
B
C
D
Av. d'Itterbeek
STADE/ STADION
ST-GUIDON/ ST-GUIDO
Rond Point du Meir
Parc Astrid/ -Park
Rue de Neerpede/ -str.
Av. du Roi Soldat/ Koning Soldaatlaan
R. de Veeweyde
Bergense Steenweg
VEEWEYDE/ VEEWEIDE
Av. M. Renard/ -laan
B.d T. Lambert/ -laan
B.d M. Careme/ -laan
Chaussée de Mons
BIZET
R. Walcourt/ -str.
Van Kalken/ -laan
Av. F.
Bassin de Battelage/ Schipperijdok
B.d Industriel/ -laan
R. de la Petite Île
B.d Paepsem/ Paapsemlaan
Rue du Charroi/ Gerijkstraat
ANDERLECHT
ST-JOSEPH
Route de Lennik
Boulevard Industriel/ -laan
B.d de l'Humanité
Quai de Veeweyde/ Veeweidekaai
U.L.B./Erasme Lennik
B.d International
R. de la Bienvenue
FOREST/
St-Denijsstr.
Tweedeleger
2ème Armée Britannique/
R. St-Denis
St-Pieters-Leeuw Anderlecht
ST-DENIS
B.d de la
Ch. de Bruxelles
Bergense Steenweg N6
Oudstrijdersstraat
Brusselbaan
FOREST-MIDI/ VORST-ZUID
R. de Hal/ -straat
Neerstalse Stwg.
Kersbeek/ -laan
Anderlecht Bruxelles
Av. de la Verrerie
Avenue
CURÉ D'ARS
ST-STEPHAAN
Vaartkant
Ring O
Humaniteits
Chaussée de Neerstalle/
Av. Kersbeek/
Chaussée de Mons/
Groot Bijgaardenstraat
Kanaal Brussel Charleroi
B.d. de l'Humanité/
Ch. de Ruisbroek/ Ruisbroekse Stwg.
ST-PA
Paul Gilsonlaan
Verlengde Stalle -straat
ST-PIETERS-LEEUW
Ed. de Baerdemaeker -straat
Groot Bijgaardenstr.
Humaniteitslaan
Nieuwe Stalle -str.
DROGENBOS
Rue de l'Étoile/ Sterstraat
Ruisbroek Drogenbos
Kuiken -straat
Kerkstraat
Stationstr.
Ruisbroeksestwg.
Gran Route/ Grote Baan
Karel Gilsonstr.
A7-E19
1:30000
0
300
600 m

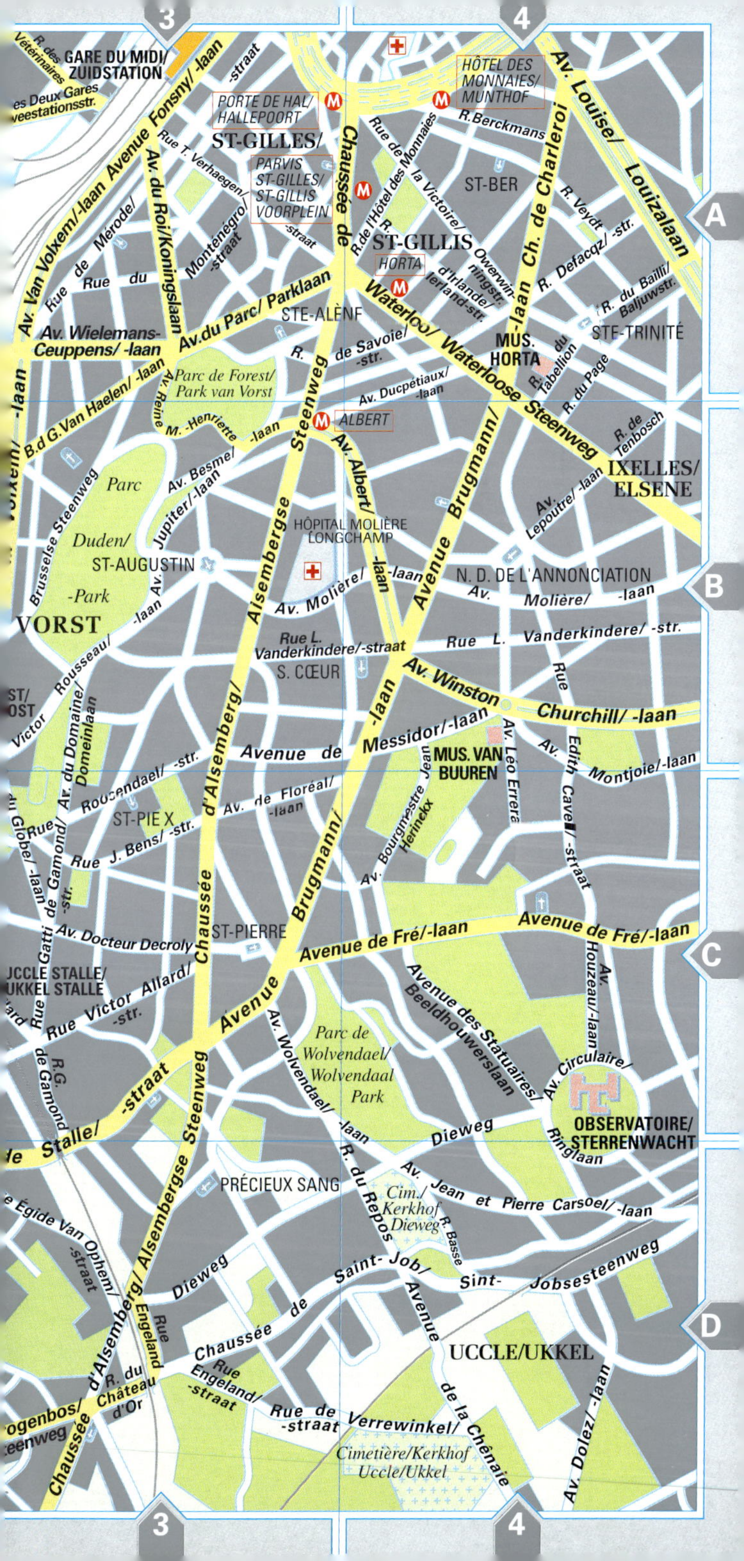

3
4
A
B
C
D
GARE DU MIDI/
ZUIDSTATION
R. des Vétérinaires
es Deux Gares
veestationsstr.
PORTE DE HAL/
HALLEPOORT
HÔTEL DES
MONNAIES/
MUNTHOF
ST-GILLES/
PARVIS
ST-GILLES/
ST-GILLIS
VOORPLEIN
ST-GILLIS
HORTA
ST-BER
Av. Louise/
Louizalaan
R. Berckmans
Ch. de Charleroi
-laan
Rue de la Victoire/
Overwinningstr.
R. de l'Hôtel des Monnaies
R. d'Irlande/
Ierland-str.
R. Veydt
R. Defacqz/ -str.
R. du Bailli/
Baljuwstr.
STE-TRINITÉ
MUS.
HORTA
R. du Tabellion
R. du Page
Waterloo/ Waterloose Steenweg
Chaussée de
Steenweg
Av. Van Volxem/-laan
Avenue Fonsny/ -laan
-straat
Rue T. Verhaegen/
Av. du Roi/Koningslaan
Monténégro/
-straat
Rue de Mérode/
Rue du
Av. Wielemans-
Ceuppens/ -laan
Av. du Parc/ Parklaan
STE-ALÈNE
R. de Savoie/
-str.
Av. Ducpétiaux/
-laan
ALBERT
B.d G. Van Haelen/ -laan
Parc de Forest/
Park van Vorst
Av. Reine M.-Henriette
-laan
Av. Brugmann/
R. de Tenbosch
IXELLES/
ELSENE
Av. Lepoutre/ -laan
Parc
Duden/
-Park
Brusselse Steenweg
Av. Besme/
Jupiter/-laan
ST-AUGUSTIN
Av.
Alsembergse
Av. Albert/
-laan
HÔPITAL MOLIÈRE
LONGCHAMP
Avenue Brugmann/
N. D. DE L'ANNONCIATION
Av. Molière/ -laan
Av. Molière/ -laan
VORST
Rousseau/
Rue L.
Vanderkindere/-straat
Rue L. Vanderkindere/ -str.
S. CŒUR
Av. Winston
Churchill/ -laan
ST/
OST
Victor
Av. du Domaine/
Domeinlaan
Avenue de Messidor/-laan
MUS. VAN
BUUREN
Av. Léo Errera
Rue Edith Cavell/ -straat
Av. Montjoie/-laan
Roosendael/ -str.
Av. de Floréal/
-laan
d'Alsemberg/
ST-PIE X
Rue du Globe/ -laan
Rue de Gamond
Rue J. Bens/ -str.
Av. Bourgmestre Jean Herinckx
Av.
Rue Gatti de Gamond/ -str.
Av. Docteur Decroly
ST-PIERRE
Chaussée
Brugmann/
Avenue de Fré/-laan
Avenue de Fré/-laan
UCCLE STALLE/
UKKEL STALLE
Rue Victor Allard/
-str.
Avenue
Avenue des Statuaires/
Beeldhouwerslaan
Av. Houzeau/-laan
Parc de
Wolvendael/
Wolvendaal
Park
Av. Wolvendael/
-laan
R.G.
de Gamond
de Stalle/
-straat
Steenweg
Av. Circulaire/
Ringlaan
OBSERVATOIRE/
STERRENWACHT
Dieweg
PRÉCIEUX SANG
R. du Repos
Av. Jean et Pierre Carsoel/ -laan
Cim./
Kerkhof
Dieweg
R. Basse
Rue Égide Van Ophem/
-straat
Alsembergse
Dieweg
Saint- Job/
Sint- Jobsesteenweg
Chaussée de
Avenue
Rue
Engeland
UCCLE/UKKEL
d'Alsemberg/
R. du
Château
d'Or
Rue
Engeland/
-straat
Rue de
-straat
Verrewinkel/
de la Chênaie
Av. Dolez/ -laan
ogenbos/
eenweg
Chaussée
Cimetière/Kerkhof
Uccle/Ukkel

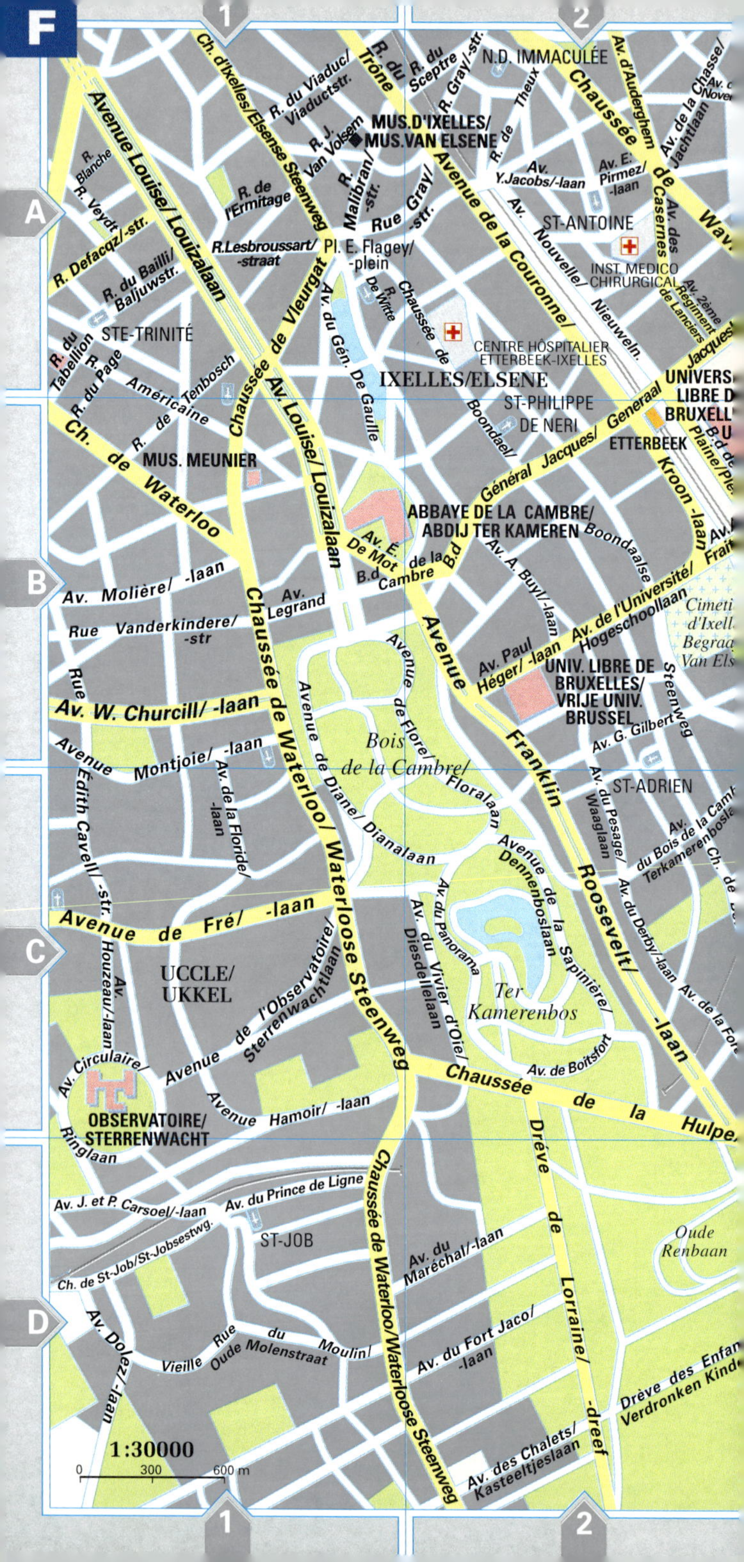
F
1
2
A
B
C
D
N.D. IMMACULÉE
MUS.D'IXELLES/
MUS.VAN ELSENE
Avenue Louise/ Louizalaan
Ch. d'Ixelles/Elsense Steenweg
R. du Viaduc/ Viaductstr.
R. du Trône
R. du Sceptre
R. Gray/-str.
Chaussée de Wavre
Av. d'Auderghem
Av. de la Chasse/ Jachtlaan
R. J. Van Volsem
R. Malibran/ -str.
Rue Gray/ -str.
Avenue de la Couronne/
R. de Theux
Av. Y.Jacobs/-laan
Av. E. Pirmez/ -laan
Av. des Casernes
R. Blanche
R. Veydt
R. de l'Ermitage
R. Defacqz/-str.
R.Lesbroussart/ -straat
Pl. E. Flagey/ -plein
R. du Bailli/ Baljuwstr.
ST-ANTOINE
INST. MEDICO CHIRURGICAL
Av. Nouvelle/ Nieuweln.
Av. 2ème Régiment de Lanciers
STE-TRINITÉ
R. du Tabellion
R. du Page
R. de Tenbosch
R. Américaine
Chaussée de Vleurgat
Av. du Gén. De Gaulle
R. De Witte
Chaussée de Boondael/
CENTRE HÔSPITALIER ETTERBEEK-IXELLES
IXELLES/ELSENE
ST-PHILIPPE DE NERI
UNIVERS. LIBRE DE BRUXELLES
ETTERBEEK
Général Jacques/ Generaal Jacques
Kroon -laan
Ch. de Waterloo
MUS. MEUNIER
Av. Louise/ Louizalaan
ABBAYE DE LA CAMBRE/
ABDIJ TER KAMEREN
Av. E. De Mot
B.d de la Cambre
Boondaalse
Av. A. Buyl/-laan
Av. de l'Université/ Hogeschoollaan
Av. Molière/ -laan
Av. Legrand
Rue Vanderkindere/ -str
Chaussée de Waterloo/ Waterloose Steenweg
Avenue Franklin Roosevelt/ -laan
Av. Paul Héger/ -laan
UNIV. LIBRE DE BRUXELLES/
VRIJE UNIV. BRUSSEL
Cimeti d'Ixell Begraa Van Els
Avenue de Flore/ Floralaan
Av. W. Churcill/ -laan
Avenue de Diane/ Dianalaan
Bois de la Cambre/
Av. G. Gilbert
Steenweg
Avenue Montjoie/ -laan
Av. de la Floride/ -laan
Avenue Édith Cavell/ -str.
Av. du Pesage/ Waaglaan
ST-ADRIEN
Av. du Bois de la Camb Terkamerenbosla
Avenue de la Sapinière/ Dennenboslaan
Av. du Panorama
Av. du Vivier d'Oie/ Diesdellelaan
Av. du Derby/-laan
Avenue de Fré/ -laan
Av. Houzeau/-laan
UCCLE/ UKKEL
Avenue de l'Observatoire/ Sterrenwachtlaan
Ter Kamerenbos
Av. de la Fo
Av. de Boitsfort
Chaussée de la Hulpe
Av. Circulaire/ Ringlaan
OBSERVATOIRE/ STERRENWACHT
Avenue Hamoir/ -laan
Drève de Lorraine/ -dreef
Av. J. et P. Carsoel/-laan
Av. du Prince de Ligne
ST-JOB
Ch. de St-Job/St-Jobsestwg.
Chaussée de Waterloo/Waterloose Steenweg
Av. du Maréchal/-laan
Oude Renbaan
Av. Dolez/-laan
Vieille Rue du Moulin/ Oude Molenstraat
Av. du Fort Jaco/ -laan
Drève des Enfan Verdronken Kinde
Av. des Chalets/ Kasteeltjeslaan
1:30000
0
300
600 m

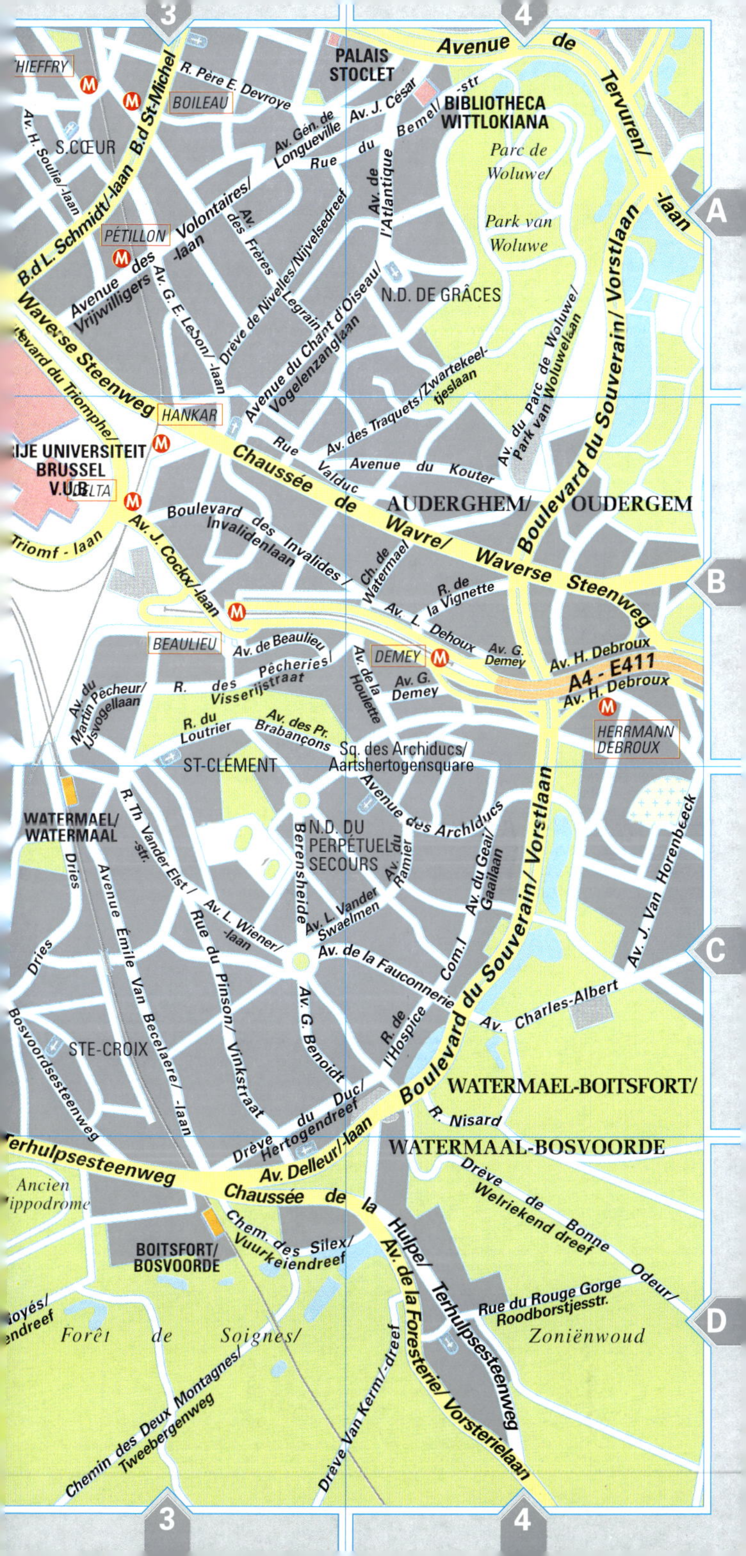
3
4
A
B
C
D
Avenue de Tervuren/-laan
PALAIS STOCLET
BIBLIOTHECA WITTLOKIANA
THIEFFRY
BOILEAU
R. Père E. Devroye
B.d St-Michel
S.CŒUR
Av. H. Soulie/-laan
Av. Gén. de Longueville
Av. J. César
Bemel/-str
Rue du
Av. de l'Atlantique
Parc de Woluwe/
Park van Woluwe
B.d L. Schmidt/-laan
PÉTILLON
Volontaires/-laan
Av. des Frères
Avenue des Vrijwilligers
Av. G. E. Lebon/-laan
Drève de Nivelles/Nijvelsedreef
Legrain
N.D. DE GRÂCES
Avenue du Chant d'Oiseau/ Vogelenzanglaan
Av. du Parc de Woluwe/ Park van Woluwelaan
Boulevard du Souverain/ Vorstlaan
Waverse Steenweg
Boulevard du Triomphe/
HANKAR
Av. des Traquets/Zwartekeeltjeslaan
VRIJE UNIVERSITEIT BRUSSEL V.U.B
DELTA
Rue Valduc
Avenue du Kouter
Chaussée de Wavre/ Waverse Steenweg
AUDERGHEM/ OUDERGEM
Triomf - laan
Boulevard des Invalides/ Invalidenlaan
Ch. de Watermael
Av. J. Cockx/-laan
R. de la Vignette
Av. L. Dehoux
BEAULIEU
Av. de Beaulieu
Av. G. Demey
Av. H. Debroux
A4 - E411
DEMEY
Av. de la Houlette
Pêcheries/
R. des Visserijstraat
Av. du Martin Pêcheur/ IJsvogellaan
HERRMANN DEBROUX
R. du Loutrier
Av. des Pr. Brabançons
Sq. des Archiducs/ Aartshertogensquare
ST-CLÉMENT
R. Th. Vander Elst/-str.
Avenue des Archiducs
WATERMAEL/ WATERMAAL
N.D. DU PERPÉTUEL SECOURS
Berensheide
Av. du Ramier
Av. du Geai/ Gaailaan
Av. J. Van Horenbeeck
Dries
Avenue Émile Van Becelaere/-laan
Av. L. Wiener/-laan
Rue du Pinson/ Vinkstraat
Av. L. Vander Swaelmen
Av. de la Fauconnerie
Com.
Av. Charles-Albert
Bosvoordsesteenweg
STE-CROIX
Av. G. Benoidt
R. de l'Hospice
WATERMAEL-BOITSFORT/ WATERMAAL-BOSVOORDE
Drève du Duc/ Hertogendreef
R. Nisard
Terhulpsesteenweg
Av. Delleur/-laan
Ancien Hippodrome
Chaussée de la Hulpe/ Terhulpsesteenweg
Drève de Welriekend dreef
Bonne Odeur/
Chem. des Silex/ Vuurkeiendreef
BOITSFORT/ BOSVOORDE
Av. de la Foresterie/ Vorsterielaan
Rue du Rouge Gorge Roodborstjesstr.
Forêt de Soignes/ Zoniënwoud
Chemin des Deux Montagnes/ Tweebergenweg
Drève Van Kerm/-dreef

Each street name is followed by a bold letter (A, B, C, D, E or F) indicating which map to refer to, and a grid reference.

Street Index

See pages 6–15 for practical information about getting there, getting around and getting by.

General Index

With thanks to OPT Wallonie-Bruxelles, Toerisme Vlaanderen, Arnaud Février, Alex Kouprianoff and all the organizations mentioned in this guide for their cooperation.

Picture credits

1 and front cover ill. (Hôtel de Ville) Jean-François Péneau. The vignettes on the cover are taken from the inside pages of the guide and credited below, except: Daniel Fouss (yellow trademark), Le Falstaff (flower), Gallimard (beer, chocolates), L. Milledrogues (street sign)
6 Arnaud Février
8 Arnaud Février (Thalys reception, Thalys logo), Lucie Milledrogues (station, Thalys)
9 Arnaud Février
10 Alex Kouprianoff (airport), Gallimard (highway)
11 Gallimard (road sign)
12 L. Milledrogues (taxi), A. Février (bus)
13 L. Milledrogues (tram sign), A. Février (subway sign)
14 Gallimard-P. Léger (banknotes, newspapers), A. Février (mailbox)
15 Arnaud Février
16 Jolly Hôtel du Grand-Sablon
18 De Tuilerieen, Prinsenhof, ILA, De Orangerie
19 1 L'Amigo
21 2 Hôtel Sema, 3 Mozart, 4 Hôtel Aris, 5 Matignon
23 8 Dix-septième, 9 Arenberg, 10 Le Méridien
24 12 Royal Windsor
25 13 Radisson SAS
27 14 Hôtel Welcome, 15 Atlas, 16 Astrid, 17 Roger Begine
28 19 Le Plaza
29 J. Evrard and C. Bastin
30 24 Sheraton
31 25 Crowne Plaza
33 Brighton, Knight (suit of armor)
34 31 Hilton
35 32 Les Bluets, 34 Conrad International, 35 Manos
36 37 Montgomery
37 39 Roger Begine, 40 Dorint
38 Arnaud Février
41 1 t'Kelderke, 3 La Maison du cygne, 4 La Roue d'Or, 5 Chez Jean
43 7 Le Pou qui Tousse, 8 and 9 L. Milledrogues, 10 Les Quatre Saisons-Royal Windsor, 12 L'Épicerie-Le Méridien
45 13 La Truite d'Argent, 18 La Moulière, 19 In 't Spinnekopke
47 20 OPT, 21 Les Petits Oignons (postcard), L. Milledrogues (street frontage)
49 26 Sheraton-Crescendo, 27 Metropole-Alban Chambon, 28 Arnaud Février, 30 Lucie Milledrogues
51 32 and 33 Lucie Milledrogues, 34 Au Vieux Saint-Martin, 36 La Tour d'y Voir
53 39 Chez Callens, 40 Stirwen, 41 Perry's Grill, 42 L'Atelier
55 46 Adrienne, 47 Maison du bœuf, 49 La Quincaillerie, 50 La Porte des Indes, 51 Maison Felix
57 53 La Truffe Noire, 54 Gri Gri, 58 La Villa Lorraine
59 59 Serge Brison (frontage), Bruneau (dining-room, postcard)
60 4 Roland Cols
62 2 André Mollekens, 4 À l'imaige Nostre-Dame
63 7 Lucie Milledrogues, 8 OPT-Christian Berthold
65 9 Le Cercueil, 12 Lucie Milledrogues, 14 De Skieven Architekt, Edit. Thill, 15 Lucie Milledrogues
67 16 Edit. Thill, 17 OPT-A. Lorgnier, 18 Le Public, 19 Michel Theunissen
69 24 Arnaud Février, 25 Denis Magniette, 26 Kaaitheater-Johan Jacobs, 27 Peter De Bruyne
71 29 Archives of the Théâtre Royal de Toone, 31 Lucie Milledrogues
73 35 Lucie Milledrogues (sign), Nova (auditorium), 36 Rachid Neffati, 38 Arnaud Février
75 40 Les Jeux d'Hiver, 41 Claridge1935, 43 Fuse, 45 Who's Who's
76 Daniel Fouss
78 Arnaud Février, OPT-B. Boccara, Alex Kouprianoff
79 OPT-Jean-Paul Rémy, Sominex, OPT-Christian Berthold
81 1 Lucie Milledrogues (bronze), OPT-Alex Kouprianoff (façade), OPT-P. Oliosi (Maison des Brasseurs), 2 and 3 Lucie Milledrogues (bronze), OPT-Alex Kouprianoff (frontage)
83 4 OPT-Jean-Paul Rémy, 5 and 6 Lucie Milledrogues
85 9 Lucie Milledrogues (detail), Alex Kouprianoff (exterior), 10 and 11 Alex Kouprianoff
87 14 OPT-Christian Berthold, 15 OPT-Hanssens, 16 OPT-Jean-Paul Rémy (statue), OPT-Bodson
89 OPT (Mont-des-Arts), 18 Bibliothèque Royale, 19 Lucie Milledrogues
91 20 OPT-Musées Royaux des Beaux-Arts de Bruxelles, 21 Musées Royaux des Beaux-Arts de Belgique, 22 OPT-Esthérazy
93 23 Alex Kouprianoff, 24 OPT-Christian Berthold, 25 Lucie Milledrogues, 26 Alex Kouprianoff
95 esplanade OPT-Boccara, OPT-Jean-Paul Rémy, OPT-A. Kouprianoff, 28 OPT-P. Oliosi, 30 Musée Royal de l'Armée et d'Histoire militaire
97 32 European Parliament
99 34 Musée d'Ixelles, 36 MRAH-KMKG, 37 Musée David et Alice Van Buuren
101 38 Maison d'Erasme, 39 Brasserie Cantillon-Patrick Huyberechts, 40 Alex Kouprianoff
103 41 Sominex, 42 Mini-Europe-Brupark, 43 OPT-Balister, 44 MRAH-KMKG
105 47, 48, 50 and 52
106 OPT-J.-P. Rémy
108 3 Edit. Thill, 5 OPT-château de Rixensart, 9 OPT-Jean-Paul Rémy, 17 Vernin, 19 Jardin botanique National de Belgique
111 1 Bastin-Évrard, 3 Edit. Thill 4 Africa Museum Tervuren
112 5 OPT-Philippart (view), OPT-château de Rixensart (courtyard)
113 6 OPT-Jean-Paul Rémy, 7 OPT-Expedo, 8 G. Dal Mas
115 Reconstruction of battle
117 13 FTPBW, 14 and 15 Fédération du Tourisme de la province de Hainaut-Christian Carpentier, 15 ASPL-Hugo Maertens (garden)
119 16 Association Royale des Demeures historiques de Belgique, 17 Vernin
121 19 Jardin botanique national de Belgique, 20 Mémorial national du Fort de Breendonk, 21 Zoo de Antwerpen, Rob Doolaard-IZP
122 Dandoy
125 1 ASBL-Sablon quartier des Arts et du Commerce (carriage), Alex Kouprianoff (terrace), 4 New de Wolf, 6 Lucie Milledrogues
127 8 TIB (N & B), L. Milledrogues, 9 OPT (bird market), Lucie Milledrogues (flower market, 10 OPT-Jean-Paul Rémy
129 13 L. Milledrogues, 14 Elvis Pompilio, 15 Dans la presse ce jour là (detail), Lucie Milledrogues (store), 16 Dandoy, 18 Au Grand Rasoir
131 19 Patrick Anciaux, 20 Delvaux, 21 L. Milledrogues, 24 Maison Brand
133 25 Philippe D., Nathalie R., 26 Stijl, Ann Demeulemeester (model), 27 Les Précieuses, 28 Idiz Bogam, 30 Laurent Lekime
135 32 Senteurs d'Ailleurs, 33 Olivier Strelli, 34 Gérald Watelet
137 38 Baltazar, 42 Philippe Dejobert
138 45 Sans Titre, 46 Zigourat, 47 Brüsel
139 48 Librairie Schlirf book, 49 The Skull, 50 Slumberland-Centre belge de la bande dessinée
140 L. Milledrogues